PRAISE FOR
The Sell Your Novel Tool Kit:

"Every novelist . . . should own this gem."

—KATHLEEN DOUGHERTY, novelist and
editoral associate for Writer's Digest School

"[Not] just another how-to puff, this is an
operations plan. Read it."

—DONALD E. McQUINN, author of eight novels

"A pragmatic marketing guide written for and about real
writers in the trenches. It's like having a five-star general
drop into your foxhole to not only show you a map of the
entire battlefield, but to give you tips on marksmanship
and battlefield survival."

—M.K. WREN, author of eight *Conon Flagg* mysteries

The Sell Your Novel Tool Kit

Everything you need to know about queries, synopses, marketing & breaking in

ELIZABETH LYON

A Perigee Book

A Perigee Book
Published by The Berkley Publishing Group
A division of Penguin Putnam Inc.
375 Hudson Street
New York, New York 10014

Copyright © 1997 by Elizabeth Lyon
Text design by Dennis Stovall
Cover design by Charles Bjorklund

Previously published by Blue Heron
First Perigee edition: December 2002

Perigee ISBN: 0-399-52828-8

Visit our website at www.penguinputnam.com

The Library of Congress has catalogued the Blue Heron edition as follows:

Lyon, Elizabeth.
The sell-your-novel toolkit / by
Elizabeth Lyon.—1st ed.
p. cm.
Includes bibliographical references and index.
ISBN 0-936085-40-1
1. How-to. 2. Book proposals.
3. Queries. 4. Marketing.   I. Title.

Printed in the United States of America

10 9 8 7 6 5 4 3 2

Dedication

Dedicated to my parents, Don and Ella Redditt,
who taught me to believe that anything is possible,
and to my brother, Jim, for cheering me on.

Contents

Acknowledgments

A book like this gets written not by a village but by a megalopolis of supporters. This book is a direct result of what I have learned from my students, clients, and the writers in my critique groups who generously shared their lives and their works, teaching me as much by their failures as by their successes. With gratitude and affection, I thank every writer in my four critique groups, including: Pat Swope, Patsy Hand, Milt Cunningham, Kathleen Cunningham, Patty Hyatt, Therese Engelmann, Trish Bradbury, Fran Toobert, Ellen Spear, Julie Mathieu, Elsie Rochna, Carolyn Kortge, Mabel Armstrong, Maura Conlon-McIvav, Kiernan Phipps, Cynthia Pappas, Geraldine Moreno-Black, DeLora Jenkins, Gerry Drew, Chuck Hitt, Mary Alice Moore, Dean Scovill, Jo Chambers, Dwight Fairbanks, Chris Bell, Nowell King, Shirley Foster, Jerry Wolfe, John Dewitz, Bill Lynch, Sarah Vail, Elaine Stec, Laine Stambaugh, Charley Snellings, Carol Craig, Candy Davis, and other group members of years past.

Most of all, I relied upon a triage team. Best friends, gifted writers, excellent editors, they have been examples of support and caring I can only hope to one day reciprocate in kind. Thank you Patty Hyatt, Carolyn Rose, and Stew Meyers.

Special thanks must go to the writers who allowed me to tell their stories and share their queries and synopses. Rainer Rey, David Wilkinson, Charley Snellings, Patty Hyatt, Paul Cody, Gregg Kleiner, Marne Davis Kellogg, Melissa Jensen, Martha Lawrence, Valerie Brooks, James Axtell, Micah Perks, Wendy Brown, Carolyn Rose, DeLora Jenkins, James Hughes, Milt Cunningham, Patsy Hand, Candy Davis, Bill Lynch, Pat Swope, Therese Engelmann, Trish Bradbury, Kent Tillinghast, Carol Craig, Sarah Vail, and Jane Maitland-Gholson.

I wish to acknowledge the perspective and expertise provided by literary agents Elizabeth Wales, Mary Alice Kier, Anna Cottle, Denise Marcil, Irene Kraas, Michael Vidor, and Anne Sheldon. The book is far richer for the addition of your thoughts and experiences. A special thanks must be extended to Peter Sears for his insights on the nature of writing for self-expression and art versus writing as entertainment and commercialism; and also to Lyndon Duke, language analyst, writers' consultant, and my friend.

Two additional resources have served the creation of this book and my body of knowledge. First, I am deeply grateful for Colonyhouse, a writer's haven on the northern Oregon coast where miracles happen. For this wonderful place, thank you Oregon Writers Colony. Second, I wish to thank the groups that have sponsored the conferences I have attended for decades, gleaning extra insight into marketing and meeting a host of "book people." Pacific Northwest Writers, Surrey Writers, Cuesta Community College, Write on the Sound, Willamette Writers, Klamath Writers, and Society of Children's Book Writers.

It never ceases to amaze me when people I barely know respond to my requests for support. To those novelists, agents, teachers, and editors who know me personally and to those who don't know me at all, thank you for being willing to read this book and endorse it: agents Denise Marcil, Mary Alice Kier, Anna Cottle, Jonathan Lazear, Jean Naggar, and authors M.K. Wren, Chuck Palahniuk, Kathleen Dougherty, Gail Provost, Kevin O'Brien, Don McQuinn, Liz Engstrom, and Margarita Donnelly.

I am lucky to have the support and love of family who endured the final weeks of book production.

My deepest appreciation and thanks to Dennis and Linny Stovall, my Blue Heron publishers, who had faith in my ideas and committed their resources to launch my publishing career.

Last of all, I thank Meredith Bernstein, my friend and agent, who ignited the interest of Perigee editor Jennifer Repo and kept this book alive.

Introduction

Many authors emerge from the safe cocoon of writing a novel into the foreign realm of marketing, a realm that seems hostile, confusing, and mercenary. At one time or another, nearly every novelist I work with complains, "I don't like marketing. If only I could focus on writing my novels and have someone else sell them." Or, "Why can't I just send in my book?"

Marketing seems like a daunting task. It demands the best of *nonfiction* writing. A query letter (a letter of inquiry) and a synopsis (a summary of the novel) demand thinking in terms of sales, not stories.

Almost no agents or editors forego reading the query or synopsis in favor of reading an entire manuscript. Why? Too many new writers; too few hours in the day.

The problem for many unpublished novelists is that while their tool kit for writing a novel contains many techniques of novel craft—characterization, plots, themes, dialogue, viewpoint, and settings—their tool kit for marketing stands empty.

This book equips you with everything you need to successfully market your novel, including eight distinct ways to sell it and a more common ninth way. The book illustrates how to write and master two major nonfiction documents, the query letter and the synopsis, in all its variations.

Here, you'll find dozens of examples of successful queries and synopses crafted by novelists, writers like you, unpublished when they began marketing their books, without insider connections or preexisting fame. You'll also read breakthrough and foot-in-the-door stories and see the individual path of each writer's journey.

I will introduce you to some of my clients who doggedly stuck by their dreams and, against long odds, succeeded. Clients like D. Marion

Wilkinson, whose 1100-page manuscript scared away agents and editors until he found editor Tom Southern, owner of Boaz Publishing Company. David's Texas epic, *Not Between Brothers*, sold out the first edition of 5500 in three months and was selected as one of three finalists by the Western Writers of America for a Spur award as "Best Novel of the West." You'll meet Rainer Rey, whose medical virus thriller was repeatedly rejected. Agents said the writing wasn't good enough. Editors said viruses had been done; he'd missed the peak of the trend. But, a year later, Rainer found an enthusiastic agent. Published in 1997, Fawcett-Ballantine printed 96,000 copies of his mass-market paperback, *Replicator Run*, and major television networks considered its movie potential.

Through *The Sell Your Novel Tool Kit*, you'll gain insight into the complex business world of publishing. This book seeks to demystify this world and make it accessible to everyone. You'll learn about author-agent relationships and why they are important. You'll learn about marketing strategies and why they are essential. You'll avoid the lost time, spent money, and diminished self-esteem suffered by aspiring novelists who begin marketing with little more preparation than wishful thinking. By book's end, you should know exactly what you want and how to achieve it.

As a published author, an independent book editor, teacher, workshop presenter, writer's coach, and literary consultant, I have helped many writers on the journey from writing to marketing to publication. Marketing often baffles and frustrates writers because it involves an entirely different set of skills and way of thinking.

My professional study of successful query letters included deciphering the unique structure, style, and content that would interest a literary agent or publisher. My collection grew as my editorial clients and novelists in four critique groups I lead queried, amassed rejections, analyzed criticism, rewrote, tried again and again, and finally succeeded.

As my clients, students, and I pooled our information, we learned what tools a novelist needs in this day of mass communication and stiff competition, where word processors have made everyone "a writer." We started to beat the odds. Students and clients began to win contests, secure literary agent representation, and sell. My novel-selling tool kit for authors continued to grow and was nearly complete.

I, too, have grown from a writer with a dream to becoming a published author. Looking back, the stepping-stones seem obvious: a fierce desire to write and publish, endless practice, and immersion in the writer's world, from critique groups to conferences. I enjoyed contest awards in fiction and nonfiction, article publications in *Writer's Digest Magazine*, and development of a community of supportive writers. My first book, a self-published nonfiction book, *Mabel—The Story of One Midwife*, sold out its 2500 copies. In 1995, Blue Heron Publishing published *Nonfiction Book Proposals Anybody Can Write*, and in 1997 the company published the first edition of this book.

Over the years, while my own files expanded until bulging with instructional material, client experiences, and effective samples from the successes of my clients, I kept waiting for someone to write a book wise in advice about marketing fiction, rich in query and synopsis examples. In over a decade, no such book has filled the specific needs of aspiring novelists. This, then, is that book.

Follow the steps I present in this book. I'm confident you can achieve your marketing goals. I have developed a great love of being midwife to the birth of new novels, then turning coach and critic, and finally fan. I will never lose the deep pleasure of holding in my hands the published books of those writers whose journeys I have shared.

Let *The Sell Your Novel Tool Kit* help you crack the insider's codes, clarify the techniques of writing query letters and synopses, and provide the tools for successfully marketing your book. My belief is that knowledge is power, and sharing knowledge empowers us all.

Good luck on your writer's journey.

Elizabeth Lyon
www.4-edit.com

CHAPTER ONE

How Novels Get Sold

- ◆ Eight Ways to Sell Your Novel
- ◆ The Ninth Way
- ◆ The Challenge of Sales
- ◆ Breakthrough: "Investing in People" by Rainer Rey

You must write what you must write.

Your first obligation as a novelist is to write the story that calls to you in the night, that pours from your heart and cannot be denied. The very fact that you have brought a story into existence for which there is no duplication, is in itself a gift to the world deserving of respect. However, the creative act is separate and distinct from the published work. It is only part of the writer's journey. In the end, the trick is to maintain your individual voice. When you decide to publish, you enter the public and become an active part of the culture.

Your marketing success depends upon your correct assessment of what you've written and where it fits in the publishing world. When you have a book ready to sell, finding a publisher closely resembles a job search. You wouldn't think of approaching a company about which you know nothing. Nor would you fail to match your skills with the company's needs. Success in marketing your novel depends on understanding the industry, beginning with knowing the many ways books get sold.

Eight Ways to Sell Your Novel

Just as some people find jobs through tips from friends, and others go knocking door to door, and still others read classified ads, selling a novel takes place through many avenues. While the manner in which each novel sells is unique, most are but a variation upon eight primary ways. In the section that follows this one, I'll introduce a ninth way.

1. Insider Connections

Your sister marries a literary agent. Your former attorney is John Grisham and he promises to introduce you to his editor. It happens. For instance, Judith O'Brien, author of a first time-travel romance, *Rhapsody in Time*, asked her friend Linda Marrow, an editor at Pocket Books, to read her novel. Judith was an editor herself—of *Seventeen* magazine. Or, consider Martha Lawrence, a former editor of Harcourt Brace, who contacted an agent with whom she'd done business. The result: representation followed by a sale of her first mystery, *Murder in Scorpio*. Do you think being the older sister to Anne Rice helped Alice Borchardt sell *Devoted*, her debut novel? If you have insider connections, use them.

2. Celebrity Status

Chances are you won't be reading this book if you are famous. Instead, you'll know you are a celebrity and will simply rely on this to create an inside connection if you don't already have one. Like Robert McNeil of *McNeil Lehrer News Hour*. He submitted his 1200-page historical novel to his literary agent, Bill Adler, who passed it on to Nan Talese at Doubleday, who helped Robert cut and shape it. Published as a Dell paperback in 1993, *Burden of Desire* was McNeil's first novel. If you question whether celebrity status affects acceptance and publication of a novel, ask any literary agent what they would do if queried on a 1200-page historical novel by...you, for instance. Let me know what happens.

3. Contest Winners

Win St. Martin's Press Malice Domestic Contest and you'll receive book publication plus a $10,000 advance against royalties. The same arrangement goes for St. Martin's Best First Private Eye Novel Contest. Many writers' conferences sponsor contests. To win or place can grant the visibility and prestige that leads to a contract. For instance, Billie Letts entered and won the Walker Percy Award at the 1994 New Orleans Writers' Conference and then went on to sell her debut novel *Where the Heart Is* to Warner Books, also selling film rights to 20th Century Fox.

4. SHORT STORIES

Many editors make a regular habit of reading short stories published in magazines and journals in hopes of discovering fresh new voices. For example, British writer, Kate Atkinson, wrote short stories and managed to win the 1993 Ian St. James Award for them. No doubt writing short stories honed what *Publishers Weekly* described as the "insistent voice, breezy delivery, and ebullient narrative style" that characterizes her first novel, sold to St. Martin's and titled *Behind the Scenes at the Museum.*

5. WRITERS' CONFERENCES

Every year, aspiring novelists meet their future agents and editors face to face at hundreds of writers' conferences around the country. Many conference organizers arrange for appointments between writers and agents or editors. Jean Auel met her literary agent, Jean Naggar, at Willamette Writers Conference and by Naggar's request subsequently submitted the blockbuster success, *Clan of the Cave Bear.* Over the years, nearly all of my writing students or clients have left conferences with invitations from agents or editors to send their novels or sample chapters. The Resource Directory offers information for finding conferences, and in later chapters of this book, you'll learn how to pitch your book at conferences.

6. SELF-PUBLICATION

Many editors with large publishing houses report keeping an eagle eye out for rising stars among self-published novels. In the last few decades, several self-published novels found meteoric success. James Redfield's *The Celestine Prophecy* and Richard Paul Evans' parable, *The Christmas Box,* both inspirational novels, began as self-published ventures. Redfield had already sold 90,000 copies of his new-age novel before Denver sales rep Mary Ann Johnson brought the book to the attention of Warner editor Joann Davis, who bought it for $800,000. Although the first printing of *The Christmas Box* was only twenty copies, Evans' fans urged him to submit his book for publication. Rejections abounded. Undeterred, Evans kept going back to press to meet local (Utah) demand, which soon became demand from across the West. From twenty copies to 700,000, Evans finally earned a mention in *People Magazine,* which caught Laurie Chittenden's attention at Simon and Schuster, eventually netting Evans a $4.2 million deal.

7. SLUSH PILE SUCCESS

Last on everyone's desirability list is what is called "the slush pile." By some accounts, slush refers to the stuff that washes over the transom (the edge) of a boat bringing a slurry of sea garbage to the deck. Used in the context of publishing, slush piles describe the totally ill-regarded stacks of manuscripts (not query letters) that uninformed writers send unsolicited. A Bantam editor once described to me how she motivated her staff to read unsolicited manuscripts. At pizza parties held "over" the slush pile, everyone gives once-overs to first pages, stuffing manuscripts back into self-addressed stamped envelopes. On the rarest of occasions, editorial assistants happen upon something—between anchovies—that catches the eye. If a writer omits the all-important return postage, the manuscript lands in File 13 (perhaps today it's a recycle bin). If rumor is correct, Taylor Caldwell's books met this fate for ten years as she sent in manuscripts, mostly not addressed to any specific editor. She never heard back. She didn't know better. You will.

8. QUERY LETTERS

Although you have seven other options for selling your novel, query letters (letters that invite agents or editors to request the novel or part of it) remain one of the most common and successful ways to match novels with publishers. For instance, a short well-written query by Robert Ferringo sparked interest from literary agent Sandra Dijkstra, enough for her to request a few chapters of his first novel, *Horse Latitudes*. She immediately signed him on and auctioned (sold to the highest bidder) his book for a six-figure amount. Although he now works with a different agent, this first sale certainly launched his career in style. To succeed at the query method of selling your book, however, you must craft a well-written letter and carefully select potential agents or editors from one of many directories. This book shows you how to do exactly that.

The Ninth Way

As you read these chapters, you'll encounter stories of published authors and writers who have advanced in the marketing process. Some have succeeded through one of the eight ways that I have just outlined, but most have followed a technique I call "the Ninth Way." The Ninth Way refers to pursuing a combination of the eight ways. If the label sounds slightly esoteric, I meant it that way. Scientist Rupert Sheldrake coined the term "morphogenic field," an activated territory that exists in a state of energy. When the field becomes sufficiently energized, it "morphs" from potential into matter.

Most of the writers with whom I have worked succeeded through The Ninth Way. They queried, they attended regional writer's conferences and met agents and editors face-to-face. They entered contests and sought publication of short stories. They tapped connections for referral and recommendation. While no one method guarantees publication, this comprehensive approach to marketing increases the synergy that eventually leads to the right connection.

In practical terms, if job applicants check the classified ads, network with friends, attend job fairs, schedule information interviews, float resumes, and send follow-up letters, one of these avenues will eventually morph into a job. Perhaps it is not so esoteric after all.

The Challenge of Sales

In the world of marketing books, as you grow from a novitiate into an apprentice and then a professional, you'll develop a belief system about how books are sold. In only a brief conversation with a writer, I can identify which of three belief systems a person holds to be true. See if you can find yourself in one of the following descriptions.

1. INTENTIONALLY IGNORANT OR PERPETUALLY PERPLEXED

Like many novelists, I began my career as a writer in contented ignorance, blithely writing my first novel with minimal awareness of craft or standards of marketability. There is nothing wrong with beginning a writing career in a state of ignorance. What's disastrous is staying there. Some writers keep themselves in a state of ignorance by sticking their heads in the sand. They don't read, join groups, listen to criticism, or rewrite, and yet they yearn for publication. Maybe they send out a few queries or manuscripts once in a while.

The perpetually perplexed are like the intentionally ignorant, only they know more; they just don't apply it. They attend writing classes, conferences, and critique groups but avoid undertaking the hard work of change—changing their writing and the perceptions of self that would help them grow into professional writers. Their secret desire is to be publishing exceptions, the lucky ones who put in a quarter and win a million dollars. The perpetually perplexed have no lack of rejection letters to prove they are going through the motions. So what are they doing wrong? Confusion is a clever self-deception.

The philosophy of sales for the intentionally ignorant or the perpetually perplexed seems to be: Publishing must be a matter of luck or politics and I'm an unlucky outsider. If only they knew that a small but steady amount of effort could replace lady luck with reliable accomplishment and turn this outsider into an insider.

2. The Numbers Game

According to Jeff Herman's *Writer's Guide to Book Editors, Publishers, and Literary Agents*, literary agents reject 99 percent of all queries and manuscripts they review. Most add only 1 to 3 previously unpublished novelists to their client list each year. Of the nearly 50,000 books published each year, only about 5000–7500 titles are fiction. About half of the mass-market paperbacks published each year are romance novels (about 1800 titles). Science fiction, fantasy, and horror account for another 350 or so titles. That leaves, give or take, 2850–5350 slots for all other types of fiction, including: children's, mysteries, westerns, historicals, mainstream, literary, Generation-X, action/adventure, thrillers— you get the picture. Of course, previously published authors claim most of these slots.

Find someone who lives his life by statistics and you will not find an optimist. The overwhelmingly negative statistics about an unpublished novelist's break-in chances are like a smoggy inversion layer. If you breathe too much of the stuff, you'll make yourself sick, and you may abandon your quest to get published.

But, find a first-time novelist who has gained agent or editor interest *and sold* his novel, and you'll find a writer with a vision and life-support system to traverse polluted territory mostly unaffected. Ask my clients mentioned in the introduction—D. Marion Wilkinson with his so-called unsalable 1100-page historical epic sold after years of practice in writing and with skillful marketing. Ask Rainer Rey with his so-called unsalable virus thriller that was supposed to be a good idea too late. Had these and other writers believed in statistics, they would have given up before they had ever begun. But they didn't and they succeeded.

The philosophy of sales for believers in the numbers game is: The odds are overwhelmingly against me. A different way of looking at it could be: If even one novelist of average skill without insider connections or celebrity has made it, so can I.

3. The Inevitability School

I admit that I am a proponent of The Inevitability School. This philosophy of book sales maintains that success is inevitable—if a writer will adhere to a number of "laws." Lyndon Duke, owner of a firm, Adversity Research, uses language analysis to problem-solve for corporations, groups, and individuals. He recommends that writers embrace the Law of Practice, which states that at whatever you practice, you grow more skilled. The Law of Know-How states that repetition produces skill and, assuming that what one practices is correct, over time leads to mastery.

I remember the man who consulted me about why he was unable to sell a novel despite the fact that he had written thirteen. A review of several told me exactly why. Among many craft problems, he had narrated the entirety of every novel, as if writing a long letter summarizing his books' events. Through the Law of Practice, he had become highly skilled at a bad habit. He would never break into print until he had learned the craft requirement to "show, don't tell."

Just as Realtors boast the cliche' "Location-location-location" to describe the most important aspect of sale of a property, writers can rely upon, "Repetition-repetition-repetition." But, repetition of good habits. The Law of Habit states that it is inevitable that you will be published if you cultivate good habits and break bad habits. There is no mystery about cultivating a good habit: Practice. There is no mystery about breaking a bad habit: Stop!

The Inevitability School supporters invest their energies in differences they can make in themselves, rather than in statistics or external opinions. These writers trust that when their skill level is high enough, when they command the tools of novel craft and marketing, they will publish. They'll never see success as a fluke or worry about whether they can write a second or fifth or fifteenth great novel. They've worked hard, know what they are capable of. Continued success is inevitable.

The Inevitability School philosophy of sales is: *It's not a matter of if you'll succeed; it's only a matter of when.*

The best antidote to ignorance is knowledge, and the best remedy for inadequate skill is practice. Chop wood; carry water, says the Zen adage. Only in The Inevitability School can writers enjoy being masters of their fate.

As Lyndon Duke also states, "Whoever has the tools holds the power." Toward the goal of becoming a master of marketing, in the next chapter I'll introduce the first tool that you'll need to open doors to the publishing industry.

BREAKTHROUGH

"Investing in People"
Rainer Rey, author of a medical thriller

As owner of a Seattle advertising and marketing firm, Rainer Rey wrote only ad copy, video scripts, and large brochures. Writing the novel he dreamed about for ten years made him feel as though he'd gone back to school.

"I was an English major at Yale," Rainer recalls, "but I got poor grades in writing. My college professors didn't like my style." Even so, Rainer believed that he would be a novelist one day.

When he finished his first draft of *Replicator Run* one year after he had begun it, a friend offered to introduce him to literary agents Mary Alice Kier and Anna Cottle, co-owners of the agency, Cine/Lit Representation, now in Santa Clarita, California.

"Frankly, had I queried them out of the blue with a sample of my writing," Rainer says, "I doubt they would have given me the same attention and help." Anna critiqued the novel and, not unlike his Yale professor, felt the manuscript needed substantial work. She suggested that Rainer work with a freelance editor, recommending my services among several others.

After three full rewrites, Rainer resubmitted his novel to Cine/Lit. Again they rejected him. "To my question of where I stood on a scale of one to ten, with ten being publishable, they said seven," Rainer recalls.

Rainer revised and rewrote then queried other agents, sending out about thirty letters in all, a few with sample chapters. "Some liked it," Rainer says, "but most didn't, and I was getting told the same thing everywhere: Virus stories are dead." He began writing another thriller.

Changing tactics, Rainer attended Seattle's Pacific Northwest Writers Conference and met with agents and publishers. He secured several requests to see his second manuscript, including one from Diane Gedymin, then west-coast acquisitions editor and vice-president of Putnam. He also submitted the first 100 pages to me for review.

I felt it was not ready to market, so Rainer called Diane to say that he would be delayed sending his thriller pending another revision. However, he used the opportunity to pitch his first book.

"Three days after she'd received *Replicator Run*," Rainer reports, "she called me to say she was sending it on to New York." While waiting for a response, he sometimes dropped Diane a note and sometimes left voice mail, keeping her up to date on his rewrites of the second book. Rainer also kept in touch with Mary Alice and Anna.

The New York senior editor at Putnam rejected Rainer's manuscript for Putnam's hardback line, but felt the story, with some changes, was appropriate for a paperback sale. Then came the unexpected: "At this point, Diane surprised me completely by telling me that she was making a career change and had decided to become an agent. She offered to represent me."

Diane's offer came a day after Rainer heard from one of the agents he'd met at the conference who also wanted to represent him. With both agents courting him, Rainer decided to meet with Diane Gedymin again to help him make up his mind. He knew a new agent was a gamble, but intuitively, he felt right choosing Diane.

By this point, Rainer had rewritten *Replicator Run* as many as a dozen times, incorporating the suggestions from the Putnam editor and from a thorough editing by Diane. As a new agent with lots of strong publishing connections, Diane took the high-risk road and put Rainer's medical thriller up for auction. While some publishers echoed the idea that virus stories were a fad that had passed, a few others indicated that they had become so popular that they might even become a sub-genre.

The book sold to Fawcett-Ballantine with a modest but better-than-average advance. Only four years from the first day Rainer had cast the first words of *Replicator Run,* Ballantine printed a confident 96,000 copy print-run and the mass-market paperback showed early strong sales.

In the midst of negotiating Rainer's contract with Ballantine, Diane Gedymin accepted an offer to become an editor at a large west-coast publishing house. Rainer was orphaned, but not for long. Believing that Rainer's first and subsequent novels have great film potential, Diane made a call on his behalf to an agency strong in both literary and film rights. None other than the Kier and Cottle team at Cine/Lit, the same agents who had first met with him and since become his friends.

"Face-to-face contact is so important," Rainer says. "Putting myself in front of people accounted for a quarter of my success. Of course, nothing will ever take the place of producing the kind of writing that an agent or publisher wants. But, business is still a people-to-people kind of thing. Communication, voicing your goals, and sharing your future wants and needs are very important, and then the agent and publisher have a good feeling of what you are made of. If you don't believe in yourself, you have no basis at all in wanting to write."

Having learned how to write a novel and demonstrated the success of good communication and relationship skills, Rainer's career is launched. Fawcett-Ballantine bought his third novel, *Day of the Dove,* a thriller. Rainer is still rewriting book number two, the book that initially led him to Diane Gedymin.

Summing up his philosophy about success as a writer, Rainer says, "In the long run, what you are is as important as what you write. When nearly everyone was discouraging me, I still believed in myself."

CHAPTER TWO

Beginning Your Marketing Tool Kit

- ◆ Overview of Publishers
    - Small and Regional
    - University
    - Canadian
    - Mid-sized
    - Conglomerates
- ◆ Product Lines
- ◆ The Jobs of Agent, Editor, and Writer
- ◆ Coping With Trends
- ◆ Money Matters
- ◆ A Foot in the Door: "Getting an Agent; Firing an Agent" by Charles H. Snellings

Overview of Publishers

The size and diversity of the publishing industry is astounding. *The Wall Street Journal* in a 1997 article reported the existence of over 49,000 publishers in the United States alone, and some 140,000 books released by these publishers in 1996. If the public can't find a book to read in that lot, they can turn to the 1.3 million books previously written and still in print.

Practically speaking, however, novelists trying to sell their manuscripts can limit their search to about 100 publishers, because only 10–15 percent of all books published are fiction. We are mostly a nonfiction-reading culture. To really put everything in perspective, about seven media conglomerates and a dozen independent publishing conglomerates account for 75 percent of all publishing in the United States, including the 5000 to 7500 novels published each year.

SMALL AND REGIONAL

Publishing less than a dozen titles per year, most small or regional publishers are owned and staffed by a single proprietor. With the assistance of part-time or volunteer help, this owner/publisher selects projects, edits, designs, arranges printing, and handles all promotion. The more successful small publishers will have sales reps and national distribution, but they must also rely heavily on author promotion and word-of-mouth sales.

A large print run for a small publisher is 5000 copies. However, a large publisher's first print run for some types of novels may also number only 5000, especially for a first novel.

Small publishers are just as selective as large publishers, more so if they only acquire a few novels in a year. In that respect, your chances for acceptance are just as high—or low—with Oregon's Story Line Press as with New York's Simon and Schuster.

So, why consider a small publisher?

The small or independent press movement has long been the defender of the literary and the alternative. By alternative, I'm referring to alternative lifestyles, leading-edge ideas, experimental and literary fiction, and books of interest to a minority of readers. Often publishing at a loss, subsidized in part by grants, occasionally asking the author to ante up, the small literary press, nevertheless, remains a viable starting point for many authors. And, more than the larger publishers, the *successful* small publisher who has learned to survive may offer more satisfaction, in both money and prestige. This is because every book is important to small publishers. There is no such thing as needing a tax write-off. A terrible failure could put them out of business.

The small publisher aims to recoup expenses, make a modest profit, and launch the next printing. A book published by a successful small publisher is likely to stay in print longer, often for decades. Satisfied with a meager but steady return, a small publisher will continue to reprint a book in small print runs, as long as it continues to sell. In contrast, the overhead and bottom-line needs of a large publisher often require minimum print runs of 10,000 copies. Also, because of state laws, most publishers pay taxes on warehoused books. A large publisher may find it more cost-effective to burn "leftover" books than to hold them over from one fiscal year to the next, especially in the larger quantities they are likely to handle.

What about the small publisher of *non*-literary novels, such as mysteries, romances, sci-fi, horror, thrillers, and other books written in a commercial style targeted at the general reader?

I believe that small, independent, and regional publishers of fiction are the unpublished novelist's under-recognized treasure. The focus of big dollars, advertising, and acclaim is constantly bestowed on a select number of bestsellers and on New York, still the center of gravity for publishing in North America. Small publishers and regional presses, though now recognized and respected within the industry, are still mostly overlooked by aspiring novelists who may get fixated on securing an agent and seeing their book published under a big-name house.

In Sidebar 2-1 I've selected a sampling of small publishers whose needs for fiction rival many larger houses' acquisitions. To find out more about small, independent, and regional publishers, consult with *The International Directory of Little Magazines and Small Presses*, with *Novel & Short Story Writer's Market*, and with *The Small Press Record*. Contact information is provided in this book's Resource Directory.

THE UNIVERSITY

In terms of quantity of *novels* published per year, the 100 or so university presses of the United States can be considered on a par with small, independent publishers. Most university press titles are nonfiction and scholarly. However, many universities are broadening their publishing programs to include fiction and more commercially lucrative types of books. Recently, the University of Colorado, for instance, is seeking Women's Novels of the West. Perhaps the most famous fiction success story springing from a university press is Tom Clancy's *Hunt for Red October*, first published by the Naval Institute Press.

In their favor, the university presses are more financially secure than small publishers, or for that matter, many large publishers. Although the university presses publish little fiction, this option may be perfect for some novelists. In the interest of leaving no stone unturned, you can explore the university press option by looking at listings in *Novel & Short Story Writer's Market* or *The Association of American University Presses Directory*. Find contact information in this book's Resource Directory.

Sidebar 2-1

A SAMPLING OF SMALL PUBLISHERS OF FICTION: AN UNTAPPED RESOURCE

(Source: *Novel & Short Story Writer's Market*, 2001)

Publisher	# fiction/yr	Average print-run	Types of fiction published; special conditions
Advocacy Press Santa Barbara, CA	3–5	5,000–10,000	juvenile; preschool; feminist/nontraditional messages
Alyson Publications Boston, MA	25	8,000	all categories; lesbian- or gay-related
Arte Publico Press Houston, TX	4–6	2500–5000	contemporary, ethnic, feminist, literary, short-story collections; contemporary U.S. Hispanic literature
Frederick C. Beil Pub. Savannah, GA	4	3,000	historical, literary, regional, short-story collections, translations
Fountainhead Productions Matawan, NJ	7	N/A	adventure, ethnic/multicultural, fantasy, historical, horror, literary, main stream, mystery/suspense, romance, sci-fi, thriller/espionage
Graywolf St Paul, MN	4–6	2,000–3,000	literary, short-story collections
Four Walls Eight Windows, New York, NY	9	3,000–5000	literary
The Nautical & Aviation Pub. Co. of America Baltimore, MD	1–4	n/a	military/war novels; 15% royalty, negotiable advance
Peachtree Publishers, Ltd. Atlanta, GA	1–2	3,000	contemporary, literary, mainstream, regional, children's
Write Way Publishing Aurora, CO	10–12	2,000	genre, soft sci-fi, fairy tale/fantasy, horror/thrillers

CANADIAN

Do not overlook Canadian publishers as a viable option for first-book rights, especially if your novel features a Canadian setting or characters, or even the setting or characters of the British Commonwealth countries, such as Great Britain, India, or Australia. Many directories that list publishers and what they seek include sections on Canadian publishers. Most of these publishers are small to mid-sized and serve a loyal readership one-tenth the size of the American market.

MID-SIZED

The spotlight almost continuously shines on the giant conglomerate publishers that dominate 75 percent of the market. However, the smaller the publisher, the more likely that a novelist can make direct contact—without a literary agent. In fact, literary agents will rarely represent a writer whose work best matches mid-sized or small publishers. This is because advances (money paid to the author out of future royalties) will be lower and the chances for a blockbuster remote. Agent commissions—15 percent of all author income—will be so low, the agent might incur a loss. If your book doesn't sweep an agent off her feet because it's not big-publisher material, don't assume you're out of luck. Publication with a mid-sized or small publisher is respectable and no less a feather in your cap.

Who are the mid-sized publishers? Chances are, if you don't recognize one by name, it could be a mid-sized publisher. For instance, read this list: 1) Bantam Doubleday Dell, 2) Academy Chicago, 3) Penguin USA, or 4) City Lights. The giants are numbers one and three, Bantam Doubleday Dell (BDD) and Penguin USA, and the mid-sized publishers are numbers two and four, Academy Chicago and City Lights. You're not alone if you've never heard of these. Most writers would not recognize most mid-sized publishers, even if the *Jeopardy!* grand prize depended on it.

Learn to identify and distinguish mid-sized publishers as major or minor players by reading *Publishers Weekly, Novel & Short Story Writer's Market, Writer's Market* and *The Writer's Guide to Book Editors, Publishers, and Literary Agents.* See contact information in this book's Resource Directory.

THE CONGLOMERATES

Suppose you've written a novel with mass appeal and you would like to be published by a New York house. Is there a way for an unpublished novelist to break into print with one of the top media conglomerates and dozen other independent conglomerates that dominate the market? Yes! These giants are, in reality, like the octopus. The head represents the owner, usually an international, entertainment corporation group. The arms of the octopus represent divisions that were formerly independent publishers who still maintain substantial editorial and identity autonomy.

Researching agents and publishers will help you ferret out which divisions are directly accessible to new writers. Sidebar 2-2 lists the top media conglomerates, who owns them, and their divisions.

Some of the other big players who are considered lesser giants by size include: Houghton Mifflin, W.W. Norton, Grove/Atlantic Inc., Beacon Press, Workman Publishing, New Left Books, The New Press, The Library of America, Andrews and McMeel, Disney, Hyperion, Thomas Nelson Publishers, and Reader's Digest.

The advantages of getting into print through a giant publisher are, *generally*, more overall prestige, a higher advance, greater promotion, larger distribution, and more sales. If you aspire to become a household name, i.e. Koontz, Steel, Grisham, Kingsolver, you are more likely to achieve this name recognition through a giant house. Besides, the really big money can be found only with the conglomerates.

However, all that glitters is not gold. There may be disadvantages to being an author with a conglomerate. You may be but a speck in the sea of titles carried by your publisher, not special at all. For writers who thrive on warm, close relationships, a mid-sized to small publisher may prove more satisfying. With a giant publisher, if your first book's sales don't jump out of the chute like a rodeo bull, you may fall from grace. The hoof prints on your back may brand you as a first-time failure and block fair consideration of your future books. Even a modestly successful first book may go quickly out of print—in months, not years.

On the other hand, thousands—yes thousands—of authors enjoy positive and financially acceptable relationships with giant publishers. A very helpful book to apprise you of the perils and promises of big-time publishing is *The Career Novelist* by literary agent Donald Maass.

TYPES OF PUBLISHERS

An entirely different way to look at publishers is not in terms of size, but in terms of types of books they publish. If your novel concerns military events, for instance, it makes more sense for you to research who publishes this specialized kind of novel (Presidio Press or Nautical and Aviation Publishing Company, for instance) than to worry whether that publisher is small or large. The same holds true for other specialty fiction, including the entire realm of inspirational and Christian publishing, which is like a parallel universe to the secular commercial publishing industry. There is a publisher, or branch of a publisher (called an "imprint"), that specializes in virtually any kind of subject niche one can think of. Lesbian- or gay-related fiction, for example, has its own niche publishers.

Independent of size or type, publishers vary dramatically by the style of books they publish. Like the individuality (or lack) of designer clothing, publishers seek to project an identity that distinguishes them from others who publish the same kind of novels. When I say, "mystery," do you think of St. Martin's or Mysterious Press or Berkley? When I say "romances," do you think of Harlequin, Silhouette, or Bethany House? What publisher comes to mind for literary writing?

If no particular publisher comes to mind, take that as a clear sign to bone up on who, in broad terms, publishes what. Otherwise, you risk mailing your category romance to a publisher who doesn't handle any.

Product Lines

For one publisher of romance, like Silhouette Desire, explicit sexual scenes are required and for another, like Bethany House, euphemistic sensuality is the limit. Publishers develop definite preferences for the content of novels and codify them into specific written guidelines. It's like any other kind of business. They work to maintain certain images with their readers that define them apart from their competitors.

The romance publishers, capturing 50–60 percent of the paperback mass market, are renowned for their product lines. Their specific guidelines ensure a kind of quality control so that readers get exactly what they expect. Thus, if you are writing a romance, you would certainly want to know a "Homespun" from a "Love and Laughter" from a "Heartsong," all individual product lines requiring different handling of characterization and plot. Sidebar 2-3 reprints an example of one guideline from Harlequin, one of the largest and oldest romance publishers. Writer's guidelines

Sidebar 2-2
SEVEN MEDIA CONGLOMERATES THAT CONTROL TODAY'S PUBLISHING

Conglomerate/Ownership	Imprints
News Corporation C.E.O. Rupert Murdoch	*HarperCollins Publishers*—Access, Amistad Avon, Cliff Street Books, Ecco, Eos, Perennial, HarperBusiness, PerfectBound, Quill, Rayo, Regan-Books, William Morrow; Harper Large Print, Harper Resource; HarperAudio; Harper San Francisco, HarperCollins, Harper Entertainment, HarperLibros, *HarperCollins Children's Books Group*—Avon, Green-willow, Joanna Cotler, Laura Geringer, Tempest, HarperCollins Children's
Pearson PLC	*Penguin-Putnam Group: Viking Penguin*—Viking Portable series, Viking Critical Library, Pen-guin Classics series, Penguin-Putnam, Penguin Poets, Arkana, Penguin Ediciones, Viking-Penguin, *Penguin USA Children's Division*—Cobblehill, Dial, Dutton Children's, Lodestar, Puffin, F. Warner & Company, Viking Children's; Viking Studio; *Dutton*—Signet, Onyx, Topaz, Plume, William Abrahms, Roc; *Putnam & Grosset Book Group*—GP Putnam & Sons, Philomel, Sandcastle, Grosset & Dunlap, Platt & Munk; Price Stern Sloan, Tarcher, Berkley Books, Dor-ling Kindersley; Jove, Ace, Perigee, Riverhead, Rough Guides
Viacom C.E.O. Sumner Redstone	*Simon & Schuster: Simon & Schuster Trade*—Simon & Schuster, Touchstone, Fireside; *Simon & Schuster Children's*—Aladdin, Atheneum, Little Simon, Margaret K. McElderry, Nickelodeon, Rabbit Ears, Simon & Schuster Books for Young Readers; *Pocket*—Pocket Books, Pocket Books for Young Read-ers, Archer/Minstrel/Pocket Pulse; Star Trek, Washing-ton Square Press, Paradox Graphic Mysteries; *Scribner*—Lisa Drew, Rawson Associates; Simon & Schuster Interactive; The Free Press, Brassey's USA, Jossey-Bass, The New Lexington Press, Pfeiffer & Co., Prentice-Hall, Silver Burdett Ginn, Allyn & Bacon, Computer Curriculum, Macmillan USA, Aguilar, Libros en Espanol

Bertelsmann AG Privately held; controlled by Reinhard Mohn	*Random House, Random House Trade Publishing Group*—Modern Library, Villard, AtRandom, Random House Paperbacks; Random House Large Print, Random House Value Publishing; Random House Information Group; *Random House Children's Books*—Knopf Delacorte Dell Young Readers Group: Knopf, Bantam, Crown, Fickling, Delacorte Press, Dell Dragonfly, Dell Laurel-Leaf, Doubleday, Wendy Lamb; Random House Reader's Group; *Bantam Doubleday Dell*—Bantam Classics, Bantam Double Day Dell Books for Young Readers; *Ballantine Publishing Group*—Bantam Ballantine, Bantam Reader's Circle, Del Rey, Del Rey/Lucas, Fawcett, Ivy, One World, Wellspring; *Bantam Dell*—Bantam Hardback, Bantam Trade Division, Bantam Mass Market; Crimeline, Domain, Fanfare, Spectra, Delacorte Press, The Dial Press, Delta, DTP, Dell Island; *Crown Publishing Group*—Bell Tower, Clarkson Potter, Crown Business, Harmony, Stage Arehearst, Three Rivers; *Doubleday Broadway Publishing Group*—Broadway, Currency, Doubleday, Doubleday Image, Nan A. Talese, Main Street Press; *Knopf Publishing Group*—Alfred A. Knopf, Everyman's Library, Pantheon, Schocken, Vintage Anchor Publishing; Prima; Bantam Trade, Bantam Mass Market, Crimeline, Domain, Fanfare, Spectra; *Dell*—Delacorte Press, The Dial Press, Delta, DTP, Laurel, Island; WaterBrook Press
AOL Time Warner Ted Turner, TCI chairman John Malone, The Capital Group	*Time Warner Communications: Warner Books*—Warner, Hyperion, Time Warner Audio, Warner Aspect, Hyperion; Little Brown & Company—Bullfinch Press, Little Brown & Co Books for Children and Young Adults; Christian Division—Warner Faith, Walk Worthy; Mail-Order Books—Book-of-the-Month Club, Time-Life Books, Oxmoor House, Sunset Books
Holtzbrinck Privately held by Dieter Von Holtzbrinck, president	*Farrar, Straus & Giroux:* Hill and Wang; North Point Press, Noonday Press; *St. Martin's Press*—A. Wyatt, Bedford, Buzz, Orb, Picador USA, St. Martin's Griffin, St. Martin's Scholarly & Reference, St. Martin's Press Trade, Stonewall Inn Editions; A Thomas Dunne; *TDA (Tom Doherty Associates)*—Tor Books, Forge Books; *Henry Holt & Company*—Henry Holt & Co. Books for Young Readers; Henry Holt Reference, John Macrae, Metropolitan, Owl, Times, 21st Century; Farrar, Straus & Giroux Books for Young Readers

are freely available from most publishers for the inclusion of a self-addressed stamped envelope. Or, check publisher websites.

Romance publishers aren't alone in projecting an image. One of the most certain ways to know which publishers match your novel's style and content is by broad reading of the same kinds of book you are writing. Pay attention to who publishes what. Most publishers print seasonal catalogs of their product lines. You can often find these catalogs at libraries and at trade shows, but you can also write to publishers and request copies.

As you follow the marketing half of your writer's journey, remember the inspiration that led you to translate your dream into a story. Your search for a publisher is really a search to find the person who can see and sense your dream through its representative, your novel. Books aren't really sold to conglomerates, or to large or small publishing houses. They are sold to people. They are sold to one person at a time. An assistant or reader, the agent, the editor, other editors, sales personnel, production people, reviewers, booksellers, the customer who buys your book. One person at a time. As you may know, the most effective sales are by word of mouth.

The Jobs of Literary Agent, Editor, and Writer

In most cases, the first two people who must become enraptured by your dream incarnate, your novel, are the literary agent and the editor. You'll save yourself much confusion by understanding the jobs and interdependency of agents, editors, and writers.

One of the big decisions faced by any writer is whether to approach publishers directly or through the author's representative, the literary agent. There is no cut-and-dried answer that applies to all writers. Many individual as well as marketplace considerations go into this particular decision. Make up your mind after you have read this book. I'll address the nuances of this choice in later chapters.

WHAT LITERARY AGENTS DO

Literary agents represent authors in the sale of their books and the related subsidiary rights, such as foreign translations, movies, and book clubs. Every agent has the best intention to "respond to query letters in two weeks, or to manuscript submissions within one month," as agent directories so often cite. Few are the agents who actually meet these self-

Sidebar 2-3
WRITER'S GUIDELINES—AN EXAMPLE*

Harlequin® Enterprises Ltd.

ROMANCE™, 50,000 words Editorial Dept.,
Query   Harlequin, Mills & Boon Ltd.
                                       Eton House,
                                       18–24 Paradise Rd.
                                       Richmond, Surrey, TW9 1S4 U.K.

Written in third person, from the heroine's point of view, each book should focus almost exclusively on the developing relationship between the main protagonists. The emphasis should be on warm and tender emotions, with no sexual explicitness; lovemaking should only take place when the emotional commitment between the characters justifies it. These heartwarming stories must be written with freshness and sincerity, featuring spirited, engaging heroines portrayed with depth and affection—as well as heroes who are charismatic enough to fulfill every woman's dreams! Readers should be thrilled by the tenderness of their developing relationship, and gripped by romantic suspense as the couple strive to overcome the emotional barriers between them and find true happiness in the romance of a lifetime!

* Reprinted with permission from Harlequin® Enterprises Ltd.

imposed deadlines. One major reason is because "acquisitions," the search for new writers, falls to the bottom of the list and ranks down there with items such as "clean the desk top."

As harsh as this sounds to aspiring writers, the reality is that agents eat when agents sell, not when they acquire. Those books that they are actively engaged in selling at any given moment take priority over just about everything else. Their next highest priority is calls and correspondence with author-clients for whom they have previously sold a book. Mornings are largely spent on the phone, pre-selling books, talking and negotiating with editors, reporting back to authors on upcoming deals, and faxing, phoning, and emailing.

Most agents use part- or full-time assistants to handle the mail, which every week may bring 100 queries and dozens of manuscripts. The effective assistant selects the promising book ideas, according to the tastes and criteria of the individual agent, who approves or rejects the selections.

Form rejections expedite a reasonably speedy response. As time allows, agents may jot short notes to authors whose manuscripts almost, but not quite, made it. While writers long for more than a brief paragraph in response, from the agent's point of view, even this short paragraph is an act of generosity, rarely appreciated for the level of sacrifice of time and energy. In afternoons, evenings, and vacations, agents must read the manuscripts they requested and in which their assistants see promise. When they find a book they love and believe they can sell, often it still needs tweaking—just one more revision. If so, the agent dons the editor's cap in directing the writer where to make changes.

Then, there are numerous phone calls with writers discussing needed changes, explaining editorial response or lack of, translating contract details, and sharing existential angst over the craziness of the industry.

Agents located outside New York must plan trips to this mecca of the publishing world, which means lining up appointments and making travel arrangements. Agents who live in New York may have more in-person meetings with editors and other agents, for business as well as social ties, and these meetings take a bite out of busy days. All agents must keep tabs on their accountants, stay on top of taxes, royalty payments, and bookkeeping. Many spend evenings returning e-mail, perusing writer chat rooms on the Internet, and canvassing literary journals for new clients. In their spare time, they must keep current with *Publishers Weekly*, *The New York Times Book Review*, or *Horn Book* (for children's literature), other newspapers and trade magazines, and read their clients' books as they get published.

Most agents track their authors' book promotions, and follow through on subsidiary sales, that is, sales of foreign rights, movie rights, book-club rights, and others. If a relationship between an author and editor turns less than harmonious, an agent may also serve as confessor and counselor, buffer and buttress against a broken relationship or contract. Believe it or not, they do more than all this.

No wonder agents don't appreciate phone calls from non-clients wondering if they have the time to discuss a few unpublished book ideas!

WHAT EDITORS DO

The job description of most editors is obvious; they edit. They correct manuscripts and make suggestions on the story and its execution. However, at giant publishing houses, this function may be the least of what an editor does. The editor who reads your query and manuscript sample may be an editorial assistant, a gatekeeper who decides whether a submission deserves consideration by a senior editor. The person who negotiates the contract and buys your book may primarily serve as an acquisitions editor. You may be turned over to a line editor who works intensively with you on conceptual or content changes, but your typos, mistakes in the hero's eye color, and creativity in spelling likely fall to a copy editor. Finally, making corrections to the galleys may fall to a freelance editor.

In a small, or even mid-sized, publishing house, the editor who opens the mail, acquires, edits, and corrects copy may be one and the same person who also handles your book promotion, cuts your royalty check, and sends you a Christmas card.

Larger publishers have larger staffs and more division of labor. For instance, at a larger house, the editor with whom you bonded, because she wishes to acquire your book, may do any or all of the following in one day: read memos from assistants; write short descriptions on prospective books; estimate costs and income for the in-house book-production forms; formally present books to review committee; return calls to agents and authors; talk with staff in production, art, contracts, law, promotion, publicity; sort telephone messages; initiate correspondence; sign papers; write memos; delegate; attend meetings; talk with media; work late; take home manuscripts to read. As you can see, editors are busy people, with much more to do than read prospective books.

WHAT SHOULD WRITERS DO?

You know that your first job is to write the book that you feel compelled to write. Your second job is to rewrite it, over and over, until the written word matches the dream. While chapter three in this book addresses several other steps before marketing your book, you'll be less frustrated if you fully realize the diversity and demand of the jobs of agent or editor. And, from their point of view, you'll avoid becoming a pest or pariah.

As a helpful member of the agent, editor, writer team, you should learn how to follow the rules and when to be assertive. Following the rules refers to how to submit queries and manuscripts, remembering to include return postage and envelopes, and a dozen other conventions that will be fully covered in this book. It also refers to not mis-using an agent or editor's phone, fax number, or e-mail address. It means calling your agent in the afternoon rather than in peak hours of doing business with editors—especially true for west-coast agents. It means that you learn how to distill your purpose in calling or writing into a succinct form that can be responded to easily. The ideal writer also seeks to make the job of the agent or editor easier. After all, once you have finished with revisions and sent your manuscript to an agent or editor, your job is done until promotional efforts begin. Meanwhile, you can be more productive than waiting by your phone and fuming—you can be writing your next book.

Literary agents Anne Sheldon and Michael Vidor, co-owners of The Hardy Agency in San Luis Obispo, California, sum up what they look for in writers with a list called "Our Ideal Clients," in Sidebar 2-4.

Coping With Trends

One good way to spook your creativity is by worrying about trends. As a veteran conference-goer, I listen to the VIPs from New York as they talk about what is "in" and what is "passé." One year, every one of two dozen editors and agents said they were looking for thrillers. The nonviolent adventure story was out (never mind *The Celestine Prophecy*—an anomaly). For several years running, the experts gave thumbs-up to female sleuths in mysteries; thumbs-down to Mickey Spillane-like writing. While these experts admit that strong female protagonists have an undeniable place in mysteries, they also predict a peak in the trend. Or that courtroom thrillers are done and overdone, unless your name is John Grisham. Sometimes publishing pundits will announce the exile of an entire type of novel, such as horror, Gothic romances, and Louis L'Amour-type westerns.

If the predictions prove true and the very story you've spent a decade writing has no purchasers, what should you do?

The best thing is to listen to what is allegedly popular and passé, but primarily stay focused on writing the book you want to write in the very best way that you can. If an agent tells you, "One could practically track what is not selling by what you are writing," then use that information for adjusting your marketing strategy. The recipient of this remark was one of my writer-clients. He decided it might not be true, but all the same, he shifted his marketing efforts to small and regional publishers, where his book is currently gaining serious consideration.

The only way you can anticipate or verify trends is to immerse yourself in the information stream. Read newsletters, newspapers, trade journals. Attend writers' events and keep your ear to the ground. Talk with published authors of the kind of book you are writing. Attend writers' conferences and confer directly with editors and agents. Trends are hard to distinguish from rumors, and they may be blown like so much chaff to the wind with the next blockbuster hit that defies all predictions. Keep abreast of reported trends but don't let them interfere with your number-one job: writing the best novel—of your choice—that you can.

Sidebar 2-4

OUR IDEAL CLIENTS*:

- Call to tell us what *they* are doing to further their careers, not to ask what *we're* doing to further their careers.

- Continue to study their markets, and contribute to the process of identifying potential buyers for their works.

- Demonstrate a true understanding of the realities of the writing/publishing business, rather than a perception of how things should go.

- Nonetheless, remain determined to succeed.

- Recognize that the combined effort being made is what will lead to success.

- Realize that our entire reputation with publishers is based on the quality and appropriateness of the work we submit. If we choose not to submit work to a particular publisher, writers must trust us in that choice.

- Don't assume that those who reject their books must have missed the point or are just plain stupid.

- Act professionally, yet personably.

- Are dedicated beyond all expectation, and realize that most people in this business are as well.

* Revised and reprinted with permission from Anne Sheldon and Michael Vidor, The Hardy Agency, www.booklogic.com.

Money Matters

At some time or another, the thought of money will flicker across your awareness. Advances. Royalties. You'll wonder what you can expect, what is typical. Rightly so. You deserve to be paid for your artistic vision and hard work. For a first novel, however, the pay may be less than the glamorous figures you read about in your newspaper or in *Publishers Weekly.*

I couldn't help but cringe the day I got a call from a client who had just read that some first-time novelist's book had been auctioned off for an incredible quarter of a million dollars. "Why not me?" my client demanded to know. He wanted to circumvent all of the waiting, rewriting, skill curves, and usual channels, and he failed to understand why I kept throwing ice on his plans to jet to this or that conference or personally call this or that agent. Although marketing miracles do occur, this writer had yet to learn how to write well enough to get published. The dollar signs of exceptional success kept flashing in his way.

So, what can you reasonably expect to earn for your mystery, young-adult novel, or international thriller? What about literary or mainstream?

First of all, payment for novels falls into two categories: the advance and the royalty. An advance is exactly what it says: borrowed money from the future sales of your book. An advance is money paid soon after a contract is signed by all parties, though the advance may be paid in two or three spaced increments. A royalty is a percentage rate of the retail, or list, cost of your book; in some contracts it is a percentage of "net" sales.

Let's say you are offered a $5000 advance. When the book sells well enough that your royalty income equals $5001, you have just paid back your advance and earned your first royalty buck.

As you can see, you must know more than your advance and royalty rate to see a clear picture of your novel's earning potential. In the long run, the number of books printed and distributed and the length of time your book stays in print become even more important considerations than the advance and royalty rate. After all, if only 3000 books are printed and then your book falls out of print, your $3000 advance may not be as lucrative as no advance and a first print run of 10,000 books.

National Writers Union keeps tabs on typical advances, royalties, and print-runs and publishes this information in *National Writers Union Guide to Freelance Rates and Standard Practice.* Here are some of their findings:

ADVANCES	RANGE: LOW-HIGH	AVERAGE
Trade Books		
Fiction Hardcover	$5,000–$100,000	$19,745
Fiction Paperback	$1,500–$56,000	$14,135
Mass-market Paperbacks		
Mystery	$5,000–$50,000	$13,900
Romance	$1,000–$40,000	$ 6,400
Science Fiction	$3,500–$40,000	$19,900
Western	$1,500–$35,000	$ 5,700
Young Adult	$1,000–$14,000	$ 6,100
Other Original Paperback	$1,500–$35,000	$10,500
Children's Books	$0–$53,000	$ 5,061

ROYALTIES	PREVALENT RANGE (OF BOOK'S RETAIL PRICE)
Trade Books	
Fiction Hardcover	
First 5,000 books	5–10%
Next 5,000 books	10–12%
Thereafter	12–15%
Fiction Paperback	
First 10,000 books	5–10%
Thereafter	8–15%
Mass-Market Paperbacks	
Mystery	
First 150,000 books	6–15%
Thereafter	8–15%
Romance	
First 150,000 books	4–10%
Thereafter	7–15%
Science Fiction	
First 150,000 books	7–10%
Thereafter	8–15%
Western	
First 150,000 books	2–10%
Thereafter	4–15%

Young Adult
    First 150,000 books   1–10%
    Thereafter   1–12%
Other Original Paperbacks
    First 150,000 books   5–15%
    Thereafter   7–15%

AVERAGE PRINT RUNS	RANGE: LOW–HIGH
Trade books	
Fiction Hardcover	500–72,000 books
Fiction Paperback	750–500,000 books
Mass-Market Paperbacks	
Mystery	5,000–150,000 books
Romance	10,000–500,000 books
Science Fiction	5,000–150,000 books
Western	5,000–100,000 books
Young Adult	10,000–150,000 books
Other Original Paperbacks	3,000–250,000 books

As you look over these statistics, you'll probably be hoping to land in the mid- to upper-range of all these figures. That's natural. Just remember, many factors determine each book's advance, royalty, and first print run.

In general, the larger the publisher the more likely of an advance (many small presses pay no advances), and larger advances as well as larger print runs. The royalty rate, however, varies little when compared to small publishers.

The size of your print run may also determine your degree of success, independent of almost anything else, including the perceived quality of your writing. The reason for this is that large publishers spend practically no promotional dollars on low–average print runs. As Marne Davis Kellogg expresses in her breakthrough story at the end of chapter eight, a print run of 10,000 for mysteries with her publisher seemed to be the low-end cut-off for promotional dollars. Those promotional dollars, well spent, can create a publishing success, if not ensure a bestseller. Some people call it hype, but when publicity moves customers to buy books, the publisher and the author profit. When it's a good book, the reader profits, too. Small presses often do very short runs solely because of expense and plan to quickly reprint in more short runs to satisfy demand.

Another key player in the money picture is the literary agent. If you retain one to represent you, the standard agent commission is 15 percent—of all monies. So, before you figure out how much royalty you stand to receive from 7 percent royalty on your $6.00 mass-market mystery if all 50,000 copies sell in the first print-run, don't forget to first subtract your agent's commission. For the mathematically challenged like myself, the math goes like this: .07 X $6.00 = $0.42 royalty per book sold. On 50,000 books, you would earn 42 cents X 50,000, or $21,000. Since your publisher sends your royalty checks to your agent, she'll deduct her 15 percent. That's .15 X $21,000 = $3150. Your check will equal $17,850.

But not if your advance was, say, $25,000 ($21,250 after deducting your agent's 15 percent). In this case, your actual royalty income on the first print run is zip. The $21,000 earned royalty still falls short of the $25,000 they advanced you. You owe $4000. National Writers Union's book reports that about 50 percent of all novels published fail to earn back the authors' advances, much less turn a profit. So, why would a publisher be so foolish as to offer a high advance for a print run when there is a 50:50 chance he'll suffer a $4000 shortfall?

In the example I've given, if all 50,000 copies sold, before the last book left the warehouse, the publisher would follow through with what it had planned all along: a second printing. And, in all truth, publishers in general hope that each book they invest in will fall within the 50 percent that do make money. You, however, won't see a penny in royalty until that $25,000 advance has been earned out. Not until 59,524 books have sold.

Another source for paying back your advance is any monies earned by your publisher for the sale of what is called subsidiary rights. Sub rights (as they are called) include sales of foreign and translation rights, book-club rights, movie rights, and others. If a publisher has negotiated to acquire these rights, then it will apply revenues from subsidiary rights sales toward your debt, your advance. However, if your agent has negotiated to retain these rights on your behalf, the publisher still must wait for the sale of your book to pay off the advance. After your agent deducts her 15-percent commission, you can directly receive the monies from the sale of translation rights of your book into Lithuanian.

Another factor that strongly affects sizes of advances and first print runs, as well as the initial book purchase, is economics—global and local. As the publishing industry weathered the closing years of the twentieth century, no question but that a mood of caution and belt-tightening prevailed. The trickle-down effect on first-time novelists has been lower advances, smaller print runs, and thin promotional budgets.

However, you can easily get ahead of yourself by borrowing trouble from the future. Until you secure an agent or get an offer on your book, keep the matter of money secondary. Your primary job: learn to write well; stock your marketing tool kit.

The foot-in-the-door story that completes this chapter features one writer's struggle with trends. With this overview of the publishing industry, its trends, money matters, and the function of its principal players—the agent, editor, and yourself, you're ready to take a last critical look at the offspring of your imagination, your actual book.

A FOOT IN THE DOOR

"Getting an Agent; Firing an Agent"

Charles H. Snellings, author of horror novels

In November of 1991, Charles 'Charley' Snellings emerged from a "dark night of the soul" with the realization that what he most wanted to do in life was write. A middle-aged, disenchanted insurance salesman and single parent of two children, Charley began a first draft of a horror novel on seven yellow legal pads and then borrowed a friend's computer to prepare the book for sale.

In 1992, he learned from library books that sales in the book field were mostly initiated by a query with a synopsis, his first version of which was ten pages long. As a salesman, he was undaunted by the first sixty rejections and heartened when two agents requested the manuscript. Before sending it out, he connected with my Wednesday-night critique group and hired my editing services. "I thought I needed an editor to help me polish the beginning. Otherwise, I thought my novel was ready for publication," he recalls.

Charley remembers the manuscript after I finished editing the first sixty pages. "It came back looking as if someone had hemorrhaged all over it." Even with revision, the two agents rejected the book and advised considerable rewriting. Finally, Charley stopped marketing.

By 1994, after complete revision of the book, he decided it was at last finished and sent out a revised query and a substantially shorter synopsis, contacting publishers as well as agents. After several dozen rejections, Charley decided to alter his query. His new submission included a one-page query, a three-page, double-spaced synopsis, a color photocopy of himself as a whitewater river guide, and a selected one-page excerpt of his story formatted like a page in a published book and labeled as an excerpt from *The Hidebehind.* "I figured the unconventional query would set me apart from the thousands that cross desks every day," he says.

Through one friend's connections to an agent, he received a referral to an agent from whom he had received a form rejection years earlier. Figuring that this agent wouldn't remember the former query since Charley had by this time changed the book's title, he sent the new query package. The agent requested his novel, loved it, and agreed to represent him. Charley adds, "He told me it was unprofessional to send my photo unless I was marketing nonfiction. He also expressed confusion over the excerpt, not understanding what I hoped to accomplish with it. But, despite his complaints, apparently my approach worked.

"At first, I'd think that any day the phone would ring and he'd have sold it. I was naive. Not even a good salesman can sell everything." For two years Charley waited for the phone to ring, but the only time he heard from his agent was if he made the call. He never saw a progress report or even a copy of a rejection letter. In the meantime, Charley continued to write, pouring out five more novels, two of them in horror.

A turning point came after he'd read Dean Koontz's out-of-print book, *Writing Bestselling Fiction.* "I decided to write to him both to thank him for all of his books and to ask him several questions about writing horror. Dean wrote back a personal letter supporting my career and answering my questions, but he cautioned me that the horror market had died for all but established authors like himself. It came as a complete surprise. I felt I should have heard it from my agent."

Meanwhile, Charley checked with two publishers who had requested to see his novel, leads he'd turned over to the agent. The publishers found no record of receiving the manuscript. He decided to terminate the verbal contract with his agent.

Looking back, Charley says, "Knowing what I know now, I wouldn't have waited so long to terminate." Even so, through all the rejections and then the disappointment of his first experience with an agent, he never considered giving up.

"I made a deep-level commitment to myself that this is what I want to do for the rest of my life," he says. His advice to other writers: Read. Take courses on writing. Find a good independent editor. Find a supportive critique group, not one that slashes and burns. "When you finish a novel, put it away for two to three months, and then come back fresh."

Charley has decided not to market *The Hidebehind* and his other horror novels until he gets word that the horror market has rebounded. In the meantime, his mainstream adventure story has one agent's blessing and the interest of a small publisher who has recommended it to a movie producer. And, Charley is almost finished with a thriller.

"I've always been a storyteller, but I needed to learn how to write," Charley adds. "It's just now that I feel capable of writing a bestseller."

CHAPTER THREE

Ready to Market?

- First—Finish
- Diagnostic Checklists
- Writer's Critique Groups
- Professional Editors
- Categorize Your Novel
- Sixteen Ways to Describe Your Novel
- Tempting Titles
- Breakthrough: "Long Deserved; Long Overdue" by Paul Cody

I like to tell my writing students the story of a novelist who, using the wishful-thinking tool kit, garnered 124 rejection letters before an agent said those magic words, "I love your book." One hundred and twenty-four rejections! I assume that you are asking yourself whether or not you could emotionally withstand so many rejections. Could you stay the course?

Before you jump to any conclusions, consider the rest of this novice's story. He patterned the main character after himself and the other characters after his friends. He had barely researched books on writing; instead, he thought he could win the day with the marketing skills he already possessed and used in his sales work.

Had he known more, he would never have sought publication of those early versions. In my opinion, 120 of those 124 rejections were well-deserved. Although he could take pride in having written a novel, it was far from any standard of professionalism—and he didn't know it. The last four rejections came after he had rewritten the book half a dozen times and the first chapter about twenty times—per the suggestions of the critique group he joined, from my editorial recommendations, and after he'd taken some classes in how to write novels.

Although many novelists get rejected because they lack the expertise supplied by this book, most market too soon—before their manuscripts are polished. In fact, I believe that only one percent of the novels submitted for publication are both structurally correct and appropriately polished.

If you were to call me on the phone and ask me, sight unseen, whether or not you should begin marketing your novel, I would not miss a beat predicting: "Your book's not ready." In fact, in my fifteen years as a freelance editor, I have *never* received a book that was ready to sell. My literary agent friends tell me that such a thing is as infrequent as a snow storm in mid summer.

You, the novelist, it seems, are the last person able to judge market readiness. After all, your story has sprung as if Athena from the head of Zeus. You've loved, loathed, and lived with your characters and story for months or years. You've created, examined, rewritten, and typed every word. Isn't it silly for you to believe that you could, after all of that, be objective about your writing? Like all writers, I, too, face this problem, which is why I rely upon a bevy of writer-editors to keep me on the straight and narrow.

Some of you may assume, erroneously, that this is where your literary agent or editor comes in. Some of us carry images of famous editors of the past, editors like Maxwell Perkins, who did in fact make substantial contributions to the finished products of some of our most revered writers: Thomas Wolfe, Ernest Hemingway, Taylor Caldwell, and others. While you may get editorial help from your literary agent and eventually from an editor, they are unlikely to devote time to your development unless your novel is all-but-ready to go to press. Because it's a buyer's market, your product—your novel—is easy to pass over if it isn't nearly ready to be placed on the shelves. Obviously, the problem is that most writers assume their manuscripts *are* perfect.

Although the focus of this book enables you to attract agent or editor interest by writing a compelling query letter and scintillating synopsis, this chapter emphasizes having a manuscript worthy of marketing in the first place.

First—Finish

It may come as a surprise that to sell your book you must first have written your entire novel. In stark contrast, previously unpublished *nonfiction* book writers can secure a contract having submitted as little as one finished chapter, although three chapters is more typical. They must also produce a comprehensive report called a book proposal outlining all kinds of market considerations and a comparison of their book idea with existing competitive titles. This subject is covered in my book *Nonfiction Book Proposals Anybody Can Write.*

So why this apparent discrimination against first-time novelists?

A nonfiction book can be written fairly quickly. Fiction, on the other hand, may take years to develop and complete. Also, it's one thing to write a terrific first three to five chapters of a novel. It's entirely another to carry the excitement and characterization and plotting through the vast troubling middle section of a novel to a nail-biting conclusion. Over long, bitter experience, publishers and literary agents have recognized that unpublished authors must prove they can deliver an entire, well-crafted novel. Only then will a publisher risk its money. This avoids potential disappointment and legal sticky-wickets all around.

Exceptions abound. I enjoyed a workshop with Robert Ferringo, whose first thriller made bestsellerdom. I asked how he had marketed *Horse Latitudes* and was surprised when he said he'd written a brief query letter and enclosed the first few pages of the novel. His first agent, Sandra Dijkstra, recognized his outstanding writing from the sample and sold the book *based only on a partial* (part of a book); he had not yet finished his novel. As I said, exceptions abound, and the marketplace provides direct feedback for self-confident writers testing whether they can join this elite minority.

The trends and styles of novel writing often demand that you alter the way you conceived your book. You will be asked to rewrite. It will be up to you to define how much these changes improve your book or to refuse changes that would compromise your vision.

To become a member of "the one-percent club," those one percent of writers whose works are truly ready for sale, first, check your manuscript against one or all of the following objective sounding boards:

- diagnostic checklists
- a writer's critique group
- a professional editor

Diagnostic Checklists

Any number of checklists exist to self-diagnose problem areas. Some books are entirely checklists, such as *The 38 Most Common Fiction Writing Mistakes* by Jack Bickham. Others identify areas of craft from which writers can make their own checklists, such as *Dare to Be a Great Writer: 329 Keys to Powerful Fiction* by Leonard Bishop. Others will show you how to edit your own manuscript, such as *Self-Editing For Fiction Writers* by Renni Browne and Dave King.

The Resource Directory of this book lists books that offer diagnostic checklists and others that are great overviews of the essentials of novel craft.

Writer's Critique Groups

Occasionally, writers, some published and famous, will say that writers should never show works-in-progress to another soul. These isolationists believe that opinions from others could contaminate their crisp original vision and reduce their stories to a pile of limp spaghetti. I suspect these old-paradigm people still live as though every man is an island and you can't trust anyone. Or, they've never recovered from their experience of having been chewed up and spit out by a cannibalistic critique group.

I see the art and skill of critique very differently. A compatible writer's group of mature adults can help you grow, develop, and reach your goal of getting published years sooner than you would have on your own. A writer's critique group provides a forum of peers to listen to, respond to, and critique your writing. They support both you the writer and you the person.

You don't have to be in Mensa to recognize a group running contrary to your best interests as a writer or to your sanity as a person. A group must meet your personal and professional standards. Effective critique is a give-and-take process. In general, look for (or assemble) a group of writers who embrace these fundamental guidelines:

- All members cooperate with and support all group members.
- The majority of group members enjoy a similar level of development, with most displaying comparable levels of skill and knowledge of craft.
- All members act to help all others reach their full potential as writers, as defined by each member.

Adopt the good attitude that the success of each member of your group enhances the success of every other member. There is plenty of room for everyone in your group to succeed.

Once you and your friends agree on the guidelines, make sure you establish other agreements, to the effect that:

- All members commit to learning how to give and take constructive criticism.
- All members remain active in their writing, able to fulfill three deadlines per ten-week interval, with exceptions for occasional "sabbaticals" at appropriate times in the writing process.
- All members commit to "continued education," to taking classes, attending conferences, and reading novels in their own category and instructional books on novel craft.

Although I've met writers who shrink in fear from the "exposure" involved in sharing a work with a group of like-minded aspiring writers, I view critique groups as a chance to save face, such as when a group advised me recently about the start of this book. "No, Elizabeth, we don't think the image of unpublished novelists as floundering deep-sea divers awaiting rescue will encourage writers." Too negative. Too scary. I agreed.

A good critique group must master the fine art of critique. We benefit from the insight of others because we can't always see our own work objectively. On balance, of all the criticism and praise I have received about my writing, at least 80 percent was accurate and 100 percent was helpful.

Save yourself postage. Save yourself the emotional expense of rejection. Find a good critique group and rewrite based on their recommendations.

Professional Editors

Since I work as an independent book editor, I am necessarily biased toward the advantages of working with one. You may question what an editor can add that you won't already know from the use of diagnostic checklists and feedback from a savvy critique group. It's true that some novelists write so well they may not receive enough help from professional editing to warrant the expense. They are the talented and gifted few who occupy the far end of the bell-shaped curve; bless their lucky stars.

The critique process is as helpful as the critique group's collective level of skill, and as the writer's ability to take criticism and revise. However, one of the limitations of most critique groups is that a novel is read chapter by chapter (or in lesser portions) over a prolonged period of time, making it difficult for group members to critique continuity, unity, and relevance of every section to the whole.

In contrast, a professional book editor combs through a manuscript looking at it as one complete unit as well as individual parts. Editors, like all professionals, vary in experience and skill, but a competent editor will identify your strengths as well as weaknesses and help you through multiple revisions, if necessary, until your book is ready to sell.

Rewriting according to the suggestions of an independent book editor can shorten your learning curve and get you published years ahead of the decade or more a first novel usually takes. The downside is the cost for editorial services. The risk you take is trusting an unknown editor.

The cost of professional editing of a novel varies from lows of $2 per page to highs of $10 per page, although I know of an editor of a very famous novelist who charges the equivalent of a down payment on a home to edit a novel. You'll probably pay higher-per-page amounts to editors who live in large cities, especially in the Big (Publishing) Apple, and you'll pay higher fees to editors who have been in business longer. Beware, just because an editor lives in a big city or has been in business for a long time does not guarantee your happiness or a job well done.

Like most services, you take less chance of making a poor choice if you select someone recommended by those who have used the service. Ask writing friends for recommendations. Write to literary agents. Many maintain lists of freelance editors to whom they refer clients. Check with writers' organizations. Some editors list themselves in *Literary Market Place*, a resource book you can find in your library.

From editors you contact, request the names of writer-clients and contact them. Ask editors for a sample critique. Request a contract that clearly states what money you will pay and when, and what you'll get for that investment.

Let's assume that you use diagnostic checklists to edit your own novel. You rewrite and get feedback on the book from your critique group friends. Maybe one of them offers to read the entire book. You rewrite again. When you wouldn't change a word, when the novel is the best you can make it, you invest in your future career and hire a freelance editor. Your perfect creation comes back bleeding with red ink, but you agree with most of the suggestions. You rewrite again. Now what? Are you ready to market?

If you can afford the cost, send it back to the independent book editor for a second edit. Chances are that your story will have transformed from an Edsel to a Mustang but is not yet a sleek Jaguar. Take the criticism and write again. Perhaps, again and again. Now—maybe—you're ready to query a literary agent or editor. Or, you may want to hire an editor one more time. If your editor has already seen the manuscript three times, send it to a new book editor for a fresh-eyes' edit.

Today's readiness standards are much higher than at any other time in history. Even so, every writer reaches the day when it's time to let the child of their imagination venture into the world, to be judged worthy or unworthy of publication.

Categorize Your Novel

The creative process demands that you write your novel without concern or care about what you've written or where it fits among the diversity of fiction. However, once written, you must categorize your novel in order to sell it. Otherwise, you chance confusion and rejection. For example, suppose you describe your novel as a romance when it is really a contemporary mainstream story that happens to include a romance. You are sure to get rejections from agents who don't represent category romances. Getting a request for your thriller, when what you have actually written is undiluted horror, wastes both your time and that of an agency that doesn't represent horror. Not to mention your emotional cost.

Like it or not, to market effectively, you must categorize your novel in ways that match current labels. Although many of these labels remain fixed, others are in flux. For instance, you might get rejected if your query said that you had written a *western*, but be welcomed with open arms if you've written a *Novel of the West*.

To sensitize you to these labels, this section explains and defines the three large categories of fiction and some of the dozens of subcategories. I'll discuss what to do if your novel really doesn't fit a category. Also, Sidebar 3-1 gives the average length for different types of fiction.

Broadly speaking, all fiction falls into three main categories:

- Genre Fiction
- Mainstream Fiction
- Literary Fiction

GENRE FICTION

Genre fiction is the stock-in-trade of most publishing. Also referred to as category fiction, genre novels can be easily pigeonholed. Produced as mass-market paperbacks and stocked everywhere from bookstores and libraries to pharmacies, gas stations, and one-stop-shopping megastores, genre fiction has traditionally included: romance, westerns, mysteries, science fiction, fantasy, and horror.

According to *The Concise Oxford Dictionary of Literary Terms*, "a literary genre is a recognizable and established category of written works employing such common conventions as will prevent readers...from mistaking it for another kind." To determine whether your novel fits a genre, ask this key question: Is your novel a lot like others in its plot, style, and characterization? If your answer is yes, then you might be writing to the specifications of a genre.

Genre fiction is notorious for having more rigid structural expectations and guidelines for its plot, characterization, length, and writing style than the other two broad categories of fiction. That's because avid readers of a particular genre want to be guaranteed a comparable experience to the last book they read. No left-field surprises for them!

This doesn't mean that genre fiction is any less original or excellent in craft—although it sometimes takes a bad rap for mediocrity. What's true is that the form is more prescribed—much like ballet or opera, for instance. Within the requirements of form, however, genre writers enjoy as much freedom of expression as the next writer.

As particular genre writers gain confidence and stature, many seek less rigid rules and constraints. These writers "break away" or "break out" with single titles that no longer fit the genre. Although category, or genre, romance commands about 45 percent of the mass paperback market and 20–25 percent of all fiction sales each year, these break-away writers carry loyal readers with them. Writers like Nora Roberts, Rosamunde Pilcher, or

Julie Garwood. Using their former readers as a word-of-mouth base, their new work builds an even larger readership.

The same break-away process is true for writers in every genre, and these writers graduate, in income and fame, if not also in literary expression, to the next category of fiction.

MAINSTREAM FICTION

What makes breaking into mainstream fiction versus genre fiction more difficult for unknown and first-time novelists is the pressure to gain name recognition. Readers of mainstream fiction ask their local bookseller for a book by its title or author name. A mainstream reader says, "I would like *Airframe*" or "I would like Crichton's newest thriller." Although genre readers also develop fierce loyalties to specific writers, they are primarily lovers of the type of novel, i.e. the genre, and instead say, "Where is the mystery section?"

Mainstream fiction, also often referred to as commercial fiction, is expected to make money for all concerned, and more money than a genre novel. In fact, publishers are under tremendous pressure to turn their commercial fiction into bestsellers. The *New York Times* bestseller list is a lineup, primarily, of mainstream fiction. In fact, you could say that this prestigious list is dominated by F.W.G.s (pronounced "fwigs"), Famous White Guys—like Clancy, Crichton, Grisham, King, Koontz, and Sheldon. Sometimes their names appear several times in the top ten or fifteen. Like these famous men, women authors who make this elite list have often come up through the ranks of genre authors and created enough reader recognition to become bestselling break-away authors. Women authors such as Rice, Cornwell, McMillan, Steel, or Grafton, for instance. Or, they will be literary writers whose commercial appeal has been great enough to make the list, authors such as Esquivel, Smiley, and Didion.

Mainstream fiction is expected to explore a larger literary landscape than genre and include and develop more characters in greater depth. Its greater length allows its authors to explore the full range of the craft.

LITERARY FICTION

While literary fiction may sell well and have recognizable if not famous authors, its most outstanding feature is the writing style, or voice, of the author. Evaluating this is such a subjective decision, the lines between the label of literary and mainstream writing are easily blurred. In truth, there are only opinions, no objective criteria.

Literary fiction demands the most of its readers, because it may not entertain or care about entertaining the reader. By genre and commercial standards, a literary novel may be too long, or too short, plotless and seemingly pointless, and still win a Pulitzer Prize. It may also be read and appreciated by fewer readers, perhaps thousands rather than tens of thousands or even millions. Even so, an appreciative reader of a literary work is unlikely to forget the book, the author, or the style. Successful literary writers who have reached far beyond a small audience include Toni Morrison, Umberto Eco, Margaret Atwood, or John Updike.

Literary fiction has more original everything; it develops characters in greater depth and it features greater and more profound use of symbolism, imagery, theme, and voice. Some literary writers manage to combine the best of all worlds, incorporating the plot finesse of commercial writers with outstanding individual style. The results can be literary novels that make the bestseller lists. Novelists like Barbara Kingsolver, Anne Tyler, Larry McMurtry, Jane Smiley, or Pat Conroy.

BROAD CATEGORY CONFUSION

As you may have guessed, some authors cross over the lines of these three categories. A genre writer stretches and begins to introduce mainstream elements. A commercial writer affects such a touching character portrait and uses so many wonderful metaphors, a reader wonders how the work differs from literary. A literary writer includes such a hard-driving plot, are you sure it isn't mainstream?

Because genre writing has the most definite requirements, if you suspect that you may be writing a genre novel but aren't sure, you must do two things: read widely in the genre for which you may be writing, and seek writer's guidelines from publishers. Remember, with genre writing, the form, the specifications, cannot be overlooked.

Among my clients, the greatest marketing damage comes in mistaking mainstream for literary writing. To proclaim oneself a literary writer—and then not to be categorized that way by agents or editors—involves a loss of face. Because the distinction between literary and mainstream is subjective, if you are uncertain whether you are a literary writer, describe your book as "serious mainstream" and let an agent or editor correct you. In this case, I would not advise you to use the word "commercial" because of its connotations of entertainment over art.

Sixteen Ways to Describe Your Novel

In addition to the three broad ways to categorize your novel, you'll also want to be versatile with other categories and subcategories, including the following sixteen.

1. Mystery, Suspense
2. Thrillers, Espionage
3. Western, Frontier; Novel of the West
4. Action and Adventure; Military
5. Science fiction; Fantasy; Horror
6. Romance; Women's fiction
7. Ethnic; Multicultural
8. Humor
9. Children's; Young adult
10. Gay, Bisexual, Lesbian; Feminist
11. Generation X, Off-beat Mainstream, Noir
12. Experimental; Erotic; Magical realism
13. Inspirational, Religious; New-age, Mystical, Spiritual
14. Historical or Contemporary
15. Crossovers
16. Blockbusters, High concept

1. MYSTERY, SUSPENSE

Approximately 850–900 *new* mystery titles are published annually. What at one time was a limited category of genre mystery has multiplied and divided into many subcategories and spread out into mainstream and literary writing. When you contact an agent or editor about the mystery you have written, be specific. Is your story a police procedural, a cozy, a puzzle, a private eye, a caper, a malice domestic, an amateur sleuth? Is it a who-dun-it, how-dun-it, or why-dun-it? Before you make claim to having written any of these, learn what they are by studying the unique requirements for each mystery subcategory.

Another defining element of mysteries is a strong protagonist, one so distinctive that he or she can become the sleuth for a series. Like M.K. Wren's Conan Flagg. Like Sue Grafton's Kinsey Millhone. Like Ed McBain's Matthew Hope.

The easiest way to distinguish suspense from mystery is to know when the crime occurs. Mysteries focus on crimes that have already been committed. Reader interest comes from figuring out the who-dun-it and why. New crimes may be committed, but the story will focus on bringing to justice the criminal who committed the crime that opens the book. In contrast, suspense novels feature criminals and crimes as yet to be committed, although the criminal may be known to have committed terrible

---

Sidebar 3-1
HOW LONG SHOULD MY NOVEL BE?

* The average lengths of different types of novels

Genre	Words	Pages
Young readers	10,000–15,000	40–60
Middle readers	20,000–37,500	80–150
Young adult	45,000–62,500	180–250
Adult literary	65,000–85,000 and up	260–340
Genre mystery	65,000–75,000	260–300
Mystery/Suspense	70,000–90,000	280–360
Thrillers	85,000–100,000	340–400
Science fiction	65,000–85,000 and up	260–340
Fantasy	80,000–120,000	320–480
Historical	100,000–110,000	400–440
Mainstream	85,000–110,000	340–440
Genre romance	read publishers' guidelines	
Most genre romance	50,000–85,000	200–340
Regency romance	70,000–75,000	280–300
Contemporary Women's	80,000–100,000	320–400

*Page lengths are based on double-spaced manuscript pages with 250 words per page. Consider the length of printed pages to be the same as manuscript pages. First-time novelists may be asked to be more conservative in their books' lengths.

acts in the long-ago past. Reader interest comes from anticipation of a heinous crime and fear for the life of the hero or heroine. Thus, suspense novels include subcategories such as women-in-jeopardy, romantic suspense, and psychological suspense.

2. THRILLERS, ESPIONAGE

In some cases it may be difficult to draw the dividing line between a suspense novel and a thriller. That said, thrillers are likely to involve more action, violence, weaponry, and a multitude of interlocking and exotic settings, characters, and plot twists. The evil is known and crimes will have been committed in the past and continue throughout the book.

Thrillers are a type of action and adventure novel, but this genre has developed a whole set of subcategories of their own such as: techno, medical, serial killer, psychological, courtroom, international, and espionage.

3. WESTERNS, FRONTIER; NOVEL OF THE WEST

The white-hat, black-hat traditional western made famous by the late Louis L'Amour seems destined for Boothill. In its place, a more realistic novel has taken root with greater character depth and respect to all the people of the West: women, African Americans, Mexicans, Asians, Native Americans, as well as white men. Taking a more thoughtful approach, these frontier novels, also called Novels of the West, tend to be mainstream rather than genre westerns like their predecessors. A recent break out from the category of this latest category is called Woman's Novel of the West.

4. ACTION AND ADVENTURE; MILITARY

Although adventure stories are a label given to novels with lots of fun, friendship in the face of adversity, and pure adventure, they are not the same as what is called "action and adventure" novels.

Action-and-adventure novels are considered "male" novels, typically x-rated for violence and sexuality. Men at war. Men brandishing Uzis, M-16s, and combat weapons. Paramilitary men. Tough men stopping terrorists, neo-nazis, cult-killing crazies.

5. SCIENCE FICTION; FANTASY; HORROR

Sibling to action and adventure, science fiction places more emphasis on exploration of ideas, new frontiers, than on techno-weaponry—except for military sci-fi. Science fiction has as many subcategories as mysteries. If you think you're writing this type of novel, you'll need confidence in placing your novel among such categories as: space opera, hard sf, science fantasy, sociological (i.e. soft) sf, dystopian sf, and humorous sf. Since the '80s, a new subcategory emerged in the sci-fi world: Cyberpunk features futuristic worlds dominated by computers.

Similar to mystery and suspense, fantasy and science fiction are oriented in opposite directions in terms of time. Fantasy looks to the past while science fiction generally looks forward. Furthermore, one might classify science fiction as commanding more of the realm of the logical left brain, whereas fantasy dwells in the land of the irrational, the fantastic, the magical and intuitive—the right brain. Whereas science fiction extrapolates from reality, fantasy never pretends to have ever been there. Fantasy, too, has its subcategories: dark, high, traditional, urban. Before you begin marketing, learn the differences between one subcategory and another.

Horror, the once-new genre on the block, is the evil twin of science fiction and fantasy. Ranging from horror's subcategories of splatterpunk, vampire, popular, and literary horror, this genre has seen roller-coaster ups and downs. It soared into high-dollar heights in the eighties, a time that made King, Koontz, Straub, Rice, and Barker household celebrity names. It plummeted in the mid-nineties, dead as a zombie, except for the established stars and teen king of horror, R.L. Stine. Like the vampire that returns to rest in its coffin, horror remains in repose, but I doubt it can be killed. Horror novelists having a tough time selling their novels as horror have been advised to market them under other labels, such as suspense, dark fantasy, or dark paranormal romance. Horror is a great example of how a label can work against an aspiring writer, and also of how capricious but important categorization may be. While you are waiting for horror to rise again, accumulate some short-story credits by selling "dark" stories to the still-active fanzine, and magazine, and e-zine markets. Join Horror Writers of America. Bide your time. Keep writing.

6. ROMANCE; WOMEN'S FICTION

Although the formula for all romances remains the same through the ages—boy/man, girl/woman, attraction, misunderstanding, happy ending—a romance today might take place in a former life (reincarnational), through a time-gate (time-travel), involve ghosts (paranormal), or take place in various historical periods, including in the Regency period in England (1811–1820), or in modern times and places. The heroine and hero might be almost any age of consent, and they need not be virginal. Nowadays, the heroine might be "with child," or be a single parent. Nearly anything goes, as long as it's, well, romantic. Without doubt, romances remain the most popular of all the genres, claiming one out of every two paperbacks sold. Publishers abound, as do imprints. If you are a writer of romance or women's fiction, you will do yourself a favor to read *Romantic Times*, a magazine covering publishers, guidelines, agents, and support organizations. Available only to members of Romance Writers of America, I recommend you join a local chapter. The only romance categories that are now defunct are bodice-rippers—now seen for what they portrayed: humiliation, subjugation, and rape; and the passé Gothic romances, with their dark, windy castles or mansions and dark, suspicious, threatening heroes.

Women's fiction, including women's romantic fiction, describes non-genre, mainstream writing. That means formulas, tip sheets, and guidelines no longer apply, and the stories must display greater scope and characterization than their cousins in category romance. Women's fiction focuses on issues and situations of interest to women, but it may not have the tied-in-a-bow ending of traditional romance. Many authors of women's fiction are break-away genre writers who have found a larger playground, larger royalties, and more readers.

7. ETHNIC; MULTICULTURAL

A reflection of several decade's emphasis in our educational systems on "diversity," the ethnic or multicultural novel has finally wedged a permanent place in "mainstream" publishing. Supported by grants, foundations, and sales to educational institutions, ethnic and multicultural publishers have had a chance to sink roots. This category's novelists typically belong to the ethnic, racial, or cultural background that they portray through their stories' settings and characters. These new voices have increasingly gained the attention and acclaim they deserve. Some of the better-known authors include Amy Tan, Alice Walker, Isabelle Allende, and from my home town—Eugene, Oregon—Chang-rae Lee for *Native Speaker*.

8. HUMOR

The humor novel is an endangered species. Only a handful of agents list "humor/satire" as a category of novels they are willing to consider. One explanation offered by an agent I spoke with was that humor has been usurped by movies and visual mediums. When consumers feel in a mood for comedy, they trot down to their video stores and rent Steve Martin. Were they to visit their local bookstore and say, "Hey, I'd like a good humor novel," they might draw furrowed brows. Humorists like Dave Barry and Bill Cosby write funny nonfiction. But wherefore the section on humor novels?

If you have that unique capacity to make people laugh, you may have to infiltrate another category and add a humorous twist. Write a romantic comedy for Harlequin's romantic comedy imprint. Write a mystery caper or a mystery with twisted humor like Carl Hiaasen or light humor like Carol Higgins Clark. Write science-fiction humor. But, don't try to write a humor novel, or worse yet, a humor novel with a romance and a mystery set in cyberspace. Unless you're Tom Robbins. Too tough a sale.

9. CHILDREN'S; YOUNG ADULT

The most important decision to make when categorizing your writing for children is determining the age of your readers. Seven- to nine-year-olds begin reading novels, referred to as "chapter books," that average only 6,000 words in manuscript form. By ages eight to twelve, readers have progressed to "real" novels that average 25,000 words. The last category for children's books is the young-adult novel, averaging about 200 manuscript pages, about 50,000 words.

If you seek to write for children, you should not rely solely upon the number of words in your manuscript. Age-appropriate language, character behavior, and themes figure strongly in successful children's writing, in addition to mastery of the craft.

10. GAY, BISEXUAL, LESBIAN; FEMINIST

The categorization of a novel into gay, lesbian, or feminist is more a matter of setting the work apart from others to reach the intended audience than it is any matter of form. Thus, you can have a lesbian romance, a gay mystery, a feminist mainstream novel. The distinction is only one of shared values, or sexual orientation of the characters, not of craft. Especially now that homosexuality is no longer a skeleton in our collective closet, the literature has found support among niche publishers, whose mission is to publish and support gay or lesbian writers. The same is true for feminist writing for which niche publishers have dedicated their efforts. A measure of the growing success of gay, lesbian, and feminist fiction is the expansion of what is called specialty or niche book lines within large publishers.

11. GENERATION X, OFF-BEAT MAINSTREAM, NOIR

It is natural that the offspring of the baby-boom generation, the so-called "Generation X," would seek its own form and voices. The most distinctive characteristic of these novels is main characters that are twenty-something, disillusioned, and extremely quirky. In fact, a Gen-X novel shares a great deal with other "experimental" fiction by emphasizing oddball characters in oddball and alternative settings and scenarios, sometimes to the omission of plot. Also called "off-beat mainstream" (perhaps a less scary label to oldster agents and editors than "Gen-X"), many of these novels qualify to be called "noir," a literary translation of what commercial writers call "dark." A noir novel, for any generation of reader, plays out its themes through the shadow nature of the human being—through violence, masochism, and symbolic countercultural acts, none of which are gratuitous, as they might seem in the commercial action or military novel. Like Chuck Palahniuk's debut novel *Fight Club*, noir novels make statements about life and culture, and they include layers of meaning and symbolism. This kind of novel is extremely difficult to write well.

12. EXPERIMENTAL; EROTIC; MAGICAL REALISM

Yesterday's experimental fiction is today's new category. What distinguishes experimental fiction from all other types is its departure from traditional structure and style. Perhaps the writer decides to experiment with point of view, addressing the audience directly, and shifting willy-nilly between the audience, first person, third-person, and omniscience. Also known as "avant-garde," experimental fiction is difficult to write, and just as challenging to read. In contrast to traditional fiction, the author of experimental fiction may not "care" about the reader's involvement or seek to create what is called "verisimilitude," the illusion of reality. Instead, the writer's intent is to experiment with form, structure, or style. In the earlier part of the twentieth century, writers like James Joyce and Gertrude Stein experimented with new methods of fiction writing—stream-of-consciousness, automatic writing, and absurd juxtapositions of images.

At one time, noir as well as erotic fiction were considered experimental but have since developed into categories of their own. The most distinctive characteristic of erotic fiction is a more realistic portrayal of sex than in romances, for instance, and an absence of euphemisms. Like writers of humor, writers of erotica may write suspense, mystery, mainstream, thrillers, or other types of novels. It's not the form as much as how the authors imbue the inherent sexuality of life into their stories.

A sub-type of experimental fiction that has emerged with substantial popularity is called magical realism. According to *The Concise Oxford Dictionary of Literary Terms*, magical realism is "a kind of modern fiction in which fabulous and fantastical events are included in a narrative that otherwise maintains the 'reliable' tone of objective realistic report." Nowadays, this form of writing is mostly associated with writers from Central and South America, though its earliest roots trace to literature in Germany in the 1950s. *One Hundred Years of Solitude* by Gabriel Garcia Marquez and *Like Water for Chocolate* by Laura Esquivel are two of the more famous recent examples.

13. INSPIRATIONAL, RELIGIOUS; NEW-AGE, MYSTICAL, SPIRITUAL

Religious fiction, also called Christian fiction, used to be a weak David next to the secular Goliath of publishing. Religious fiction often showed less excellence in craft. It has always been dogged by a top-heavy, scripturally supported message weighing down the story. With the revitalization of religious publishing, more fiction is being published and more religious writers are writing. Competition among talented writers has spurred growth in writing excellence until published religious novelists are on a par with secular novelists. Because different publishers adhere to different religious beliefs, it is all-important to follow publisher guidelines before marketing.

Inspirational writing, a more expanded label than religious fiction, formerly embraced denominational writing as well as nondenominational and even nonreligious writing. Inspirational fiction today is synonymous with religious or Christian publishing.

Nonreligious, inspirational writing has a different label. When the novelist conveys spiritual ideas—uplifting messages that do not in and of themselves belong to any particular religious creed—he is probably writing spiritual, "new-age" or "mystical" fiction. A recent bestselling example is James Redfield's *The Celestine Prophecy*.

14. HISTORICAL OR CONTEMPORARY

It's easy to categorize a novel set in ancient Greece or in 1997, but what about a story that takes place during World War I or II? According to Persia Woolley, author of *How to Write and Sell Historical Fiction*, "historical fiction [is] set in a time other than that of the reader, with characters that react in some degree to historical events of their eras." According to my teenagers, the sixties would be historical and the fifties ancient history. Technically, fiction based on these decades could be called nostalgia novels. One rule of thumb uses the memory of those alive today as the criteria for what is historical and what is not. Since few people alive today can remember World War I, it's history! Because many people do recall World War II, that time period is within contemporary times, just barely. For clarity involving decades within the last fifty to sixty years, make sure to describe the time period: set in World War II; set in the fifties; and there will be no confusion.

A variation on the historical mainstream novel is the epic. Epic novels encompass a larger span of time and cast of characters and involve seminal historical events. These are big books, like D. Marion Wilkinson's *Not Between Brothers* that covers the birth of Texas.

Another popular subcategory of historical novels is the family saga. The distinguishing characteristic is a family of strong characters that can be traced from volume to volume, generation to generation, in an interesting setting and time period. The best family sagas revolve around a core conflict or theme that integrates the entire body of work.

The biographical novel is historical mainstream fiction based on real lives and people. These are most difficult to write because they demand historical accuracy yet literary license to novelize the story, characters, and chronology.

15. CROSSOVERS

Having spent a large portion of my youth in Arizona, I became familiar with a popular postcard of a species of animal indigenous to Arizona humor, whose purpose was to amaze naive east-coast friends and family. The postcard featured the photograph of a "jackalope," a rabbit with a rack of antlers. Truly unique; neither fish nor fowl, neither bunny nor beast. So, what is it?

This is the question asked about crossover novels. That is, novels that seem like a jackalope, a crossbreed between two or more other categories. Romance and mystery. Science fiction and horror and mainstream and romance. Dean Koontz? Right? Most agents and editors shy away from crossover novels out of fear that instead of gaining more readers, they will lose more. Readers, they say, tend to be loyal to certain categories and the crossover novel is too hard to market and risks loss of readers who would like the elements of the novel that appeal to their favorite genres but dislike other elements. Dean Koontz has fought long and hard to defy categorization, having begun his career writing science fiction under a pseudonym. However, I am one of those readers who loves his suspense, sci-fi, romance, and mainstream writing, but can't stand the horrific elements. Because I also enjoy and admire Koontz's writing, I am in a quandary and almost always wait until someone else has read one of his books and can give me a violence rating.

If your writing is good enough, you will eventually find a buyer for it, but know ahead of time that writing crossover novels adds obstacles to your writer's journey.

16. BLOCKBUSTERS; HIGH CONCEPT

The novel that jumps off the charts and is the talk of the town—on nearly every talk show and read by every other person on airplane flights—is a blockbuster. It is as New York agent Albert Zuckerman says, "a Big Book." It is characterized by high stakes, such as the loss of a child's life, 350 airplane passengers, an entire nation, or all life on earth. Blockbusters also have bigger-than-life characters: Scarlett O'Hara and Rhett Butler (*Gone With the Wind*), Nurse Ratched (*One Flew Over the Cuckoo's Nest*), Jack Ryan and Ramius (*Hunt for Red October*), Ayla (*Clan of the Cave Bear*). Most blockbusters are "high concept" novels. Zuckerman defines high concept as: "a radical or even somewhat outlandish premise." *Jaws. Clan of the Cave Bear. Jurassic Park. Airport. Outbreak.* Usually the blockbuster also features strange, exotic, or technically specific settings, though rarely historic time periods. Dramatic conflict is complex and relentless. The story is typically told in multiple points of view, often from an omniscient point of view. If your novel boasts most of these features, all that remains is strong writing, a great agent, and blind luck. A fabulous book on how to create a story that captures the imagination is *Writing the Breakout Novel* by Donald Maass.

Tempting Titles

Titles sell books. "It's the first thing that draws a person to your book," says Jessica Faust, editor with Berkley Publishing. "If it doesn't clearly stand out, it might not be bought. Ask yourself, 'Would I pick up this novel?' "

You may have used one title while writing your book. Now's the time to choose a title to market your book—even though many titles chosen by the author eventually get changed by the editorial committee or the marketing department. "Don't get too wedded to your title," says Sarah Pinckney, editor with Simon & Schuster.

Titles cannot be copyrighted. Nothing is stopping you from naming your book *Roots*, *War and Peace*, or *Bridges of Madison County*. However, don't expect to get an open-hearted response from agents or editors if you do. On the other hand, identical titles sometimes happen simultaneously, without anyone knowing ahead of time. An agent told me the story of a client whose novel of women's fiction was published concurrently with another author's novel by the same title. To prevent confusion, this agent and the author sent out postcards alerting booksellers around the country. The end result was even stronger sales, simply by having brought the book—and the mix-up—to everyone's attention.

You can check your titles with *Books in Print* and *Forthcoming Books in Print*, available at your library or through some online databases.

So what makes a hot title? "The more visceral the title, the more impact on editors," one agent told me. Certainly it's got to be catchy— *Moonlight Becomes You* (Mary Higgins Clark); easy to pronounce—*The Ranch* (Danielle Steel); evocative of an interesting story—*Animal Dreams* (Barbara Kingsolver); probably short—*Airframe* (Michael Crichton).

Most important, titles must arise from your book and reflect its theme. Titles must come from within rather than from without. One of my students, Carol Craig, has selected one such a title for her book *Chocolate Soldiers*, featuring a friendship between two girls of different races during the sixties.

Jessica Faust recommends that authors keep an open mind. "It's not a bad idea to think of more than one title," she suggests. "Have four or five titles and run them by other people."

My editorial client Rainer Rey seems to be starting a pattern of alliteration with his thriller titles; *Replicator Run* and *Day of the Dove.*

Some titles contain meanings that trigger deeper emotions and may stir a reader to buy them solely because of that reason. For me, titles that do this include *Abyss* (Orson Scott Card), *Misery* (Stephen King), and *Beloved* (Toni Morrison).

Make sure that your title sounds like it matches the kind of book you are writing. It's more difficult, for instance, to include the words "love" or "heart" in a title and not have associations to the category of romance. Study the titles of books in your genre. You'll quickly notice that styles differ from mystery to suspense to thrillers to literary.

Another observation made by one agent is that a great title usually has two or three meanings. *Vital Signs* (Robin Cook). *The Left Hand of Darkness* (Ursula Le Guin). *The Maze* (Catherine Coulter). If a book is literary, the title may be allusory rather than explicit. The reader may not know what the book is about, but the possibilities draw him in.

Foreign words and phrases may be tricky as titles if your reader does not share your breadth and exposure to the particular language. *Shōgun*, for instance. With the line over the 'o' as well, what does it mean? Clearly, we didn't let the term get in the way of sales, but for a first-time author, foreign words hold a greater risk.

Countless writers, stuck for title inspiration, have turned to the Bible, poetry, famous quotes, Shakespeare (I actually have a category romance novel titled *To Be or Not to Be*), even to clichés or lullabies. How about *When the Bough Breaks?* Don't feel stuck with the original; twist it, turn it. Substitute a new word for an old word to get a fresh feeling. *Where Devils Fear To Tread* creeps me out just thinking about it!

To sharpen your ability to select a market-worthy title for your novel, I highly recommend two magazine articles. The first, "An Untitled Column," by Nancy Kress appeared in the December 1994 issue of *Writer's Digest* magazine. She discussed practical techniques for combining parts of speech in different ways as a method for creating titles. The second, "Titles," by Barnaby Conrad appeared in the February 1996 issue of *The Writer*, and discusses sources of inspiration for finding titles. As always, read *Publishers Weekly* and notice what titles seem most effective to you and why.

* * *

Let's assume you are finally ready to market. You've heard you may need a synopsis, but you've never written a query or a synopsis. In the chapters that follow, you'll learn everything you need to know about these marketing tools. Once mastered, you'll stand a much better chance of joining the one-percent club.

BREAKTHROUGH

"Long Deserved; Long Overdue"

Paul Cody, author of literary novels

Those who don't know Paul Cody might think success came easily. After all, Baskerville Publishers offered him a dual-book contract and in 1995 and 1996, he enjoyed the publication of his literary novels, *The Stolen Child* and *Eyes Like Mine*. The reviews of his first book glowed with praise, and portions of the book were excerpted in *Harper's* magazine.

His life has always involved writing, and reading. At age nineteen or twenty, he sold a short story to a St. Louis magazine. At twenty-two, he sold an article to the *Boston Globe*.

"Virtually every day of the twenty-odd years since then, I've wondered if I'm a crazy masochist. I considered going to law school or any number of things that would pay better and be interesting," Paul reflects. But writing continued to have a pull he couldn't resist.

As a graduate of Cornell University's Masters in Fine Arts program, Paul built a supportive community of writers in Ithaca, New York. He'd written three or four novels by the time he began marketing *The Stolen Child* and *Eyes Like Mine*. One of the Cornell faculty members recommended him to agent Georges Borchardt, who represents Nobel laureates and Pulitzer Prize winners and takes on few new clients. "When Georges Borchardt accepted me as a client, I thought I'd made it," Paul admits.

But, Borchardt was unable to sell his work. Paul asked around and found another agent, but with the same results. After two years of unproductive agent representation, Paul had an amicable parting. He says, "I think they felt frustrated and so did I." Their efforts had focused on securing a sale from the larger New York publishing houses, although a few smaller publishers had been approached.

Paul decided to concentrate on small publishers of literary fiction and turned his attention to writing a solid query letter, in which he described his writing credentials and offered a one-paragraph synopsis of his story. "In almost every case, maybe because I sounded like I'd been around the track a few times and knew what I was doing, most agents or editors I queried would request at least a portion of the manuscript. Once they got it, half would say 'not for me', but the other half would request the whole book."

Paul also credits his 50 percent success rate with researching which agents or publishers handle literary novels. He maintained a list of both and freely shares it with his friends.

"I think that sometimes you need to put in ten or fifteen years of absolutely banging your head against the wall in frustration, but if you keep the faith and keep writing, you'll eventually get yourself published," Paul says. Within a few months of pursuing his own efforts at marketing, Baskerville Publishing accepted his work.

Paul attributes some of his staying power over the last twenty years to learning how to live on relatively little money. "If you are going to go write novels," Paul advises, "don't take on a huge mortgage. Live as simply as you can and it will take pressure off your work." His wife, a poet with a book of her own newly published, is supportive. She took up the slack to allow Paul one year, in which he wrote another novel. Sold to Picador USA, *So Far Gone* was released in 1998.

Paul adds, "I've tried to get perspective and say, I take great pleasure in the writing itself and I take pride in doing something I have respect for. I feel very lucky because I get to do this thing that I absolutely love."

CHAPTER FOUR

Dissecting the Synopsis

- ◆ Content
- ◆ A Model Synopsis
- ◆ Style
- ◆ Starter Kit
- ◆ A Foot in the Door: "Learning Through Critique"
  by James Axtell

Although the most common way to market a novel is via query letters to agents or editors, the heart of most query letters is a succinct summary of the book. A synopsis. For that reason, I've put this chapter on how to write a synopsis ahead of the one on how to write queries.

For some reason, many writers who can carry off writing an intricate 500-page story with elan, are befuddled by the task of summarizing their stories. They think that being required to write a synopsis is like asking a marathon runner who staggers across the finish line to sprint fifty yards more. They'd almost rather write another novel. If you have never written a synopsis, don't let this scare you. The only hard part about writing a synopsis is not knowing how before you begin.

A well-written synopsis charms all who read it and creates a desire to see the actual book. It is a seductive summary of a novel, the fire that ignites interest in an agent, editor, book buyer, and reader. In its applications, it goes far beyond being the heart of a query letter. In the next chapter of this book, you'll learn how to vary it for eight different uses, from helping you write your book in the first place to proposing a second book. Depending upon its application, the synopsis varies in size from a paragraph to as much as ten or twenty pages.

Like any other type of writing, the synopsis has a unique purpose, structure, and style. Its main purpose is to provide a summary of an entire novel. In structure, it must overview the plot, characters, and theme. In style, it's like a preview of coming attractions at the movie theater. It packages characters, dramatic moments, and plot together—the best stuff from the movie—so the agent or editor will want to read the whole book.

Let me clarify. Although some agents and editors interchange the term "outline" with "synopsis," an outline is different in form and purpose. An outline is a chapter-by-chapter summary of a novel. In contrast, a synopsis presents the entire story, in a condensed summary, as a unit, without breakdown into chapter divisions. Often, marketing directories say an agent wants an outline to accompany a query. In most cases, the agent actually means synopsis—a summary. The only way you can know for sure is to call the agent or publisher's assistant and clarify.

Ideally, the first synopsis you create would be prior to starting your novel's first draft. Then, the marketing synopsis will merely require revision and refinement of this working version. However, whether you face writing one before or after writing your book, you'll need to work closely with the following seven parts of content and the six elements of style, allowing for many drafts until the essence of the novel is distilled.

For those of you who have never seen a synopsis, Sidebar 4-1 (page 59) provides a model.

Content

You may feel so overwhelmed by the totality of your story that you feel paralyzed about how to "condense" it into a five-page summary—never mind a one-page summary. The secret is to remember the forest but attend to the trees. There are only seven parts that comprise most synopses:

- Theme
- Setting and Period
- Plot Summary
- Character Sketches
- Dialogue
- Emotional Turning Points
- Subplots

Sidebar 4-1
A MODEL SYNOPSIS*

FAMILY ACT by Pat Swope

It is 1910, and the streets of Los Angeles throng with autos and horse-drawn trams. Suffragettes and Socialists shout from soap boxes in Central Park. Vaudeville does socko business, and a handful of movie studios crank out one-reelers on sets open to the scorching sun.

Angie Alleman, our feisty, tender, insufferably stubborn heroine, is looking for love in all the wrong places.

Olin Alleman, her father, loved her when she was small, but Angie will not conform to his new wife's Old California social code, and he rejects Angie.

Angie's beauty and passion persuade sultry, erratic Santee to be her protector, her lover, her husband. When he is accused of killing twenty people in the bombing of the *Los Angeles Times*, he betrays her, deserting her to save himself. He leaves her penniless and pregnant; she is not yet sixteen.

Angie teams up with Edward McEvoy, a cocky, demanding vaudevillian. He and his wife, Belle McEvoy, become father and mother, partner and mentor, and Angie revels in the applause of the audiences and in the warmth and energy of backstage life…until she and Edward fall in love.

Edward is the one man her conscience will not let her have. He is equally tortured by their circumstances, lusting after Angie and loyal to Belle, who is ill. They dance a fandango of advance and retreat, complicated by their switch to careers in the infant movie industry, where they become director and actress. They are involved every day in the display for the screen of an emotion they must hide from the world.

Belle dies. Through the gossip of the fledgling movie mags and scandal sheets, Santee learns that he has a son. He returns to claim him, and Angie!

Angie refuses, terrified that Santee has been crazed by his persecution by the Burns Detective Agency, a precursor of the F.B.I.

In an attempt to kidnap the boy, Santee assaults Angie.

Angie fights back, and her feistiness and stubbornness, the qualities that have gotten her into trouble all her life, now save her life and that of her beloved little boy.

Angie has lost her first love, Santee, and gained Edward McEvoy, who has seen the best of her and the worst of her, and loves her to the very depth of her soul—and his.

After two years of writing and rewriting, author Pat Swope has just begun to market, beginning with a submission of this fine synopsis and a first 50-page sample to a literary contest. Family Act was a semifinalist in the 1997 Heekin Group Foundation, James Fellowship for Novel in Progress, which receives 1200–1300 submissions. It was also a semifinalist in the Colorado Gold Fiction Writers Contest.

THEME

A theme provides a rudder for an entire novel, but the truth is, most novelists, even professionals, struggle to articulate the theme of their stories. Convey your theme in one sentence or phrase, such as: to have a friend you must be a friend; as ye sow, so shall ye reap; it's not whether you win or lose, it's how you play the game. Some writers prefer to cast their themes into single words, such as revenge, friendship, power. I believe that thematic statements are stronger than single words, which beg development into positions, or themes.

Bill Lynch, author of *Dark Nights*, devotes the first paragraph of his synopsis to presenting his book's theme. Notice the somber tone, which would also set up a reader's expectation of encountering the same tone in the actual book.

Lessons about war surface in the wake of *Dark Nights*, a tale of a World War II American bomber crew's secret nighttime missions, and in the explosive and tragic consequences of a 19-year-old French girl's part in anti-Nazi sabotage. Events blend these two stories and reveal the sad lesson that in war, victory is the reward of nations; for warriors, winning may be simply surviving.

Setting and Period

Orienting your reader to the setting or period of your book can be taken care of in a simple, opening statement. In the following example written by Candy Davis, her synopsis beginning gets right to the point with such clarity that the reader can't help but feel secure, even in the world of fantasy:

> *Three Faces of the Goddess* is a historical fantasy set in 1057 B.C. near the western edge of China in the small warrior nation of Starra Pav.

Other writers mention the setting and period later in their leads. Because there are no ten commandments about synopses with thou-shalts and thou-shalt-nots, you should know that some people believe that a statement of theme or setting has no place in a synopsis. Opinions vary, even among experts. I believe that a synopsis *is* the author explaining her story; only in the actual novel must the author become Houdini and accomplish a disappearing act. Here in the synopsis, you want to project your knowledge about theme and novel structure. Stating some of these craft elements contributes to economy and clarity. Also, no character operates in a vacuum. Context shapes values, motives, and actions, and helps explain characterization.

Plot Summary

The summary of your plot is obviously the heart of the synopsis. What some writers fail to realize is that they must summarize the beginning, middle, *and* end. Nothing frustrates an agent or editor more than a teasing end to a synopsis, such as: Will Bob escape the pit of snakes in time to save Laura?

While your synopsis necessarily leaves out many details, you must provide the inciting incident—the beginning; highlights of the protagonist's efforts to reach the story goal—the middle; and the climax and its culmination in success or failure—the end. Problem. Conflict. Resolution.

One of the tests your synopsis must pass as it is read by an experienced agent or editor is whether the plot springs from character, and whether the events of the novel happen because of who your characters are, especially your protagonist—because of his strengths and weaknesses. A synopsis fails when it only gives blow-by-blow events—and then she called the police, and then the suspect left the scene, and then…These kinds of event-driven synopses reinforce a type of structure the publishing professionals *don't* want to see, what is called "episodic structure." Plot that springs mostly from character ensures that a novel has dramatic structure.

Consider this succinct synopsis by Carolyn Rose for her mystery *Consulted to Death* and note how in her lead sentence several elements can be combined in one sentence, such as characterization and setting. Mysteries are very plot-oriented as a genre, yet notice how Carolyn uses characterization like bookends, signaling that her story does spring from character. In a longer synopsis, she would have room to weave in more dashes of characterization, showing how her protagonist's strengths and weaknesses determine, in part, the plot.

Casey Brandt is smart, self-reliant and cynical; she's also divorced, disenchanted and disgusted with the New Mexico television station where the unofficial motto is: "good news is no news." Then things get worse. Her boss threatens to fire her, she discovers the body of the consultant who's recruiting her replacement, and a police detective who was once her lover calls her a prime suspect. Fearing she's being framed, Casey uses her position as Assignment Editor to conduct a reluctant investigation that turns up a wealth of suspects—her colleagues loathed and feared the consultant, and most had the opportunity to kill.

A news photographer dies next, setting off a wave of fear, accusations and chaos at the station. The District Attorney pressures police to act, and they arrest Casey's best friend, the station's former news director. Believing he's been framed, too, she probes deeper, and someone poisons chocolates delivered to the newsroom. The maintenance man raids the box and is victim number three.

A clever attorney keeps Casey out of jail but the frame is complete—when the killer tries to strangle her, detectives insist she injured herself. Terrified, angry and alone, Casey confronts a man who seems to have no motive, and uncovers the lies, blackmail and murder he used to get the on-air exposure called "face time."

Rescued by friends, she returns to the newsroom to learn her boss has been fired, she's in charge, and it's easier to complain at the bottom than command from the top.

CHARACTER SKETCHES

The best-written and most impressive synopses are those that make it clear that a story is *character driven*. Many writers devote a healthy paragraph to profiling the protagonist in order to make clear his central conflict, his motivation, his unique psychology, and his quirks—especially the character flaws and past events or trauma that make him unique and memorable.

For most novels, the synopsis is too short to sketch all of your characters. Omit the subplot characters and limit your sketches to the protagonist, major characters, and your antagonist, giving most development to the protagonist. In general, name only four or five characters and use roles to describe less essential characters, roles such as the bartender, the detective, the mother-in-law.

When summarizing a complex story or one with many subplots and a larger cast of characters, introduce characters using a list with their basic roles, similar to the style used in the program for a play. This will help orient the reader and avoid awkward introductions in the middle of the synopsis.

In the following example of a synopsis' character sketch by Patricia Hyatt for her biographical novel *Land of Thirst* take note of the inclusion of the characters' strengths and "fatal flaws." In this example, the author has sketched her two co-protagonists and the antagonist.

Captain WILLIAM NEWTON LANCASTER (protagonist). English aviator who sets records around the world in the late 1920s. An honorable man, Bill nevertheless loses his way pursuing love and redemption. The cost—death during a desperate effort to set a solo speed record in 1933 from London to Cape Town, South Africa...

JESSIE "CHUBBIE" KEITH-MILLER (protagonist). Australian aviatrix who sets records with Bill across the British Empire, and then, in America, sets speed records in her own right in the Powder Puff Derbies. She's a woman who mistakes her love of *adventure* for love of the *adventurer.* She, too, loses her way—twice—but in the end finds redemption and happiness....

HADEN CLARKE (antagonist). American writer, dead in 1932 from a bullet to his brain. A handsome, relentless seducer, Haden lives for the moment, never glancing back or looking to tomorrow. When he decides he wants what Bill Lancaster has—namely, Chubbie Keith-Miller—he uses charm and deceit to get her. Murder—or suicide? The not-guilty verdict makes no difference. The .45-caliber bullet through Haden's brain ensures his destruction—and Bill's.

DIALOGUE

Any use of dialogue in a summary heavily emphasizes the words and character voice; therefore, use it sparingly or it will detract rather than add to your effort. It may also slow pace, and dialogue consumes space. In the brevity of a synopsis, every word must be efficient.

However, well-chosen bits of dialogue can lend flavor to the bland voice of a summary. One of my favorite uses of a character's direct voice is in the synopsis for Pat Swope's historical romance (still in progress). Notice the power of emotion and clarity of her character's story problem in the synopsis opening to *I Have Loved Strangers*:

"I will *not* be a bastard forever!" Linda Alleman wails to heaven, vowing to win the respectability she craves.

EMOTIONAL TURNING POINTS

Many years ago, in my quest to teach writers how to write effective synopses, I asked a literary agent with strong editorial skills what a synopsis should include. "Emotional turning points," she said. Every novelist knows that a story contains lots of little scenes that move the plot forward, introduce complications, and develop the characters. One couldn't possibly summarize all of these little scenes; nor should they be part of a synopsis. However, little scenes should contribute to a crescendo of dramatic suspense that culminates in crises. These big scenes turn the story, as the characters come to grips with new obstacles and conflicts standing in the way of their goals. Reread Pat Swope's synopsis for *Family Act* on page 59. Notice how most of her summary leapfrogs from one big scene to another: "he betrays her…leaves her penniless and pregnant"…. "until she and Edward fall in love"…. "Belle dies"…. "Santee…returns to claim him, and Angie." All big scenes. Emotional turning points. No precious synopsis space taken up by little scenes.

The climax of a novel is the final emotional turning point. It should be emphasized in your synopsis, along with a statement regarding how your protagonist ultimately changes by book's end.

Look back at the three-paragraph synopsis given on pages 62–63 by Carolyn Rose for her novel, *Consulted to Death*. Reread the last line to see how she summed up how her protagonist was changed.

In the next chapter, I've made notations by the parts of the sample synopses that correspond to these emotional turning points.

SUBPLOTS

You'll drive yourself nuts if you try to capture all of your subplots. You'll simply have to drop most of them, just as you have to drop most of the scenes of your book. Where you have an important subplot, perhaps one inextricably involved with the main plot, you must include it in your synopsis.

Once you understand the seven elements of structure, you can turn your attention to the six elements of style. Because the most common uses of the synopsis involve marketing, the style is radically different from that used to write your novel.

Style

The purpose of the distinctive style of the synopsis is to heighten reader interest while providing a story overview. Making a synopsis generate excitement is accomplished by special handling of the following elements:

- Tense
- Viewpoint
- Nouns and Verbs
- Length
- Story Chronology
- Variations

TENSE

Chances are, you've written your book in past tense; most writers have. "She went; she saw; she conquered." However, present-tense creates a sense of immediacy and excitement that better matches a sales pitch. "She goes, she sees, she conquers." More immediate. More exciting. Note the effect of present tense in the following example, written by novelist D. Marion Wilkinson from the synopsis portion of his query:

> *Not Between Brothers* is a novel of the clash of cultures at the time of Anglo colonization of the American Southwest, and the bloody wars that soon followed.... The novel begins in 1816 as Remy Fuqua, a Scotch-Irish/French halfbreed, is suddenly and violently orphaned. Doubly damned, he bides his time in the loveless house of his strict, abusive uncle, who sells Remy's father's land—his only inheritance and lifelong dream—to save his own.

VIEWPOINT

Because the synopsis is the author's summary, it is written from the author's perspective independent of whether the actual story was written from a first-person or third-person point of view. Reread the example given above for tense. Notice the distinct overviewing, author-as-narrator viewpoint, even though the novel was written in third-person past tense.

NOUNS AND VERBS

When you write a synopsis for yourself, to clarify your book in a nugget, you can dash off flabby sentences or use passive sentence construction. When you write a synopsis that will be scrutinized by literary agents or acquisitions' editors, every word counts. Make your nouns concrete and your verbs vivid. Querying on her historical novel, *Allah's Amulet*, writer Therese Engelmann writes this synopsis; I have italicized my favorite concrete nouns and vivid verbs:

> At her mother's *grave site* in a fictional 16th century European *duchy*, eight-year-old Ella *swears* to reach her mother's home in *Persia*, so that she can live with her people. But sixteen years later, after a journey of about 95,000 words, Ella *discovers* that *assassins* have *slaughtered* her sister and all of her relatives. The

horror of this discovery *threatens* her *sanity*, but she *accepts* what she cannot change and *realizes* the oneness of all life.

As much as possible get rid of to-be verbs and limit passive verbs. Give your synopsis a sense of action, excitement, movement.

LENGTH

How long should your synopsis be? They are like accordions that unfold into larger and larger sections. A synopsis may be as short as a single paragraph on a jacket blurb or as long as a novella. The following long, one-paragraph synopsis by Kent Tillinghast charmed one agent enough for her to request his mystery, *Firedance*.

The Florida Keys are an enchanting string of islands, a remote retreat for smugglers, gunrunning Haitians, and world-class card shark Sam Rhodes. Perhaps it's the pirate flavor of life in the islands, or simply the farthest point to which he can escape the Mob, but Sam soon discovers Key West is also the pipeline for the sadistic Panamanian Colonel Vargas smuggling diamonds into his fortress-like villa. When a boat filled with refugees is shipwrecked and a $10 million diamond stolen from the Colonel's courier, Sam finds himself trapped between organized crime and an evil smuggler with a penchant for torture. The beautiful Ava Morreno is the key to the missing jewel and both the Mob and the homicidal Vargas are looking for her. With Hurricane Andrew blowing towards them and just hours to find the stolen diamond, Sam must play a high-stakes game of bluff greater than any in his career.

Most short synopses that are used in queries are three or four paragraphs in length. One-page synopses, usually single-spaced, are an attractive length for inclusion with a query letter, although it is acceptable to send a two-page synopsis as well.

A now-standard length for a synopsis when requested by an agent or editor is five pages, double-spaced. This is also the most common length to accompany a novel sent by agents to editors. One of the most difficult realities to face as a novelist is that you must trim your synopsis to five pages, even if the novel is a 500-page historical with a cast of 50 characters. While the job is difficult, what you must leave out forces you to clearly see what *is* important. You can look forward to gaining a deeper understanding of your character's motives, the theme, and the turning points of the novel as a result of stripping away subplots and boiling the story down to its essence. This can only help you present your novel with greater clarity. It may even help you diagnose areas needing revision.

Some synopses are ten or fifteen pages or longer, but these greater lengths go hand in hand with selling books solely on the basis of a synopsis. This privilege is usually reserved for authors who have already sold a first book.

STORY CHRONOLOGY

Some novels start in the long-ago past, then jump to the present. Others begin in the intensity of the present moment and backfill the past. Others have overlapping time sequences as the author shifts the point of view to different characters. Some novels have parallel plots or parallel stories happening at the same or different time periods. Time can get quite complex.

Because a synopsis collapses a novel into such a short form, you need not try to capture the shifts in time exactly as they occur in your novel. You may also present the turning point scenes in your synopsis in a chronology that makes sense of them within the summary. When an agent or editor reads your actual manuscript, the artistry with which you handle time will speak for itself.

VARIATIONS

Good writers, like creative cooks, adjust the recipe for the standard synopsis to fit the unique needs of their stories. Here are three variations on the standard style:

- Short Summary Followed by Longer Summary
- Narrative Hook
- Short-story Hook

Short Summary Followed by Longer Summary

A short summary followed by a longer one is only used when a synopsis will be several pages in length, most commonly five or more. There is a strategic marketing reason for writing a "double" synopsis. The short form operates as a hook, a blurb, a concise overview. Rainer Rey, author of *Replicator Run*, developed a one-page summary followed by a four-page synopsis for his literary agent to give to interested publishers when she auctioned his medical thriller. Given below is the short summary. Notice the first one-line description (a synopsis of sorts), similar to what one might read in the television guide.

The story of a broadcast journalist's self-discovery during a battle against a conspired epidemic.

SHORT SUMMARY: Devin Parks, a formerly successful TV anchorman, becomes the unwilling video journalist assigned to cover a disease story in Bellingham, Washington. The multiple patients' symptoms are physically devastating—worse than Ebola, and the prognosis is hopeless.

Disappointed by divorce and professional difficulties, Devin is temporarily lost between his on-camera identity and his true self. The disease crisis and the responsibility to save a co-worker from certain death force Devin to search for answers that ultimately result in his journey toward personal rediscovery.

This adventure encompasses several other main characters: Ann Skerit, mother of the initial disease victim in Bellingham; William Galbreath, an English diplomat who discovers the true origins of "the Replicator" in Africa; Dr. Thomas Hendrix, a microbe researcher who blames himself for the epidemic, and Dr. Ginelle Hendrix, his daughter, who shows Devin that a relationship with a dynamic, self-sufficient woman can be desirable.

Faced with overwhelming odds, Devin reaches within and gradually transforms into an empowered fulfilled professional, confident in himself and the woman he now loves.

Narrative Hook

Another compelling variation begins with a narrative hook, in present or past tense, in the viewpoint of a character—as if beginning the novel itself. This hook may not correspond to the actual novel's beginning. It is created solely for the purpose of enticing agents and editors to read further. In another example of disagreements in opinion, one writer who used a narrative hook in her synopsis told me she had been "skewered" by a contest judge for using an opener for her synopsis that differed from her novel. However, when she sat down with her synopsis and first chapter, the kind of submission an agent or editor would read, even she got confused and it was her writing! As a result she rewrote it, but she also discovered when to use a narrative hook in a synopsis. "When agents read a synopsis with a query letter, rather than with a first chapter, they don't have the first chapter for comparison." Words to the wise. If you wish, use the narrative hook when querying, but when you get a request for sample chapters and a synopsis, make sure your synopsis beginning corresponds to chapter one's beginning.

After a narrative hook, the writer offers the usual summary of the plot. Here's an example of this last variation, from *Windstalker* a suspense novel by Patsy Hand:

> Merritt Walker is totally unaware that Max has followed her to the restaurant. He slides into the booth as quietly as a hunter stalks his prey. Surprise, recognition and shock register simultaneously throughout her body, riveting her feet to the floor. Merritt sits terrified, feeling splinters of wood dig in between the threads of her sweater as she presses against the tall back of the booth. She stares into thick-lashed eyes so black, so menacing the color seems to go on forever, a bottomless pit. Max smiles, tilts his head to one side, then slowly narrows his eyes into dark onyx-like slits. Merritt knows she is looking into the face of a man who intends to murder her.
>
> *Windstalker*, a suspense novel, is set in a fictional small town on the Columbia River in Oregon. The protagonist is Merritt Walker, a psychologist, whose carefully controlled life takes a sharp turn on her forty-fifth birthday....

Short-story Hook

This unconventional variation must be considered one of high risk. The only example of its kind that I have seen was written by Andrew Coburn for his suspense novel, *The Babysitter*, published by W. W. Norton. The first four pages of the synopsis read like a short story. It was written in third-person past tense and included dialogue throughout. It focused narrowly on a father's shock and immediate actions following information that his baby daughter had been kidnapped, presumably by the babysitter. The last page shifted to synopsis, including the use of present-tense, omniscient, author/narrator summary.

After watching so many writers struggle through the process of novel creation, I am convinced that the task is made easier if they use a blueprint. I strongly recommend writing a synopsis before or upon beginning your first rough draft, another halfway through, and again upon completion, before undertaking the first rewrite.

Since this blueprint becomes a way for you to talk with yourself to keep clear about your novel's structure, direction, and author intent, it may exceed five pages. It may be ten or even twenty. Later, you can revise this rough, working synopsis into one that meets all the specs for content and style mentioned earlier in this chapter.

In case you feel a need for more structure in composing this first synopsis, I've created a "starter kit," a fill-in-the-blank form into which you can plug the details of your story. It represents the basic outline of dramatic structure and I've included all of the steps in Joseph Campbell's Hero's Journey, because most commercial novels and movies reflect this mythic structure. You can find this starter kit in Sidebar 4-2.

A FOOT IN THE DOOR

"Learning Through Critique"

James D. Axtell, author of off-beat mainstream novels

Thirty-something author, James Axtell, can tell you the moment he made a conscious decision to become a writer. "It was March 29, 1989, and I was reading *Writing the Novel* by Lawrence Block. That night, I decided to become a writer."

"My first book was science fiction—not my genre, but I did market it. I quickly realized it wasn't very good. My second book was a sort of Generation-X, mainstream-literary story, but I decided it wasn't high-enough quality. So, I wrote it off as a learning experience. I did query on my third book—the same type, but my fourth book, *Berlin Café*, was my first serious attempt and something clicked. Now I'm almost done with my fifth book."

When his first efforts to gain interest for *Berlin Café* brought form rejection letters, James went to work on his lackluster query. "I got my own stationery, printed it up on good paper, and made it look immaculate. I never handwrite my envelopes." His day job involves working with computer graphics and animation for TV, making commercials. "I'd packaged other people's stuff," he says, "so I decided to package myself. It sets you apart."

After packaging himself better, he got positive responses to his query and was signed on by an agent. "I didn't send a synopsis with my query," James admits. "Synopses tend to sound ridiculous, so I wanted them to see my actual writing style. That's why I used a short excerpt from my book in my query."

While James is pleased to have an agent for *Berlin Café*, he's rewritten it more times than he can count and relied upon both selected readers and professionals to help him improve it. "Art is subjective. I believe a writer should never ever have only one person read his stuff. I like to use eight or nine people, readers with the same demographics as readers of my genre."

James is also a big believer in hiring freelance editors. In the course of polishing *Berlin Café*, he worked with me and another professional editor. "You can't write in a vacuum," James explains. "If you're serious about your writing, it's worth paying for feedback that is more honest than your friends', and much more detailed."

With wisdom beyond his years, James has planned his life around a commitment to writing. He believes in consistency, so he writes every day. James is concerned about pacing himself and not burning out. "I'm the tortoise, not the hare," he says.

It's been eight years since that night of commitment. James reflects on the time: "Although I've thought, 'I should have something by now,' I really haven't had a low point. I'm writing because I absolutely love it, rather than to get published. It's in my blood. It's not a matter of the money or fame; I don't care if I'm ever a household name. I love being a writer."

His advice to writers: "Tenacity and willingness to take criticism are the major ingredients of success. In order to learn from your mistakes, you must admit that you made them. I take my ego and put it in a closet. I want to know the truth, even if I hate hearing it. When people give criticism, I take the position of being non-defensive and totally open to what they have to say. There are more quitters in writing than failures."

James ends with musing, "Most people have one book in them. I'm just into my thirties and I've written five books. I've got an agent. I believe that if I stick with it forever, sooner or later, I'll luck out."

Sidebar 4-2

STARTER KIT FOR A SYNOPSIS

Use the following guideline to create a synopsis of your story, adjusting it to fit your book. First create a summary for your main characters as they interact with and create the story. If a subplot intrudes at one of the stages in the main plot, explain, or make a note. You may need a similar synopsis for each point-of-view character in a book that features multiple viewpoints.

If you discover that your story doesn't have some of the steps mentioned in this explanation, consult the Resource Directory to find instructional material on the classic hero's journey. Please understand that this is not a formula that will deprive your novel of its artfulness. This is an archetypal skeleton that will allow you to discover and shape the muscle of your art.

Note: Examples below are based on the book, *The Wizard of Oz* by L. Frank Baum, not on the movie. Details vary. Words are capitalized according to use in the novel.

BEGINNING

1. SETTING, PERIOD, AND THE INCITING INCIDENT/
   THE ORDINARY WORLD
   Example: On a sultry summer evening in Kansas during the early 1900s, a cyclone strikes the farm house of Aunt Em, Uncle Henry, and their orphaned niece Dorothy, who worries that her life will turn as dull and gray as the farm, the sky, and Auntie Em's eyes.
   Summary from your book:

2. CALL TO ADVENTURE/THE CHALLENGE/ELIMINATION OF EXPENDABLE PERSON
Example: Dorothy awakens in the Land of Oz and discovers her house has fallen on and killed a wicked witch.
Summary from your book:

3. THE STORY PROBLEM AND STORY GOAL
Example: Dorothy desperately needs to find her way back to Kansas but is completely lost.
Summary from your book:

4. CALL TO ADVENTURE AND REFUSAL OF THE CALL (CAN BE ELIMINATION OF EXPENDABLE PERSON HERE RATHER THAN EARLIER)
Example: When the good Witch of the North tells her that she must travel to Oz over dangerous and difficult terrain in order to ask help from the Wizard, Dorothy breaks into tears.
Summary from your book:

5. SUPERNATURAL AID/THE WISE OLD MAN OR WOMAN (OR SIMPLY, WISE ADVISOR)
Example: The Witch of the North promises assistance, kisses Dorothy on the forehead, leaving a magic mark, and counsels her about the Wizard.
Summary from your book:

MIDDLE

6. CROSSING THE THRESHOLD INTO THE SPECIAL WORLD
Example: Slipping on the Silver Shoes (not ruby slippers!) from the dead Wicked Witch of the East, Dorothy scoops up her dog Toto and finds the yellow brick road, beginning her journey to Oz.
Summary from your book:

7. THE ROAD OF TESTS AND TRIALS/ALLIES AND ENEMIES
Example: Although embraced by the Munchkins, Dorothy meets new friends: the Scarecrow, the Tin Woodman, and the Cowardly Lion, who eagerly accompany her. With allies they meet, Dorothy and her band fight off beasts, raging waters, and deadly poppies.
Summary from your book:

8. CHARACTER STRENGTHS THAT DRIVE THE STORY FORWARD; WEAKNESSES THAT SET IT BACK.

Example: Dorothy's friends seem unaware that they are demonstrating the very strengths they seek from the Wizard. Dorothy, ever resourceful and courageous is also naive, allowing the Great Oz to order her to kill the Wicked Witch of the West.

Summary from your book:

9. THE DARKEST HOUR/THE BELLY OF THE WHALE

Example: Dorothy, the Scarecrow, the Tin Woodman, and the Cowardly Lion use their strengths to fight off wolves, crows, and bees, but they are captured by the witch's Winged Monkeys and taken captive in the Wicked Witch's castle.

Summary from your book:

THE CLIMAX

10. THE SUPREME ORDEAL/LIFE AND DEATH STRUGGLE

Example: Days and weeks pass as Dorothy works as the witch's slave and sneaks food to the Lion—also imprisoned—at night. Having exhausted her other sources of power, the witch tricks Dorothy into falling. When one of the Silver Shoes falls free, the Witch snatches it, triumphant in reducing Dorothy's power by half and increasing her own. In her anger, Dorothy douses the witch with a bucket of water, unknowingly causing the witch to melt into nothing and freeing Dorothy and the lion forever.

Summary from your book:

11. THE MOMENT OF TRIUMPH/SEIZING THE SWORD

Example: Putting the Silver Shoe back on, Dorothy and the Cowardly Lion celebrate with the freed Winged Monkeys and with their help find and revitalize the Tin Woodman and the Scarecrow. As the new owner of the Golden Cap—whoever owns the cap gets three wishes from the Winged Monkeys—Dorothy calls on them to return her and her friends to the Wizard. Triumphant, they are ready to have their requests granted.

Summary from your book:

12. REFUSAL OF THE RETURN

Example: When the Wizard of Oz reveals that he is a "humbug," he decides to leave Oz and invites Dorothy to go too in his hot air balloon. At the last moment, Toto runs off and Dorothy cannot leave without him and the Wizard flies away without her.

Summary from your book:

13. THE ULTIMATE TEST, AND THE RESURRECTION (IF THE CHARACTER HAS LEARNED)

Example: Dorothy uses the Golden Cap to summon the Monkeys and uses up her second wish asking them to return her to Kansas, which they cannot do. She uses her third wish when she and her friends encounter an obstacle on their way to consult with Witch Glinda, Dorothy's last hope. Having changed from a tearful naive child into a wise resourceful young woman, Dorothy does not hesitate to give Glinda the Golden Cap. Glinda rewards Dorothy's generosity by promising to use her three wishes to return the Dorothy's friends to their new kingdoms, and free the Monkeys.

Summary from your book:

14. MASTER OF TWO WORLDS/ A BOON, A TREASURE, OR NECESSARY KNOWLEDGE

Example: Knowing that all is well in the Land of Oz and that her friends will be taken care of, Dorothy clicks her Silver Shoes three times and in a wink finds herself back home, filled with newfound appreciation for her aunt, uncle, and the jubilant feeling of having a place you call home.

Summary from your book:

CHAPTER FIVE

Studying the Synopsis

- ◆ Nine Synopsis Applications
- ◆ Medical Thriller
- ◆ Historical Mainstream
- ◆ Horror
- ◆ Generation X
- ◆ A Foot in the Door: "Running the Writer's Iditarod" by Patricia J. Hyatt

Long before I knew the term *synopsis*, it had become a part of my life as a student. There was a time when I would have traded my worldly possessions for ownership of the bestselling study-aid, *Cliffs Notes*. Synopses! We can be assured that as long as there are students, summaries of literature will never go out of print. But an effective marketing synopsis for your book is more than a simple summary of action, and it can do a lot more for you.

In this chapter, you'll learn how synopses are used and altered for various purposes. Following this section will be four complete synopses with analyses of their structures, styles, strengths, and weaknesses. The chapter ends with another author's foot-in-the-door story.

Nine Synopsis Applications

The following uses for your novel's synopsis should help you understand just how versatile, and important, this unassuming document can be.

1. As a One-line Hook
2. As a Working Blueprint

3. Within a Query Letter
4. Accompanying a Submission
5. As an Oral Pitch
6. For a Contest
7. For Agent Use
8. For Publisher Use
9. To Propose a Next Book

1. As a One-line Hook

"As the Civil War rages, a woman's passion for the wrong man blinds her to the love of the right one." That's a one-line synopsis of *Gone With The Wind*. What's your book about? People will ask you. If you don't have a ready answer, you could miss an opportunity.

I've noticed that the ease with which writers clearly and briefly summarize their novels seems to correspond with how "finished" their novels are—how ready for market. If you can't describe your novel in one line, you don't know what it's about," drones an old cliché. Cliché or not, how can your story appear in *TV Guide* if it can't be summarized in one line?

Short is always difficult. A one-line summary is a good starting point for collecting your thoughts about your book. Keep working on the one-line summary as you also create your working blueprint.

2. As a Working Blueprint

After watching so many writers struggle through the process of novel creation, I am convinced that writing from an outline and forming that into a synopsis can make the task of writing a book easier. I advocate writing at least three working drafts of a synopsis: one before or at the beginning of writing the first rough draft, another halfway through, and the third upon completion—before the first rewrite. As a working blueprint this application of the synopsis is a way for you to talk with yourself, in order to keep clear about the novel's structure, direction, and author intent.

3. Within a Query Letter

Your novel is done. You want someone to look at it. Now what? As the heart of a query letter, the synopsis should be condensed to one to three paragraphs. Generally, if you devote more than three paragraphs to the synopsis portion of a query, you risk including too many plot events.

The content you select to put in the synopsis within a query depends upon the type of novel you are writing. The synopsis within a query written by Kent Tillinghast for his mystery, *Firedance* (page 67), hits so heavily on plot and a romantic gestalt that for one agent reading it was reminiscent of *Key Largo*.

If a novel focuses on characterization, especially if it is literary or mainstream, you might choose to include more details about the protagonist than about the plot. The synopsis within the query for *Requiem for Red Hawk* by Patricia Bradbury is an excellent example of this emphasis on characterization. An excerpt from her novel won first place in the 1996 Surrey Writers Contest. Notice how this synopsis from her query gives the reader a clear sense of the sensitivity that the author brings to her story.

...At Red Hawk, the remote annex of Montana's State Psychiatric Hospital, a beautiful young piano teacher battles to atone for two deaths: that of her unborn child and her protege whom she allowed to drive the icy road home from a concert.

For Helena Boire, the abyss between sanity and insanity is treacherously narrow. Her struggle to recover and accept herself is nearly thwarted by a power-hungry psychiatrist who must destroy her, because she is the only witness to a murder. Her courage, and the healing powers of love, allow her to triumph over him and her own devastating self-loathing.

To counterbalance the dark threads of evil, *Requiem for Red Hawk* explores themes of friendship and atonement, of courage and love. In Helena Boire, readers will find both a wistful sense of humor and a grim determination to use this crazy time of craziness to explore her faith, her love for music, and her feelings for two very different men. Above all, she must learn to accept herself as an imperfect creature.

4. TO ACCOMPANY A SUBMISSION

You may also decide to submit a synopsis as an enclosure with your initial query letter. The length of this synopsis should be one-page, single-spaced (with double spaces between paragraphs).

A second synopsis that accompanies a submission occurs when an agent has responded to your query and now requests a synopsis and sample chapters. This synopsis, usually five pages double-spaced, provides the agent or editor with a greater sense of your entire story. It affords a more complete picture than could be offered within your query or from the sample chapters alone. In the hands of an astute agent or editor, this longer synopsis also reveals how well you understand novel structure.

There is some discussion among writers over whether to include a synopsis before it has been requested—if the directions in a directory for agents or editors specifically state, "query only." Sometimes it's hard to decide, especially when the listing in a directory differs from the directions given by the same agent or editor in person. One literary agent I know said that she uses what writers send her as a barometer to measure how well they can follow instructions, and therefore to how well she can rely upon them if she takes them on as clients.

For every hardtack editor or agent, you can find another who is amazed that writers ask these questions. "Just send me three to four chapters, or find a good cut-off point. A synopsis is fine. One page, two page, five page—whatever!"

I've resolved the gray area for myself and my clients by advising writers to send only a one-page synopsis with "query-only" requests, and to send up to five pages, double-spaced, to requests for a synopsis or sample chapters.

5. AS AN ORAL PITCH

You might not have thought about giving an oral pitch to sell your novel. It's true that a shy writer can arrange life to avoid pitching a novel to an agent or editor, but most writers must face this when they get up to their kneecaps in the marketing process. Pitching a novel most commonly occurs at writers' conferences, either informally or by formal arrangement. Informally occurs when you catch an editor or agent after a panel discussion with an, "Excuse me, may I talk with you a moment?" Formally occurs when the conference organizers have established a system of appointments between writers and publishing professionals.

Some conferences, like the Maui Writer's Conference, require the submission of a synopsis in the form of a fill-in-the-blank document they call a "Manuscript Resume'," to be followed with an oral pitch. Other conferences, like the well-established Willamette Writers Conference in Portland, Oregon, hold practice sessions to help attenders learn how to pitch their books. They recommend that writers bring a well-crafted one-page synopsis to all agent-editor appointments.

Whether formal or informal, one thing is true: You won't have much more than ten minutes—if that. And, you've got to leave room for hellos, goodbyes, and questions and answers. What's left is all the time available to pitch your book.

Will you be nervous? Yes. Hit a blank? Most likely. Stumble over something you memorized? Possibly. Unless you are a Barbara Walters' clone, don't expect to ad lib. Make the best impression by preparing your synopsis in writing ahead of time—and not more than one page. Plan to read it aloud, verbatim, or hand it to the agents or editors for them to read, whichever they prefer.

The short synopsis given in chapter four (page 62) about *Consulted to Death*, written by Carolyn Rose, doubled as a synopsis to send with her queries and as an oral pitch to present to agents and editors at the Surrey Writer's Conference in British Columbia.

The synopsis that follows was written specifically to use as an oral pitch at several writer's conferences and netted its author, Sarah Vail, half a dozen requests to submit her complete manuscript for her first mystery, *Fresh Powder*, a book that was represented but not sold.

Gunfire shatters the silence on a cold wintry night in a sleepy neighborhood on the edge of the city. Lieutenant Chad Atherton and Detective Sherry Crosby are sent to investigate the fatal shooting of David Matthews. What on the surface looks like a justifiable homicide, rape self-defense, quickly turns to suspicion of premeditated murder, after evidence at the crime scene is gathered and reviewed. As the police detectives proceed with their investigation, Lt. Atherton is thrown into a whirlwind of emotion when he comes face to face with the exquisite and seductive victim/suspect, Miss Victoria Connell. Suddenly, the forty-year-old detective is forced to deal with feelings he has denied himself since his divorce five years earlier.

When the investigation is only ten hours old, to add to the jumble, Atherton is pressured from within the department to tread carefully. Victoria Connell has powerful political connections and it is the winter before an election year. Candidates on all levels of government are jockeying for position, preparing to announce their intentions in the coming spring. This homicide is just what some of them need. Just what others do not. Atherton realizes quickly that he's about to open the laundry basket and whose dirty laundry is he about to find?

Soon the forensic evidence gathered at the scene eliminates Victoria Connell as a suspect, but establishes her as a woman in grave danger. Moved by overpowering feelings, Atherton begins to protect her, which only angers Sherry Crosby, his partner. He is unaware that Crosby is in love with him and has lived day to day on fantasies of one day being his wife as well as his police partner.

The mystery unravels in the Pacific Northwest's lush Willamette Valley and in the powder-sugar snow-covered peaks of the Cascade Mountains. Atherton and Crosby methodically, meticulously, and relentlessly pursue the unknown killer. Hour by hour they narrow down the suspects until there is only one: Senator Charles Strother, who has just announced his bid for the Presidency.

The thrilling climax leads the detectives to a showdown between love and death.

6. FOR A CONTEST

What can you do to bring more attention to your work? Competition in a literary contest can bring more scrutiny to an entry, including the synopsis, than from an agent or editor. In a contest, judges examine the entries, intentionally comparing each one with all others. Many contests require their judges to write critiques on all entries and ultimately select the best for awards. In contrast, agents and editors tend to have highly specific tastes or "slots" to be filled by certain types of books. Thus, you could have written an absolutely brilliant historical saga and be rejected by a publisher who only acquires one such book a year. A less-well-crafted technical thriller sent to the same publisher might fill an open slot.

Contests are wonderful whetstones for sharpening a manuscript. Most specify the page requirements for the synopsis, and most limit this to no more than five pages. Whereas you could submit five and a half pages to a literary agent, do that in a contest with a five-page limit and you will be disqualified.

Entering contests makes me, at least, far more critical of every word I write and has provided me with the impetus to learn about "deep revision." Having also worn the judge's hat, I've experienced first hand how a well-written synopsis can inspire confidence and anticipation in the story, while a poorly written one can negatively predispose me toward the manuscript.

The content and style of the five-page synopsis you write for a contest is no different from the one you send with a query, or with sample chapters or the entire manuscript. If you can find a contest that provides a detailed critique of your writing—including the synopsis—then I recommend using contests as a marketing test for your work. Contact information on contests is provided in the Resource Directory.

7. For Agent Use

Your agent calls you and requests a sizzling synopsis. Why? Many agents send out shopping lists of the properties they represent, supplying a blurb-length synopsis for each book. When your agent succeeds in generating editorial interest, off goes your manuscript, usually accompanied by a five-page synopsis you've written. While your synopsis cannot substitute for the actual manuscript in the sale of a first-time novel, it comes in handy in the busy lives of acquisitions editors and their readers. The synopsis can be used prior to reading the book to raise or answer editorial questions, and it facilitates quick review during discussions among the editorial staff.

8. For Publisher Use

Yes, publishers need your synopsis too. Long before any book's actual publication, publishers generate several versions of a synopsis. They need copy for their catalogs and blurbs for book jackets. Letters and releases will accompany copies of galleys (typeset proofs) to potential reviewers. Each of these documents includes some form of synopsis.

9. TO PROPOSE A NEXT BOOK

Most first-time novelists must demonstrate that they know how to write a decent novel by submitting the entire finished copy. Many second-time novelists, on the other hand, can be granted a contract for a next book based solely on the basis of a long synopsis. More details will be supplied about what can happen beyond the first sale in the final chapter of this book.

For those of you who learn best by example, the next part of this chapter features full-length synopses with a critical analysis of each. If you are reading this book to get an overview of queries, synopses, and marketing strategies, you may wish to return to these sample synopses when you are at your desk ready to roll up your sleeves, study the examples, and write your own.

SYNOPSIS

Medical Thriller by Rainer Rey

Title: *Replicator Run*, 85,000 words

Sold in auction by former literary agent Diane Gedymin to Fawcett-Ballantine. Published in Spring 1997. Short summary (one-page synopsis) featured in chapter 4, page 69.

MAIN PLOT SUMMARY	COMMENTS
Overnight, several dozen U.S. children contract harmless-looking blemishes which manifest themselves to be a highly contagious disease more devastating than Ebola or any other known virus. Young, ravaged patients are given little hope. Adults become contagious as an epidemic looms.	Opens with problem and what's at stake, which is most, if not all, of human life. A "high concept" story. Builds lots of empathy with children as first victims.

MAIN PLOT SUMMARY	COMMENTS
Devin Parks, a burned-out video journalist, is assigned to cover the story. Frank Freeman, Devin's boss, insists that Devin cover the event as a last chance to recover the dignity he once enjoyed as a star anchorman.	Introduces protagonist with hint of his inner problem and a statement of his past accomplishments. Supplies "refusal of call" and "wise advisor" from hero's journey.
Accompanied by an aspiring young reporter, Amy Klein, who admires Devin's past glory, Devin flies to Bellingham, Washington. After interviews with doctors and witnesses, unknown to Devin, Amy contracts the disease.	Expendable person makes the stakes personal.
Devin's national TV report is seen by Dr. Thomas Hendrix, who is shocked; the current symptoms are reminiscent of those he witnessed during his now-defunct, top-secret government, killer-microbe research project.	Second point-of-view character. Introduction of secret research project, backstory, and more sense of the thriller story structure.
Hendrix fears exposure but wants to meet Devin to make a vaccine available for "the replicator" (a term describing microbe reproduction).	Lets us know a cure does exist.
Amid national panic and now aware of Amy's illness, Devin flies Amy to Richmond in the company Lear jet to meet with Hendrix to save both their lives.	Stakes increase, especially with the protagonist's life in jeopardy. Not clear if Devin contracted the disease.
In the interim, Hendrix is kidnapped by conspirators, led by an amoral mercenary named Jaktar, who, employed by an unknown power, murdered all of Hendrix' co-researchers. In her father's absence, Ginelle Hendrix, daughter of	Kidnap increases sense of "ticking clock" and increases reader suspense. Antagonistic forces get a face, a name, and a background.

MAIN PLOT SUMMARY

Dr. Hendrix, meets with Devin and Amy. She has a single dose of vaccine, enough to save either Devin or Amy but not both. Though critical of Devin, Ginelle gives him the vaccine. He may survive whereas Amy surely cannot.

Amy dies. Devin recovers, overcome by guilt, and at odds with Ginelle, who is refined, self-sufficient, and intolerant of his manner. Still, Ginelle has few people to whom she can turn. She convinces Devin to help her find her father. Reluctant, Devin thwarts an attempt by the conspirators on Ginelle's life and begins to look upon Ginelle differently. Vulnerable, she is still more self-assured than any woman he has ever met.

His decision to help her is the turning point in his life. The crisis spurs his renewed self-awareness. Devin and Ginelle go to the National Disease Control Center in Atlanta where they witness the epidemic's devastation. Several hundred-thousand victims are affected. Devin and Ginelle meet with government officials in Atlanta, including Jonathan Swain, the National Security Advisor, and Col. Williamson, Frank Freeman's old service buddy, and are told that Hendrix has been blamed for the disease.

Disappointed, Ginelle follows Devin to San Francisco, where he goes on world-

COMMENTS

Unclear why Ginelle is critical of Devin.

Major emotional turning point. Unclear what Devin's "manner" is that makes Ginelle intolerant of him.

Reassertion of story goal. Must find Dr. Hendrix to create antidote and save lives.

Devin shows necessary heroic characteristics; summary lays groundwork for romance.

Unclear why this is turning point of his life. Could be more specific about what he is now aware of.

Takes reader to larger perspective, interesting locations. Proves the stakes are worldwide and consequences grave.

Because author offers names, we must presume these characters will play central roles in the rest of the book.

Protagonist showing heroic characteristics.

Main Plot Summary

wide television, confronting the terrorists and defending Hendrix. The courageous eloquence of his editorial has
substantial impact. Immediately after his
broadcast, Devin is contacted by British
diplomat William Galbreath, who
informs him that he has unearthed an
incredible discovery: 15-year-old photographs of native Africans with similar
symptoms to the current replicator
scourge. Devin agrees to meet with Galbreath to compare information while he
sequesters Ginelle at Freeman's beach
cabin in Monterey.

Galbreath reveals that Arthur Quail,
owner of The Maxillar Chemical Company, is also owner of an Iranian company which operated labs in the African
desert where the photographs were
found, indicating that the replicator
plague is older than once thought and
definitely man-made. Devin reminds
Galbreath that one of Hendrix' former
research partners, a man named Dr.
Ahmar Kahvahl, was a native Iranian.
This leads them to believe the disease is
a means to an end, an agent of an international plot.

With some military backup and the
photographs as bait, Galbreath and
Devin confront Quail in hopes of generating a verbal exchange that Galbreath
can tape on a miniature disc recorder he
carries in his cane. Though intimidated

Comments

Intrigue deepens and new
character, presumably an
ally, is introduced.

Stakes quickly worsen.

Unclear why Ginelle would
need to be sequestered.

Plot deepens and we meet
another antagonist, learn
more about the virus, and
clues about its origins.

Unclear why the characters
don't turn evidence over to
existing authorities and how
they are able to get military
backup without knowledge
of authorities.

MAIN PLOT SUMMARY	COMMENTS
by Quail's calculating evil, Devin gets him to verbalize his motives. Angered by Devin's intrusion, Quail wishes to hold him but is temporarily unable to do so, fearing military reprisal. Devin and Galbreath leave, pledging to meet in Atlanta with Ginelle to expedite Quail's prosecution.	Unclear why Ginelle would need to go to Atlanta.
As Devin arrives in Monterey to pick up Ginelle, Quail publicly announces that his chemical company, Maxillar, has just discovered a vaccine to save the country. Quail is hailed as a hero. Ginelle is further depressed by this development. She disagrees with Devin's plan, demanding the evidence be presented in Washington, even though her father formerly distrusted the federal government. At odds, Devin and Ginelle fall asleep in separate bedrooms.	Shows good plot twist. Shows good plot complication and moving towards "the darkest hour."
That night, they are abducted by a conspirator commando team. In the fight, Devin loses consciousness. He wakes up in a large truck to find himself in the company of Ginelle, Dr. Hendrix, an unconscious Galbreath, and Dr. Ahmar Kahvahl, who, initially a conspirator, has been betrayed and captured.	Widens the scope of the mystery part of the story and shows international settings common to thrillers.
In the semi's chamber, Jaktar abuses Devin and threatens to remove Ginelle's body parts. Previously tortured, Galbreath comes to and distracts Jaktar by attacking another conspirator. Though weak, Devin uses the opportu-	On track for a thriller and demonstrates "life and death struggle."

Main Plot Summary

nity to overcome Jaktar in a desperate fight. Jaktar, Kahvahl, and Galbreath die in this exchange, but Devin, Ginelle, and Dr. Hendrix manage to escape. Hendrix announces that, based on a deathbed confession by Kahvahl, Quail holds the country hostage. Quail's vaccine, distributed to the members of the Federal Government as well as to the public, contains a molecular cipher which will re-infect recipients with a mutated microbe causing their certain deaths unless Quail supplies a computer-generated antidote.

Hendrix disappears into his lab to find an answer. Without Hendrix, Devin and Ginelle try to avert disaster. They arrive with their recording of Quail at a congressional prosecution hearing condemning Dr. Hendrix. Quail makes his blackmail demands on the members of Congress, stating that his international business cartel intends to halt a disastrous political course for America. He reveals Jonathan Swain to be his co-conspirator. Together, they will run the government in order to alter the ultimate decline of the U.S.

Hendrix arrives with a research note. Using it as a weapon, Devin steps into the limelight, strikes Quail down, and announces that Hendrix' new research confirms Quail's molecular cipher is impotent due to chemical miscalculation.

Comments

Inner character dimension unclear.

Good plot twist. Keeps reader interested as medical mystery aspect of the story continues to unfold.

Shows that as bad as things get, they can get worse yet— great plotting

Shows the "belly of the whale" from Campbell's "hero's journey."

Corresponds to "seizing the sword" and story goal reached.

MAIN PLOT SUMMARY	COMMENTS
Swain and Quail are arrested. Devin receives praise from everyone, including the President of the United States, who wishes to elevate him to national office. Devin declines. His old TV anchor position is all he really wants, with the opportunity to remain with Ginelle. Through the crisis, she has gained respect for him.	Having succeeded, the protagonist is offered a prize, which he gives up for what he has discovered he truly desires, thus showing character growth.
The story ends as we leave Devin and Ginelle on the beach in Monterey, apprehensive in an insecure world, yet fulfilled by new-found spirituality and love for one another.	Supplies "denouement," the wrapping up of loose ends. First mention of spirituality, so unclear how this fits in story.

ANALYSIS

The strength of this synopsis is the clarity with which it demonstrates plot. It shows dramatic slope based on ever-increasing conflict and stakes. It is a good match for the thriller category and supplies unexpected twists and complexity to the medical mystery part of the story.

What is undeveloped is the character dimension of the story. Although the author has clearly written well for the plot-driven thriller style, I would have liked greater exposition of the interaction of the protagonist's character with the story. In fairness, the "Short Summary" that was sent as the first page with this synopsis (and is printed in this book's chapter four) gave two paragraphs to characterization.

Since this synopsis was sent to publishers with the complete manuscript of the novel, any questions of deficiencies of the synopsis would have been answered and supplied by the actual book.

SYNOPSIS

Historical Mainstream by Patricia Jean Hyatt
(based on the lives of real people)

Title: *Land of Thirst,* 90,000 words
Theme: Adventure is not love; nor is it a substitute for love.

Novel was a Heekin Group Foundation semifinalist; second-place winner in Colorado Gold Fiction Writers Contest (Patty's other novel took first place); and second-place winner in Pacific Northwest Writers Contest.

MAIN PLOT SUMMARY	COMMENTS
Protagonist Jessie "Chubbie" Keith-Miller grows up in Melbourne in the early 1900s, closely bonded with her twin brother. She is devastated when he is killed at age twenty. Her cold and incompatible marriage also flounders amid the grief and guilt of two miscarriages, followed by a hysterectomy. Without her twin, Chubbie loses all sense of who she is; without children, she loses the best sense of who she might have become.	Synopsis lead devoted entirely to backstory, especially traumatic past that creates the inner psychological wound. This emphasis signals readers to expect depth of characterization, which would be expected in mainstream fiction.
In 1927, thinking to honor ambitions shared with her brother, Chubbie leaves Australia. In London, she meets an English RAF pilot, Bill Lancaster, who dreams of setting a solo distance record with a flight from London to Port Darwin, Australia. Chubbie rushes to fill her emptiness with the thrill of open-cockpit flying. Bill resists taking her along as a passenger, but she makes herself indispensable to him by raising the money for his flight. He gives in.	Establishes time period and introduces secondary protagonist. Interweaves character motive with inciting incident.

Main Plot Summary

En route to Darwin, their flying exploits make them famous. They survive desert sandstorms, engine failure over shark-infested waters, the bayonets of hostile Arabs, imprisonment in Bushire. They survive a jungle crash and later, while crossing the Timor Sea, a hurricane. Though they are each married to others, the dangers they share and the obstacles they overcome create such an intense emotional bond that they become secret lovers. With each obstacle, Chubbie's determination to succeed grows stronger. With each success, her daring increases. She learns to fly; she commits herself to Bill and leaves her husband, incorrectly believing Bill can fill the emptiness left by her earlier grief and failures.

They set the distance record to Australia, then move on to America, where they achieve new records. Chubbie's husband divorces her, but Bill's Catholic wife refuses to free him. By 1932, the Great Depression completely stalls their livelihood in aviation. Finances grow so desperate, they are reduced to one meal per day. Finally, seeking to capitalize upon their renown, they engage journalist Haden Clarke to ghostwrite a book about their adventures. Shortly after Haden moves in with them in Miami, Bill flies to Mexico to scout air routes for a new airline. Although reluctant to leave Chubbie alone with Haden, Bill rejoices in his

Comments

Promises readers an exciting story with lots of danger, conflict, and passion.

Keeps reader aware of character flaw and plot that springs from deep characterization.

This paragraph covers the territory of their lives and the plot. External events conspire to pressure the characters, testing their mettle.

Unclear why he would be reluctant to leave Chubbie with Haden—the moral

MAIN PLOT SUMMARY

first work in six months. He rationalizes that at least he leaves Chubbie with food on the table.

Chubbie's greatest strength now becomes her undoing. The determination that allowed her to put her partnership with Bill together, the determination that earlier kept them in the air against all obstacles, now eats at her, frustrates her, and feeds a sense of failure and powerlessness. She has nothing to sustain her. Their desperate financial straits have kept her flightless too long; she is an adrenaline addict in need of a fix. Her sense of failure spirals her into a deepening emotional void.

In a dream, she relives the violent death of her twin brother. Her suppressed grief and longing reawaken. Haden capitalizes upon her vulnerability. He deliberately lures her into reminiscing about her flying adventures and Baghdad; she succumbs to his feigned sympathy, his booze, his bed. In the following weeks, she rationalizes her betrayal of Bill by convincing herself that she must love Haden. Haden is erratic, violent. Sexually dangerous. He becomes a new adventure, filling her void. Chubbie becomes so determined to end her overwhelming feelings of guilt that finally she accepts his proposal of marriage.

Shortly before the wedding, Bill returns. The three quarrel violently, then retire for

COMMENTS

standards of the time, or because of a weakness he has seen in Chubbie.

Demonstrates the powerful characterization dimension of the novel, making clear how the coming darkest hour is a mirror of the dark side of the protagonist, who is looking more and more like a tragic hero.

Shows road of tests and trials.

Shows a momentum of a downward spiral. Suspense additionally comes from wondering what will happen when Bill returns.

An emotional turning point.

MAIN PLOT SUMMARY	COMMENTS
the night. In the bedroom that Bill shares with Haden, Bill trumps Haden's card with secret information he's learned while in Mexico: "Either you tell Chubbie that you already have a wife, or I will." Caught in his lie, Haden further unburdens himself. They talk; Bill realizes that Haden already has not just one wife, but two. Haden is a bigamist. After Bill falls asleep, Haden lies awake. In the morning Bill will force him to reveal to Chubbie all his unhealthy secrets: Not only is he a bigamist, he has long had syphilis; he's bisexual. He knows that Chubbie will despise him. Leave him. Return to Bill. Trapped by his myriad lies, facing a tortuous death from a grim disease, Haden decides the only way out is suicide.	A "Big Scene" and major turning point. Strong drama and twist of fate.
Lying in the moonlight, Haden resolves if he can't have Chubbie, neither can Bill. He sets the scene, then shoots himself through the head with Bill's pistol. He believes he's fixed it so Chubbie will blame Bill and turn away from him forever.	Another Big Scene in the downward spiral.
Bill is charged with Haden's murder. The trial attracts worldwide headlines as sensational as the previous headlines about Bill and Chubbie's flying exploits. Chubbie stands by him, hoping her support will help clear his name. A controversial forensics expert offers his expertise; famous aviators from all over the world testify on Bill's behalf; Haden's unsavory past be-	Shows a moment of "false hope" through the acquittal,

Main Plot Summary

comes clear. Bill is acquitted. Chubbie's deterioration must raise the question whether she can be redeemed.

Bill and Chubbie return to England, but Bill realizes that Chubbie stays with him out of pity, rather than love. He cannot get work of any kind. In the eyes of society, "not guilty" is not the same as "innocent." In 1933, he decides to rehabilitate his reputation—and recapture Chubbie's love—by setting a solo speed record from London to South Africa. He crashes in a sandstorm in Algeria. The Algerians conduct a desultory search, but do not find him. Frantic, Chubbie tries to organize a search party from London. No one will participate or give her the use of an aeroplane; Bill's own father refuses to finance a search. Bill's death is thus assured.

This is Chubbie's defining moment. Because of choices she's made and the way she's lived, society views her as a lost woman—and considers Bill as not worth rescuing. Devastated, she retires to the English countryside. Forced to examine the reasons for her choices, she at last recognizes that after her twin died, she filled her emotional emptiness with adventure, mistaking its thrill for love. Facing her grief and anger allows her to more deeply love and value her family and friends. She becomes more self-sufficient, less self-involved. She devotes herself to behind-the-scenes volunteer work at a children's hospital. Three years

Comments

then how real-life events conspired to play out this apparent tragedy.

Big Scene and turning point.

When things get as bad as they can get, they get worse still.

The author swings the synopsis back to its center of gravity—Chubbie's characterization, the beginning of her redemption.

Dark night of the soul.

Demonstrates character change.

Main Plot Summary	Comments
after Bill's last flight, she falls genuinely in love and marries an RAF pilot. They live an anonymous and quietly contented life together. She never flies again.	Receives the "prize" for change.

But in 1962, twenty-nine years after Bill's last flight, French troops stumble across his disabled biplane in a desolate, untraveled part of the Algerian desert. As though still awaiting rescue, Bill's mummified body is propped against the fuselage in the shade of a broken wing. He's still wearing his aviator's jacket and leather helmet. Wired to the struts of the biplane is his death diary. In it, he recounts his crash, his injuries, the eight days he waited for death in extreme heat and cold, his acceptance of the fact that rescue will not come in time. His last wish is that his diary be returned to Chubbie.

Denouement—closure for Bill's disappearance.

She reads it. His words of love move her deeply. She weeps. It's clear from Bill's last words that he died the same way he lived—unredeemed. She understands, as he apparently did not, that though Bill didn't pull the trigger, he was guilty, and so was she. Guilty of adultery, of betrayal, deceit, reckless dishonor of their families, of deliberate disregard of society, of selfishness, all of which led Haden to a violent death. In facing the renewed publicity over the old scandals, Chubbie accepts that society will never forgive her past actions or her role in Haden's death and Bill's, but she knows that because she learned her lessons and

Author devotes considerable space in synopsis detailing the "ultimate test" and "rebirth" of her protagonist. This focus on characterization offers further "proof"

Main Plot Summary	Comments
changed, she long ago earned the right to forgive herself. She honors Bill's memory. His legacy was that for the three decades following his death, she was able to give—and to receive—love. She takes her husband's hand and realizes anew that real love is its own adventure.	of the character-centered nature of the book. Brings the synopsis back to the theme.

Analysis

In this virtually flawless synopsis—rewritten many times over many years—Patty Hyatt gives most space to four of the novel's turning points: 1) her protagonist's downfall through her alliance with Haden Clarke; 2) the night of Haden's suicide and the ensuing trial; 3) Chubbie's grief and despair over Bill's death; and 4) the working out of her redemption when Bill's corpse and diary are found. Through this lens, the author focuses reader attention more on the character dimension of the novel than on the external events, especially of their historic flights. She is thus communicating that this is a novel guaranteed to deliver deep characterization, and it should not be mistaken for a category romance or an aviation adventure story.

This is a synopsis worthy of modeling.

SYNOPSIS

Horror by Charles H. Snellings

Title: *The Hidebehind*, 105,000 words

This novel was represented by an agent but it was turned back to the author when the horror market "died." The word count is much longer than typical genre fiction, though mainstream horror novels can be this long.

MAIN PLOT SUMMARY	COMMENTS
The Hidebehind is the story of a man who is forced to face his greatest fear: responsibility for the deaths of others. Bobby Aldrich, a whitewater river guide from Oregon, is no stranger to death. By a careless oversight with loose ropes, he has caused the death of a young boater on the Upper Klamath River two months before.	Back story alerts reader to traumatic past of protagonist.
At first, winning a permit allowing him to raft down one of the most remote canyons in the United States—The Middle Fork of the Salmon in central Idaho—excites him. But because of the accident on the Klamath, he changes his mind. Only through the coaxing of his best friend, Jerry Peterson, does he acquiesce to lead the eight-day expedition. "The bad's out of the way," Jerry tells him. "What's the worst that can happen?"	Describes setting and situation.

Makes use of a snippet of dialogue and wise advisor, whose advice reader knows will be incorrect. |
| Bobby and Jerry are unaware that an entire family has been brutally slaughtered in White River, Idaho, only 150 miles from the river they are planning to float. | Deepens plot by introducing menace outside main characters' knowledge. |
| Upon launching, Bobby is back in his element and feels better. He and twelve other people from different walks of life anticipate the trip of a lifetime. Bobby alone can't relax. Besides lingering guilt from the Klamath tragedy, he suffers recurring nightmares. A beast has stalked him through dreams since childhood. Recently it has returned. He tries to ignore the dreams. | Establishes a tense, creepy mood.

Foreshadows antagonist. |

MAIN PLOT SUMMARY	COMMENTS
On the second evening of the trip, strange things occur. Bobby awakens from another nightmare only to find himself in the same scene—glowing eyes slowly fade back into the bushes. Still, he refuses to believe the dreams are anything more than a manifestation of old fears brought on by guilt. At least, until he discovers the helmeted head of a friend—one of his group—crammed into a kayak.	Shows good plot use of backstory. Major emotional turning point.
From another rafting party, he meets a courageous woman named Abigail Jones, who tells him of the carnage she and her friend, Beth, have discovered at Indian Creek Cabin. Being an assistant district attorney from Oregon, she knows the killer cannot be human.	Introduces another main character. Menace increases. Antagonist becoming known.
The canyons are steep, with hundreds of miles of wilderness in all directions. There is no way out but down what nineteenth-century prospectors called "The River of No Return." Members of Bobby's group are picked off one by one by an unseen enemy that can kill on land or in the water.	Shows use of setting to increase danger. Sets ticking clock according to number of days to go down river. Lots of deaths increases menace. Get to know range of beast's powers.
Each night they post sentries, while the creature hides just beyond the firelight …watching…waiting for the first to stray too near the edge of camp. No one ever sees a thing. It is fast, and deadly silent. In the end, only seven remain.	Implies possible beast's point of view. Plot thick with deaths. Good match for horror genre.
While Bobby and his group head down river, Earl Bohannan—the chief deputy	Another point-of-view character from law enforcement

MAIN PLOT SUMMARY

of the Salmon County sheriff's office—is investigating a murder. At a ranch along the Middle Fork, petroglyphs drawn in blood paint the walls, and dead bodies litter the grounds. Earl has never seen anything like it. Even though he is with a group of armed lawmen, he feels scared. Whoever—or whatever—killed the people at the ranch might still be there. That fear intensifies as the sun sets over the mountains while they wait for the state police inside.

One night Bobby realizes that he is psychically connected to the monster when he travels out-of-body to its location: just above the spot where they are camped. The beast is about to spring into their midst when Bobby manages to awaken and gazes directly at it. Though he can't see it, he knows where it is and realizes the beast fears him too. Bobby suspects he must find the reason in order for his group to survive.

The next day, they make it to within four miles of the confluence, their hopes running high, when the creature springs its trap. It has dammed the river in a narrow rapid using the rafts of the many boaters it has killed over the past few days. Each rafter in Bobby's group must pass directly by the beast, and not all survive. Bobby and Abigail fight back and believe they have killed the monster using the exact method that

COMMENTS

adds dimensionality to story and provides more clues to nature of the beast.

Technically, petroglyphs are drawings on rocks, not walls, by definition.

Plot shows sheriff's people in jeopardy.

Increases tension of menace.

Possibly another emotional turning point as Bobby realizes his connection to the beast.

Gives first indication of monster's vulnerability and why protagonist alone can save the day.

Would be more effective in synopsis if the days were numbered to define "ticking clock."

Big Scene and turning point.

Apparently this is the climax of the book. Could be made clearer that this is the final "life and death" struggle.

MAIN PLOT SUMMARY	COMMENTS
had accidentally killed the man on the Klamath—rope entrapment. At last Bobby releases himself of his guilt.	Good use and resolution of backstory.
At the take-out, the survivors are met by law enforcement. Earl Bohannan believes Bobby's story of the beast but will not acknowledge it publicly because of the panic it would cause.	
In the denouement, Bobby and Abigail plan marriage for the following summer. One afternoon, Bobby dozes and has the old nightmare. He realizes its meaning: the creature still lives. It will haunt his dreams until they meet for the final showdown in the sequel, *Here There Be Dragons*.	The romantic subplot could have been foreshadowed more strongly. Excellent way to set up for sequel.

ANALYSIS

In his synopsis, the author has done a good job of introducing the protagonist and the event in his past that haunts him. The story seems to be a good fit for category, or genre, horror, except perhaps in its length, which is substantially longer than the 55,000–65,000 that genre fiction usually runs. The author reveals a number of interesting and diverse points of view and focuses attention on a number of turning-point scenes. The menace grows, seems unstoppable. I would like to have had more explanation to the beast's motives and history to understand why it has suddenly appeared and why it is killing humans. Likewise, we can't help but wonder how and why this thing has been psychically linked to the protagonist since childhood.

The sense of tension within the synopsis would be heightened if the author were specific about which day this is of the eight, rather than saying "each night," "one night," "the next day." It would have also been stronger if the style had been "creepier" to convince me that in reading the book I will be afraid.

The climax seemed anticlimactic and should be rewritten to give a sense of crescendo culminating with the triumph over the beast and reaching freedom.

SYNOPSIS

Generation-X (off-beat mainstream) by James D. Axtell

Title: *Berlin Café*

This novel was represented by Jamie Forbes at Jeff Herman Literary Agency. This imaginative tale also has aspects of magical realism.

MAIN PLOT SUMMARY	COMMENTS
Wiley is in trouble. He drives his friends across the California/Nevada border going ninety miles an hour. Someone up ahead catches Wiley's eye. She is a hitchhiker, thin as a prison-camp survivor, holding out her thumb and not caring if he picks her up or runs her over. Same difference. Her name is Lola. She wants to go north because it's cold up there and she wants to be so cold she can't feel anything. Rebecca stops cleaning her gun and says hi. Rebecca is Wiley's girlfriend, a wicked combination of low self-esteem and repressed aggression.	The lead paragraph does double work; it introduces the quirky characters and manages, even though in summary, to convey the off-beat mood characteristic of the novel.

Not your everyday character.

By the end of the first paragraph, the reader has a good sense that this cast of characters would resonate with the Generation X sense of alienation, angst, but no clear center. |
| At a motel that night, Wiley wakes up to the sound of an airplane. Only he can hear it. It's been following him for hundreds of miles. He's losing his mind. | Introduces the element that will offer a touch of magical realism and injects curiosity from its mystery. |

Main Plot Summary

On the road, Wiley's friend Fritz is hitting on Lola. This bugs him. He's starting to like the hitchhiker, and he knows what Fritz can do. He pulls the car over and he argues with his friend. There's a scuffle, and Fritz gives in though he could have easily beaten him. They get in the car and move on. It seems like they are always moving on.

In a sparse motel in Fresno, they stay up late talking about how they hooked up. Wiley had flown to Germany to meet up with Fritz. He had waited at a table in Berlin and Fritz was late. An old man at the table next to Wiley introduces himself. The old man is dying and wants to talk to him, to tell him something. His name is Stephan and he's been in love only one time. Wiley is impatient waiting for Fritz. Finally his friend shows up and takes him to a club where they meet Rebecca. Later, Wiley wishes he'd listened to what the old man had said. At night, in his dreams, the old man's story comes back to him in bits and pieces and grabs hold of his imagination like a starving dog gnawing at his leg.

Wiley, Fritz and Lola have breakfast the next morning. Rebecca is asleep and they plan to bring her back something. When they return, though, she is gone. Never leave her alone. They knew that, and she'd awakened by herself, freaked out and run off in Wiley's car. She could be anywhere, but she has always come

Comments

Author uses slang, reinforcing language for this book's audience.

Seems to reinforce the feeling that the search for place or meaning might never replace always moving on. Again, fits Gen-X.

Author supplies backstory.

Should have stayed in past tense for events that are backstory.

In this mood-generating novel, the old man clearly becomes a strong image and force to the protagonist.

Another key character.

Because the backstory was erroneously given in present tense, for a moment it is unclear whether this present action is also in the past.

Offers some conflict in lieu of a clear-cut plot.

Also foreshadows a break-off between Rebecca and Wiley, although none of these

Main Plot Summary

back before, but when she does, she doesn't want to talk about it. Wiley and her have a fight over it, but they move on.

At night, Wiley has a dream about the old man. Stephan is a reporter in Berlin in 1925. It is a wild town, a town of intellectuals, visionaries, artists, Nazis, and Communists. It is crazy. It is a lot like the '90s. Stephan is at a café, The Berlin Café, and he's interviewing a female pilot. Her name is Paula and she is planning to leave the next day on a cross-country flight across Russia. She cannot live in Berlin or any city. She is planning on flying until she finds another place. She is moving on too.

Wiley and the rest go to Los Angeles. Months ago, he'd realized the insurance money he'd been squandering on aimless travel would not last forever. A friend of his from film schy work for him. He gets sucked into the Hollywood scene and ends up working as an assistant director on his friend's film.

Fritz and Lola have begun a relationship despite Wiley's maneuverings to stop it. Lola wants to leave L.A.. She and Wiley argue when he says he's "been around." She says that he's looked around, unable to commit himself to some place or some thing, or someone.

Comments

characters seems to care about each other. Incorrect grammar—Wiley and her—detracts.

Definitely asks reader to leave open what is Wiley's real life versus his dream life. The dream world has much greater vibrancy and meaning.

Good echo of one of the book's images.

Continues the mood of aimless wandering, perhaps intensifying the reader feeling that the characters are heading in the wrong direction, so in that sense creates tension.

Emotional turning point.

MAIN PLOT SUMMARY	COMMENTS
Finally, Fritz dumps her and she disappears. Wiley is crushed. Why are people always leaving him? He remembers his father who left him, and whose death and insurance settlement was paying for all the bumming around he's doing. Wiley cannot find Lola anywhere; he just has to get out of that town. He is worried about the film, but he has to go.	Story deepens. Importance of Lola surfaces.
Wiley, Rebecca, and Fritz head north into Oregon where they stay at a cabin owned by Wiley's older sister. There, Wiley dreams of Berlin again. In the dream, Paula and Stephan stay up late talking and lamenting that they didn't meet earlier. They are in love. Paula offers Stephan a seat on the plane, but he is scared of flying. The next morning she is gone. He will never meet someone like that again.	Parallels between Wiley and Lola and Stephan and Paula become stronger and the dividing line between reality and dream continues to blur. Strong symbolism and fascinating depiction of magical realism.
The plane is following Wiley. He hears it and rushes out onto the beach one night. There it is, flying low over the waves, Paula's plane. She waves at him for a minute, then flies off. Just before the vision fades, Wiley hears the engine cough, then stop dead.	Build up of tension.
Wiley's sister shows up. They do not get along. He has always blamed her for their father's death. His dad was a pilot who died in a plane crash flying home for his daughter's birthday. Thinking of that, Wiley is determined not to let Paula crash too. He comes up with the brilliant idea of waiting outside at night where he last	Another layer is revealed in Wiley's backstory. Seems laden with meaning, from the death of his father, the importance of Lola, and his own quest.

MAIN PLOT SUMMARY

saw her and signaling her with a flashlight, maybe to help her land. She doesn't show up, and he falls asleep and dreams again. He sees Stephan in a small Russian inn listening to a group of farmers talking about a plane that nearly crashed but whose engine restarted at the last minute.

In the middle of the night, Wiley gets a phone call from Lola. She had been staying with someone else who had promised to take her north but never did. She's leaving and will meet them in San Francisco. He gets her, and they try to pick up where they left off as if nothing happened. It's not that easy. Rebecca is increasingly jealous of Lola's pull on Wiley, and Fritz is frustrated that their days of idle traveling have been replaced by a strange trip taking this hitchhiker north.

In Washington, Wiley calls his friend, Sport, and finds out that the movie will never be released because of financing problems. Wiley is left with no inheritance and no job, nothing but a girlfriend who is now flirting with his best friend, Fritz. Lola wants to go farther north. She feels Wiley needs to go north more than she does, to end his dreams and stop all this running around. Wiley and Lola start falling for each other. Lola says she cares about him; she really does. Wiley sees a terrified Stephan sitting on the bed next to Lola. The hallucination, or whatever, gets up and runs down the

COMMENTS

Elimination of worldly ties, and symbolically to his father.

Turning point by some statement of truth about the protagonist's problem and character weakness.

MAIN PLOT SUMMARY

stairs with Wiley chasing after him. Wiley confronts the man and his romantic vision of a woman, Paula, he really never knew. Wiley rejects that old romantic view.

Needing money, Fritz robs a store and wants to make a run south. Wiley, having confronted his hallucinations, gives Fritz the keys to his car. Fritz and Rebecca leave together, while Wiley and Lola fly to Alaska, committing themselves to not just traveling around anymore. Committing themselves to each other. In one of his dreams he sees Stephan hiring a fisherman to take him across the Bering Strait to the same place. Wiley finds the same hill he'd dreamed Stephan finding, the hill where Paula might have crashed. Because of his fear of heights, he is unable to get up to it. He and Lola are lost in the snow and desolate cold of Alaska. Search parties will be looking for them, but it is questionable whether or not they will be found. Wiley just wants it all to end, the dreams and hallucinations. He thinks being there will do that. Lola tries to comfort him. He rests his head in her lap and she sings a song to him that sounds familiar, the one Stephan and Paula had danced to the night before she left. He realizes he's already done what he needed to do. He's learned to commit to someone, Lola, and doesn't need to find Paula and the old romanticism she and Stephan believed in so strongly.

COMMENTS

"Running from" seems to be a theme.

Giving up the car, Wiley's primary vehicle for "running from" and hapless moving, is a turning point.

Major change. Key word: commitment.

Fascinating intertwining of these four characters' lives—or perhaps two in two times and places.

This is the climax of the story, and the reader has a chance to experience the images and decisions, more than to intellectualize the meaning.

[*The writer requested that I not print the ending of the story, even in synopsis form. In terms of structure, he ends the synopsis shifting into some of the strong poetic imagery and sense of immediacy that a reader would experience by actually reading the book.*]

ANALYSIS

A story that is literary and involves magical realism, off-beat characters, and only a thin thread of plot is a very hard story to capture in a synopsis. James Axtell has done a splendid job of doing so. The strength of the synopsis is in his clarity, the well-selected key words that reflect the themes, how he conveys the book's imagery, and resonates with the Generation-X sense of reality. The only weakness is in synopsis structure: He should have used past-tense verbs to convey the backstory that was not part of the unfolding parallel story.

Whether or not you use a synopsis in your marketing package, you will now know how to write one for the body of the query. The hub of the wheel, and the main tool in your marketing kit, is the query, the subject of the next two chapters.

A FOOT IN THE DOOR

"Running the Writer's Iditarod"

Patricia Jean Hyatt, author of mainstream historical novels

"The race is not always to the swift but to those who keep on running," says the note clamped to Patty Hyatt's computer. "I can't tell you how many dark days that's pulled me through," she says.

It's a good thing Patty did not know she'd be running the equivalent of the Alaskan Iditarod, the 2350-mile dog-sled race between Nome and Fairbanks, Alaska, when in 1988 she ended her career as a legal secretary to become a novelist. Her husband, head of a university law library, showed her a transcript of the defense's 1933 closing argument in a notorious and seemingly hopeless murder case. "I was intrigued because, like the O.J. case," Patty explains, "the defense won."

The real-life subjects were aviators Bill Lancaster and Jessie "Chubbie" Keith-Miller, who first made headlines in 1927 for their open-cockpit records; then in 1933 made international news because of Bill's scandalous murder trial—and acquittal—for the classic love-triangle death of Haden Clarke.

The first 150-page version of *Land of Thirst* practically wrote itself in three months. But Patty quickly learned she'd produced a mere narrative outline, not a novel. She backed up. The project was giant in scope, so she plunged into three years of research.

Patty also took the first of many courses in writing, which led her to recast the novel from narrative outline form into scenes. "In the fourth year," she recalls, "I realized that I had bogged down because I'd chosen the wrong protagonist." Patty started over.

The next mountain on her journey cost her more than a year's time. She had started the novel so far into the story that it forced much of the dramatic action into flashback.

Five years into the project, Patty found a good starting point. "Now I was writing forward in the story, but I wrote unnecessary scenes or captured in ten pages what would now take me two pages or even a paragraph. It was a slow learning process."

When she'd completed three-quarters of her 750-page draft, I recommended that she start marketing. In 1993, as part of this initial push, Patty entered the Pacific Northwest Writers Contest and won second place. Bolstered with new confidence, Patty also entered the no-longer-available national Heekin Group Foundation contest for the exemplary novel-in-progress. She made it to the semifinals.

She secured interest from agent Denise Marcil, who said the first thing that had to go were those ninety-two patiently written—and prizewinning—opening pages. Patty says, "It wasn't until I started my second novel, which was entirely fiction, that I finally understood the difference between fiction and story, novel versus chronicle. The second novel taught me to make big leaps in time and events that made sense. I went back and fixed *Land of Thirst.*"

With Denise's generous help, Patty had compressed the novel into 550 pages. Still, the novel didn't win Denise's representation. After two years of working together through multiple revisions, they amicably parted.

Patty re-entered the marketplace, but not willingly: "To me, marketing is like visiting the dentist—something you must do. I don't mind writing queries and synopses, but I don't like being judged, found wanting, and not knowing why. You have to whistle in the dark, because marketing's a limbo place. An uncomfortable place."

Despite her dislike for the process, Patty religiously honored "Marketing Mondays," sending out queries in batches of five from her list of previously targeted agents. She tracked query statuses and kept records of rejections.

In 1996, Patty systematized her targeting of reputable agents. She sent for brochures of fifty writers conferences gleaned from the annual May article in *Writer's Digest* magazine, and compiled information about the attending agents. Her targeting led to the Rocky Mountain Fiction Writer's Conference and their Colorado Gold contest.

"It was one of the few contests which, like Pacific Northwest Writers, offered a critique. That's what I was really interested in," she remembers. "Outside feedback. I entered the synopsis and first twenty pages of my second novel. Then, what the heck, I tossed in *Land of Thirst*."

Both novels swept two out of the three finalist positions. Patty flew to Colorado to accept first place for her literary novel-in-progress and second place for *Land of Thirst*.

So what sustained Patty through her Iditarod? She says the journey was made possible by support from other writers (she belongs to two critique groups); by classes and the encouragement of mentors and teachers; by reading and independent study; by support from her husband; by the perspective of her independent book editor; and by the successes of a few contest wins.

"I was aware of the rejection rate," Patty says, "but I knew from my support groups and from my own heart that what I had written was good. Most writers don't have support groups or the persistence or the skill that I have developed, so I figure the statistics apply to someone else, but they don't apply to me."

CHAPTER SIX

Dissecting the Query

- ◆ Queries Defined
- ◆ Lead
- ◆ A Model Query Letter
- ◆ Body
- ◆ Closing
- ◆ Style
- ◆ Types and Uses
  - Query Letters
  - Query Packages
  - Unconventional Queries
  - E-mail Queries
  - Oral Queries
- ◆ A Foot in the Door: "Overcoming Marketing Block" by Patsy Hand

"My agency gets 6000 queries a year," Donald Maass said speaking at an agents' forum at a 1997 writers' conference in the Seattle area. I watched half a dozen other agents nod their heads in agreement. "The query is an art form unto itself," he added, going on to explain what he looks for in a query letter.

The volume of queries crossing agent and editor desks allows these pros to spot logical inconsistencies, convoluted plots, inadequate motivations, unpublishable lengths, and other "instant rejection" problems—problems related to marketing before a manuscript is ready. Agents and editors are also experts at spotting skillful writing, good story ideas, and promising author credentials.

They are the first to acknowledge the capriciousness and subjectivity of the selection process. To a query about a horror novel, one agent told an audience, "I don't represent horror. I don't like it; it scares me." Ten seconds to dismissal. But, regarding a query about a woman's recovery from insanity in a Montana mental hospital, the same agent responded with enthusiasm. "I like dark novels, and I am interested in mental illness in fiction. I'd be interested in seeing this novel." Ten seconds to acceptance.

You cannot control rejections based on the personal tastes of agents and editors. However, you can learn to craft queries that are well written and clear enough to attract the interest of an agent or editor who does like your ideas.

Queries Defined

On the surface, query letters look simple. After all, they are "only" letters of inquiry: Writer seeks agent or editor interested in novel. A query's sole purpose is to gain a request to see the manuscript. So simple.

Not so simple. My ex-husband, owner of a business mowing roadside brush, told me that whenever he writes a letter, he always thinks, "Not bad for a brushcutter." What's a writer going to say, "Not bad for a writer?" Writers face a unique challenge. They cannot avoid the fact that even a query letter showcases their wares. The judgment of their abilities begins with the query, even though it demonstrates nonfiction writing, as opposed to the fiction they seek to sell.

Other reference works on how to write queries have made the assumption that a query is a query, whether for proposing a magazine article, a how-to book, or a novel. After all, they have the same basic structure: lead, body, conclusion. This assumption has left novelists without help in describing content that is entirely different from nonfiction. What follows here corrects that error and outlines the structure, content, style, and variations unique to writing queries *for novels*.

Because of the 99 percent rejection rate, you should expect to see just 1 positive response in 100 letters. Most of the sample queries in this chapter averaged about a 25 percent positive response rate, 25 responses per 100. They are good examples. Every author was *unpublished* when he or she wrote and sent the query. Every author succeeded in getting a foot in the door, that is, in gaining requests for his or her manuscript. About half of the manuscripts are, at this book's publication, agent represented or published.

For a sense of a whole query letter, read the model query written by Carolyn Rose that is offered and analyzed in Sidebar 6-1. This is for her second mystery, *Consulted to Death*, published in 2001 by a small mystery press, Deadly Alibi, in Vancouver, Washington.

Lead

Leads refer to the beginning of a query letter, after the salutation. They may be as short as the first line, or as long as the first couple of paragraphs. A successful lead hooks and holds its reader's attention.

There are three basic elements in a query lead: hooks, other details about your book, and comparisons with other books like your own.

Novelists have a choice of two basic types of hooks, creative or business.

CREATIVE HOOK

A creative hook plays on the idea of showcasing a writer's skill as a writer. The goals are to rivet interest in reading on and to explain more details about the book after the hook. The creative hook involves greater risk than the business hook because of its "artistic license." However, it may be the best hook for novelists who lack publishing accomplishments and must rely solely on their demonstrated skill in writing.

The most common variations among creative hooks include:

- Direct immersion in the story
- Discussion of the period, setting, or milieu
- Presentation of the theme

DIRECT IMMERSION IN THE STORY

This kind of creative hook often makes use of dialogue to plunge the reader of the query directly into the voice and situation of a character. If you take this approach, as did Pat Swope for her historical novel *Family Act*, choose dialogue that is significant, thematic, and sufficiently unique or emotionally intense. Notice how Pat's lead quickly segues into reader immersion in the story, ending with the setting and period.

Sidebar 6-1

Model Query Letter: Mystery

LETTER	COMMENTS
Dear Agent or Editor:	
The realm of local television is a volatile one—where large egos collide, anchors fight to get their faces on the air a few extra seconds, reporters compete for major stories, and careers can be derailed if even a few hundred viewers click to another channel. Backbiting is more common than back-patting, and the words "job" and "security" are seldom used together. Controlling this tiny universe is a television consultant. As *Consulted to Death* begins, he's about to be killed.	Although Carolyn Rose chose to query only agents, the form for writing a query is the same to editors.
	This query lead emphasizes the unique milieu of television news. It demonstrates the writer's skill and voice.
	The last sentence, a power position, delivers the suspenseful punch.
The mystery novel, which runs 75,000 words, centers around Assignment Editor Casey Brandt. Divorced, distrustful, and disgusted with her boss' coverage decisions, she's a few years away from middle age and a few weeks away from being fired at the consultant's command. When he's found stabbed in the back, she thinks it's poetic justice. The police think she's the prime suspect, especially when two more people die. To stay out of jail, Casey must catch the killer. But before she can, she has to let go of the belief that she can "do it alone" and learn to have faith in those who love her.	After the lead, it's important to tell the type of novel and length.
	The body of a well-done query provides a succinct, character-driven synopsis of the story.

LETTER	COMMENTS
For twenty years, I have worked in newsrooms in Oregon, Arkansas, and New Mexico as a producer, assignment editor, writer, and researcher. *Consulted to Death* lets me combine my knowledge of the business and the dark humor of its "characters" with my love of fiction writing. I have been published in *Dogwood Tales, Ellery Queen's Mystery Magazine, Seventeen,* and *Murderous Intent.* Since 1990 I have regularly attended critique groups.	The final paragraph of the body of a query offers the author's bio, putting emphasis on any credentials related to writing and any publication credits. Involvement in critique groups indicates a writer's seriousness and willingness to self-edit.

I am seeking representation and am enclosing an envelope for your comments.
    I look forward to hearing from you soon.
        Sincerely,
        Carolyn Rose
	Concludes with a "handshake," a typical business-letter close. Telling them you've enclosed an SASE improves your chances of getting a reply.

"I'll learn what you want, Papa, so you'll love me again. And I'll behave so that woman will let me come home. But you can't make me like one damned thing about this place."

From the steps of the convent to which her father and new stepmother have sent her, ten-year-old Angie Alleman begins her "search for love in all the wrong places." When she is sent home from the convent in disgrace, she falls in love with strong, sweet-talking Santee, who marries and then deserts her, leaving her destitute, pregnant, and not yet sixteen. She vows to find a way to keep her child, and against all odds, she does. She stars in vaudeville—it is 1910—and then in the first two-reel movies made in Hollywood.

DISCUSSION OF THE PERIOD, SETTING, OR MILIEU

Author Melissa Jensen's career as a published novelist began in 1993 with a query to literary agent Denise Marcil, who subsequently represented Melissa on the sale of four Regency romances and one historical-era romance. (Her breakthrough story is featured in chapter eleven.) Read the following hook in her query about her Regency romance called *Fire and Thorn*, and notice the unique way this author leads the reader into her book's period. Also, note what covert message this lead sends namely, that this writer knows the period about which she seeks to write, and that she is an intelligent, literate person.

> Sometime in the late part of the eighteenth century, Sebastian Chamfort said, "Love, such as it is in Society, is only the exchange of fantasies, and the touch of two bodies." Among the *ton* [upper class] of Regency England, the sentiment holds just as true. Having read, reread, and studied the works of Jane Austen, and greatly appreciating her wit and talent, I still find myself wondering what sparks might have flown had Darcy and Elizabeth Bennet *touched* in full view of the reader.

Creative leads work to establish the unique milieu of the novel, displaying what the writer hopes will be a strong enough allure to draw the agent or editor into their stories. In chapter four (page 62), I included a one-page synopsis written by Carolyn Rose. Reread the first paragraph of her corresponding query, which is also included as a model query in Sidebar 6-1 at the beginning of this chapter. Her first paragraph focuses entirely on the setting and milieu of her mystery. An additional message in the lead advertises Rose's facility with language, her writer's voice, and her understanding of suspense, as evidenced with the last clause—"he's about to be killed."

PRESENTATION OF THE THEME

A description of a novel's theme at the beginning of a query announces an author's sophistication with novel structure. Theme, the story's message about life, is one of the more difficult concepts for writers to grasp. It hinges upon the ability of a writer to step back from her creation and determine its meaning. The fact that a writer knows her book's theme elevates her above other writers still groping in the dark, and whose books may therefore suffer from multiple themes, unclear or competing themes, or no theme at all.

Here is a presentation of theme in a successful query on a historical mainstream novel written by Patricia Hyatt, who said of her sixty-seven letters—and rejections—to literary agents before securing representation, "One third asked to see the novel, one third sent a form rejection, and one third never responded at all."

> Love heals grief and makes us whole. What happens, then, when a young woman is denied love in the midst of grief? In *Land of Thirst*, she suppresses her pain with the thrill of adventure. But adventure is not love, nor is it a substitute for love. This is the theme of my 460-page mainstream historical novel based upon the lives of English aviator Bill Lancaster and Australian aviatrix Jessie "Chubbie" Keith-Miller. Their lessons transcend their own colorful lives and historical period.

Business Hook

Business hooks are straightforward letters that inform a reader about a novel without any attempt to dazzle him with the novelist's writing abilities. Variations in the business lead allow writers to emphasize:

- Particulars about the book
- Author credentials and awards
- Referral or recommendation sources

Particulars About the Book

Here's an example of a query lead for a children's book, *Ice Ax*, proposed by writer Bill Lynch. When critiqued by one agent, she noted the clarity of his lead and how many agents appreciate knowing immediately the details about the type of book, length, and audience. As you can see, he quickly followed these details with his second-most important information—about a contest award.

> *Ice Ax* is a 33,000-word adventure story for fifth- and sixth-grade readers. It won the 1994 Juvenile Fiction third-place award in the Pacific Northwest Writer's Conference contest.

Bill secured representation but the agent was not able to sell his book and returned the project.

AUTHOR CREDENTIALS AND AWARDS

A different use of the business lead presents the writer's credentials first rather than particulars about the book. If you have sufficient credentials, beginning a query this way almost always initiates a request to see the manuscript, because the writer's accomplishments guarantee the professionalism and quality of the manuscript. Read this next example of a modest but confident presentation of a writer's credentials written by Paul Cody in his query that led to a two-book contract with Baskerville Publishing.

I am a writer in Ithaca, New York, have an MFA from Cornell, and am associate editor of *Cornell Magazine.* I've received a grant in fiction writing from the New York State Foundation for the Arts, as well as a Stegner Fellowship from Stanford (which I declined)…

Contest awards, grants, prior book publications (even of nonfiction), short-story publications, and work within the writing field—from teaching to television—all paint a picture of your professionalism. They are part of your portfolio. If you don't deem them important enough for emphasis in your lead, you can include them in a paragraph of author biography that comes later in the query. If, however, your award, grant, or short-story relates directly to the novel about which you are querying, this is too important *not* to feature in the lead.

Consider this lead by Jane Maitland-Gholson. Her explanation of both contest sponsors adds weight to the recognition she received but would have been a point missed by any agent or editor unfamiliar with these particular contests. Jane succeeded in gaining representation but, after six months, her literary agent was unable to sell her novel to any major houses.

Enclosed is a one-page synopsis of my literary novel, *The Ruthie Journals.* I hope that it interests you for possible representation. It won the 1993 Hackney Literary Award, a contest sponsored as part of Birmingham-Southern College's Writing Today Conference. The contest includes a $2000 cash award and attracted more than 700 authors in 1993. *The Ruthie Journals* was also a semifinalist for a Heekin Fellowship, a $10,000 award offered yearly by The Heekin Foundation for a novel in progress.

REFERRAL OR RECOMMENDATION SOURCES

A gracious mention of how you were referred to the agent or editor, or a sincere and meaningful personal remark, will acknowledge an agent or editor's humanity and individuality.

At nearly every writer's conference I've attended, some agent radiates waves of gratitude toward the unagented writers who, having read acknowledgments to them in published novels, mention that fact in their queries. "I read and loved so-in-so's novel, *xyz,* and saw your name cited in the acknowledgments." Do these writers get a form rejection? *Au contraire!* Not usually.

Patsy Hand, querying on *Frozen in Time,* a novel of speculative fiction that she has recently begun to market, opens her lead with the following paragraph:

> I have just read an article quoting you in the *Publishers Weekly* of October 21. I also finished a suspense novel by David Baldacci, *Absolute Power,* in which he states that he is with your agency. These two pieces of information tell me that my speculative fiction novel, *Frozen in Time,* might be of interest to you.

Martha C. Lawrence is an editor turned first-time novelist who recognized the value of personal connections. After composing a business lead for her mystery, *Murder in Scorpio,* an Edgar, Anthony, and Agatha nominee published in 1995, Martha wrote the following mental tickler to the agent she hoped would become her agent.

> My name might ring a bell. I began my publishing career with Simon and Schuster in New York, then served as an acquisitions editor for Harcourt Brace in San Diego. Although I left Harcourt six years ago, I do remember corresponding with you from time to time.

Acknowledge in your lead any meeting or discussion about your book involving the agent or editor to whom you are writing. Here is an example in a query lead written by Patricia Bradbury for her first book.

We met at the PNW (Pacific Northwest Writers) conference last summer where *Bandana Girl*, a YA (young adult) novel, placed in the top ten. Thank you for inviting me to send you the following material.

If you have been recommended to someone by another professional in the publishing field, that connection may be important enough to highlight by placing it in the lead. Or, mention the referral source in your query's conclusion. Some agents and editors will read queries submitted only upon recommendation of others in the field, a preference they state in the various agent directories. In this case, mention your connection in the lead or you may never have your query read at all.

DETAILS ABOUT YOUR BOOK

Like the data included by Bill Lynch in his lead to *Ice Ax* given earlier, most leads tell the reader what kind of book you've written, its setting or period, its length, and its central conflict and theme. In a sense, this pre-qualifies you—or allows instant rejection—with agents and editors who know right away whether they want that kind of book. From an agent's or editor's point of view, you're saving them time. Some writers put these details in a concluding paragraph of the body, but that is a weaker position than in the lead, since the data must be assimilated after the fact. Assuming your book does pre-qualify, the reader better connects with the synopsis of your book, which follows in the body of the query.

COMPARISONS WITH OTHER BOOKS

The minds of your query readers are busy ticking off items on a checklist, whether conscious of it or not. Agents, editors, and their readers are a busy lot, processing thousands of queries each year, hundreds each week. If your query pre-qualifies in your lead paragraph, the reader will examine it for other "qualifiers." One of those is a comparison to other published books.

Comparing yourself to other published writers is a tricky line to walk, because a writer who boasts of being "the next Harold Robbins," in half-inch letters (the lead in a real query shared with me by an agent) will receive a rejection so quickly, the envelope will be blistered where the agent pounded it shut.

Many agents advise finding at least two authors with whom you can position your novel, while remaining shy of claiming equality with millionaire novelists or Pulitzer-prize winners. For instance: "Similar to the plotting of Koontz but closer to the style of McCammon." If an agent does represent you, she'll use this positioning statement to pre-sell your book to editors, describing where your book fits in the vast array of similar titles. You can position this comparison in your lead or in your concluding paragraphs.

A positioning statement also sends a message that you read! And, that you read the kind of books that you have chosen to write. In many ways, American culture is fickle, fanatical, and fad-based. Certainly, the stories and styles that publishers supported in the past are not the same as those supported today. I am troubled whenever I meet a writer whose sole references are to long-ago classics. If you want to publish your novels, you must stay in touch with what is being published today.

Some agents suggest that you offer one comparison to a classic author and one comparison to a contemporary author. It is also acceptable to compare your book to movies that have sprung from books.

For example, in Carolyn Rose's query on another mystery, she started the second paragraph with, "The protagonist, Charlotte 'Charlie' Rogers combines the curiosity and memory of Miss Marple with the youth and tenacity of more modern female sleuths." Feeling more kinship with book-to-movie comparisons, writer Carol Craig, querying on her mainstream/literary novel, *Chocolate Soldiers*, writes, "This novel falls somewhere between *Fried Green Tomatoes* and *A Time to Kill* in style and content."

A particular form of comparison is called "a handle." Handles seem to me very Hollywood-like, but many agents like them—if they are accurate and not another version of the Harold Robbins example given earlier. They also seem to fit genre or mainstream thrillers more than they do literary or relationship-oriented mainstream books. The handle was introduced earlier as one way you can open a lead, using a formulaic-style of comparison. For instance, first novel *Meg* by Steven Alten got the handle "Jurassic Shark," because his thriller features a prehistoric shark called a megalodon.

At a recent Oregon writer's conference, literary agent Elizabeth Wales gave the example of a handle describing a literary novel as: "when John Updike's *Rabbit* meets Joseph Conrad's *Heart of Darkness*." Another agent offered the example: "When Mary Higgins Clark meets John Grisham," or "When Rosamunde Pilcher meets Susan Issaacs." A less-glitzy variation on the handle gives writers a blank to fill in: "This is a thriller in the style of *Tom Clancy* and for the same market as *Robin Cook.*"

I urge you to write several leads for your query and select the best. Some agents and editors express a forceful preference for the business lead, while just as many tell writers, "Excite me. Interest me. Make me sit up and take notice." If you don't think you can pull off a creative lead, stick with the familiar, and universally accepted, business lead. Follow this with strong writing in the body of your letter to secure interest in the novel itself.

Body

Remember, a query is unlike any other letter you may write. It does not beg, chat, demand, or pontificate. It sells. If your lead has done its job, you have secured reader attention. In the body of the query, you must deliver on the lead's promise. Here is where you describe the work that took you months, years, or decades to write.

In chapters four and five, you read several examples of what was called the "synopsis within the query." The primary element in the body of most queries is a synopsis of the story. This synopsis can take several forms with different emphasis, as follows:

- The Characterization-focused Query Synopsis
- The Story-focused Query Synopsis
- The Super Short Query Synopsis
- Query Information Unrelated to the Story
- The Excerpt-focused Query Synopsis

THE CHARACTERIZATION-FOCUSED QUERY SYNOPSIS

Across all genres and types of books, the last few decades have witnessed a strong sweep of style toward depth of characterization. Therefore, I recommend devoting the first part of the body of your query to characterization of your protagonist.

Aspire to characterize your protagonist so strongly and succinctly that your hero makes an indelible impression on the reader. Convey the story situation and terrible conflict that only your protagonist can resolve. You may sketch the past trauma and wound that scars your character and explains his weakness and strength, which you may also name. State or describe the setting and period to communicate the behavior or values of your protagonist.

Reread the query synopsis in chapter five, page 79, written by Patricia Bradbury for her mainstream/literary novel *Requiem for Red Hawk*. It is characterization-focused *and* super short. Read the first paragraph of the body of a two-page query that follows. It was written by first-time published author, Gregg Kleiner, for his literary novel. (His complete query is given in chapter seven, page 138.) If you react as I did, you'll be charmed by this paragraph, even though you've been deprived of reading his lead, which establishes the setting, the complexity of the book, and its themes.

> *Where River Turns to Sky* is the story of a half-dozen strangers who wind up living together in a rundown mansion in a small Oregon town called Lookingglass. The twist is that all these people are over eighty years old. And what brings them together is George Castor's lifelong fear of his own death, his hatred of nursing homes, and a dash of magic by a half-Paiute woman named Grace.

> As the novel opens, eighty-year-old George Castor has just discovered that his last good friend Ralph has died in a local nursing home while George was away on a fishing trip. Driving home to his farm in the rain, George makes a promise to Ralph that changes every remaining day of George's life.

Milt Cunningham selected a characterization-focused synopsis in his query for a category western, *The Killer and the Quaker*, which had been agent-represented but not sold. Notice how Milt's emphasis on the conflicts faced by his protagonist guarantees that the book will be full of suspense and clarity of motive. The use of a bulleted list is an atypical but creative choice by the author.

> Though raised a Quaker, Lash Pitkin, the nineteen-year-old protagonist, faces not only the moral frontier obligation to avenge his father's murder, but to protect his sister and himself from the crazed murderer, Silk Johnson, who has sworn to kill him and rape and kill Caroline.

Lash has four conflicts:

- The main physical conflict is with Silk Johnson, the killer.

- The second conflict is with his Quaker conscience as he tries to cope with the violence directed at him and Caroline.

- The third conflict is between himself and Caroline, his twenty-two-year-old sister, whose faith seems to grow stronger as Lash's faith weakens. The bond between them is strained as she sees him turning into just another frontier tough like the very ones that are trying to destroy them.

- Lash is also in conflict with Tyler, a powerful rancher who has driven all of the other homesteaders out of the country, and in his determination to get rid of Lash and Caroline, hires Silk, the gunslinger.

THE STORY-FOCUSED QUERY SYNOPSIS

In the body of the query, after a paragraph or less of characterization and situation, most authors summarize the rest of their novels in synopsis form (review chapter four). In order to limit your query to the preferred length of one page, you'll have to keep your basic query synopsis to about three paragraphs, no more than five.

This short synopsis must touch on all of the main elements of your story and highlight what is most important, including: the setting, the period, the story situation and central conflict, the protagonist and other main characters, the antagonist, the plot, the crises or emotional turning points, the climax, the lessons learned and the theme. All in about three paragraphs.

Can a less than ideal basic query synopsis, one that misses some elements, still win kudos and attract a request to see the book? Fortunately for the majority of writers, the answer is yes. Agents will tell you, "It's all in the execution."

THE SUPER-SHORT QUERY SYNOPSIS

The advantage of a super-short synopsis is that an agent or editor can read it quickly. If it is both short *and* well done, you earn extra points.

Anyone who has already written a query for a novel knows just how difficult that can be.

The query champions of the world somehow accomplish everything in *one* paragraph, like the one-paragraph synopsis by Kent Tillinghast for his mystery *Firedance* in chapter four (page 67). I could make an argument for breaking any long one-paragraph synopses into several, but that may be the voice of envy. Even a three-paragraph query is still some feat.

Author Paul Cody is one of those query champions, as evidenced by the following second paragraph for his literary novel. His credentials lead appears as an example earlier in this chapter (page 118). Though he has not profiled, or even named, his protagonist, his synopsis works, bearing out another maxim of writing: Rules are meant to be broken. Success can only be measured by the results. Here is the two-paragraph body of his query for his published novel, *The Stolen Child*:

> I have written a novel called *The Stolen Child*, which is about a boy who is abducted from a suburb of Boston in 1963, a month before the assassination of JFK. The book has multiple narrators, including the abducted boy—grown up, his mother, brother, and various people who met or knew the boy as a child and later as an adult. The book is about the abduction of this particular boy, but also about how he was stolen, in some way, from everyone who failed to rescue him, and how everyone who grows to adulthood has their childhood stolen from them, in one sense or another.
>
> The book is dark, and the narration complex, but it is, I think, a compelling exploration of love and loss, backlit by the death of a young president....

Query Information Unrelated to the Story

Some authors omit a summary of the plot or a sketch of the protagonist, deciding that foremost in importance is a personal brief about the author, the meaning of her work, or perhaps the reason why she wrote the novel. Omitting a synopsis within your query is a high-risk choice. However, remember the rule about rules....

The queries for *Ice Ax* by Bill Lynch and *Murder in Scorpio* by Martha C. Lawrence, mentioned for their leads earlier, are two such examples of an omitted story synopsis. In lieu of a synopsis, the body of Bill's query emphasizes the educational value of his book for nine-to twelve-year-old boys, while Martha's emphasizes her insider's connections, as well as the niche her sleuth offers to fulfill.

THE EXCERPT-FOCUSED QUERY SYNOPSIS

"Synopses tend to sound ridiculous," says James Axtell, author of a Generation-X novel. "I wanted agents to see my actual writing style." Use of the excerpt-focused query synopsis is still risky. The excerpt pulls a piece of the novel out of context and presents characters about whom the query reader knows nothing and lacks story details from which to understand or care about them. It's less risky if the writer includes a story synopsis in addition to the excerpt.

Writers who feature an excerpt hope that their writing style and voice sufficiently impress and dazzle an agent or editor to request their novels. As you can tell, the insecure or uncertain writer need not apply here. Selecting one or two paragraphs to represent and sell a 70,000- to 100,000-word novel is some kind of chutzpah.

Here is an example from a successful query written by Carol L. Craig for her mainstream/literary novel, *Chocolate Soldiers*, which gained her representation by a literary agent. I've included the two short paragraphs which precede and follow her excerpt. Notice how this query becomes a test of the author's voice and the perceived quality of the writing:

My protagonist, twelve-year-old Ruthanne, nicknamed "Spoiled" by her stepfather, must fight tooth and nail to maintain not only a friendship with a colored girl in racist Arkansas of the sixties, but to survive her childhood with her dreams intact.

As she writes from adulthood, looking back: *My friend Lacy and I used to meet at the ponds out back of where we grew up in Cave Junction, Arkansas. Over our favorite beverage, Chocolate Soldiers, we'd pour out our dreams. I was going to be a writer; she was going to Howard University and become a bigshot professor. We'd swirl our toes in the cool waters and sip on that sweet magic, imagining. We didn't know then that those Chocolate Soldiers were to be an allegory to our lives. Black, white. Bitter, sweet. Together we were unbeatable. But there was a war raging in our little town and across the nation. We were on the front lines and our dreams were the casualties.* [writer's italics]

I will not apologize for her poor grammar, born of poverty, nor for her character flaws, which are many. She is who she is. What I wanted was a book that could make people laugh, cry, and in the end think, just a little, about the meaning of family and friendships. To know that no matter the hand we're given in life, we can and must play it for all it's worth.

ADDITIONAL QUERY BODY INFORMATION

In addition to your synopsis or excerpt, the body of your query should provide other information if it is not already included in your lead. This next paragraph of the body could include a comparison of your book to other books or movies like it in style, content, or in some other way. You must include some biography of yourself, relative to writing, such as work as a teacher or writer, prior publications—both fiction and nonfiction, writing awards and residencies, and any relevant life experience to your novel. Like everything else in the query, keep this short.

I am often asked by aspiring novelists what they should write about themselves, if they have no publishing credits and their day job is unrelated to the writing field. My answer is to describe anything that shows you are a serious writer intent upon becoming a professional career novelist. You want your query reader to understand that you will write more than one book, because agents and editors alike often invest in an author's first work more than they get back in time, emotional energy, and money. They want career novelists. By the way, this has nothing to do with chronological age or how many other careers you have undertaken. Fortunately, you can begin your career at age twenty or eighty. While there may be some ageism in the publishing profession, the focusing lens is overwhelmingly on writing quality, not on age.

Include in your writer's biography a mention of writing classes, degrees in English literature or journalism, critique-group membership, years you have spent researching and writing, the number of novels you've written (even if unpublished), former work in a writing-related field, and life experience related to the subject of your novel.

Patricia Bradbury concludes the body of her query with one paragraph about the subject of her novel, *Requiem for Red Hawk*, and one with her biography.

In the hands of responsible professionals, psychiatric drugs and ECT (electro-convulsive therapy) can be powerful tools for healing. However, controversy is again stirring about the use and abuse of ECT, just as it did in the early '70s, making *Requiem for Red Hawk* timely. I did extensive research on "shock" therapy, on the use of convulsant drugs, and on the history of the Montana State psychiatric system, certainly a prime example of the barbarous conditions of many state mental hospitals less than twenty years ago.

This is my third finished novel. I've taken several writing classes and belong to a professionally led critique group.

Do *not* include the testimonials or critique comments from friends and family or "nice" rejection comments from agents or editors. You'll only succeed in making the reader cringe and brand you as an amateur. For some reason, testimonials in queries seem especially common among children's writers. Often, a grandparent, parent, or teacher will write that they "tested" their story on their children or students and "the kids loved it." As though the acceptance of children means they are also skilled judges of art and craft.

What you may do is ask someone with appropriate qualifications relative to the book you are writing to compose a letter of recommendation that you can include with your queries. For children's writers, such a person might be a school or city librarian, a teacher for the age-level you have written, but no letters or hand prints from the children, please! Many novelists ask professors, published authors, or their independent book editors to write letters of recommendation. It's best if these are included with the query and not sent separately, because they probably won't get matched up with the query.

Closing

Every query should close with a handshake. This amounts to the same type of conclusion that would appear in any business letter: "Thanks for your consideration. I look forward to hearing from you at your earliest possible convenience."

In addition, it's a good idea to make clear what you are enclosing with your query and to clarify anything in particular that you seek, beyond the obvious—representation or a manuscript request—from the agent or editor. For instance: "Please read the enclosed synopsis and initial chapters. I will gladly send the remainder at your request." Or, "I have enclosed a self-addressed stamped envelope." Or, "I have enclosed a synopsis and an SASE for your convenient reply. I look forward to hearing from you."

You may also indicate enclosures in the traditional, secretarial notation that follows your signature, such as: "enc: SASE, synopsis, first chapter." Do remember that you must *always* include an SASE—a self-addressed stamped envelope, or an SASM—a self-addressed stamped mailer. This is the writer's responsibility. Failure to do this raises the ire of the agent or editor and may cause instant rejection, no matter how compelling your query.

Style

The query for a novel constitutes a business correspondence, even if you open with a creative hook. Therefore, the style should conform to that of any business letter by being clear, straightforward, and serious, at least where you deliver information rather than showcase your talents as a novelist. Even if your novel leans strongly toward humor, avoid trying to make a query reader laugh or even smile. It really is a "just the facts, ma'am" type of document, although it is perfectly fine to state that your novel is a "romantic comedy" or that your "sleuth demonstrates a fine sense of humor."

When you write the body of your query, adopt synopsis style; summarize the story using present-tense verbs. When you depart from the synopsis and talk about the novel or yourself, use the past tense, as you normally would, i.e. "I have finished my 90,000-word contemporary mainstream novel...."

The query for a novel is, as writer James Axtell said, "the single most important piece of paper a novelist writes." Rewrite and revise it thoroughly. Because the query puts your writing on display, you must proofread your copy for typos, passive verbs, and grammatical errors. Read it aloud for cadence, color, and voice. Better yet, ask several eagle-eyed friends to critique it.

Another aspect of query style is length. Everyone prefers one page, but don't consider it a tragedy if your query runs into a second page. Especially if you use letterhead stationery, the header design combined with the conclusion, signature, and enclosure notations may consume one-third to one-half of the page. Absolutely use a second page over compromising one-inch margins or skipping the line space between single-spaced paragraphs.

And, like any business letter, use single space for the text.

Types and Uses

While some writers mail queries, others talk with agents or editors on the phone or in person and follow up these first contacts with a written query. Many writers pursue all avenues, written and oral queries.

Every writer should know about the following five types of queries and when they can be used.

- The Standard Query Letter
- Query Packages
- Unconventional Queries
- E-mail Queries
- Oral Queries

THE STANDARD QUERY LETTER

The earlier part of this chapter focused on the standard query letter. As a one- or two-page document, it includes a lead to hook the reader, a body with a synopsis and author biography, and a closing. Its purpose is to secure a request to read part or all of the novel and ultimately to secure agent representation or editorial purchase. It is the most common query. Full-length examples of standard query letters follow in the next chapter.

QUERY PACKAGES

The query package features a one-page standard query but also includes other materials, such as a one- or two-page synopsis, a separate author biography, and sometimes a letter of recommendation.

Writers who prefer query packages believe that the entire one-page standard, but short, query serves as the hook and is appreciated for its brevity. Then, if the query reader is still interested, he can read the enclosed synopsis, where the writer has more than three paragraphs to develop the book's essence. Or, the agent or editor can read more details about the author than allowed by the typical one paragraph in a standard query. Also, the materials may be reviewed in any order.

I haven't heard any agents or editors object to the query package. However, I have several reservations about it from a writer's point of view. I would not want to see writers using it as a substitute for thorough editing to achieve a concise standard query letter. Sometimes, the query package appeals to a writer's lazybone or to writers who err on the side of verbosity. Yet, a writer may improve his marketing results—suffer fewer rejection letters—by working harder to produce a succinct standard query letter.

Another risk with the query package involves the expansion of the typical, single paragraph of author biography into a full page. The writer must have enough relevant author qualifications to warrant a full page. Otherwise, the separate author biography may lead the query reader to see the writer as self-absorbed and not respectful of an agent or editor's time.

With these reservations aside, the query package offers a good marketing strategy. The writer focuses on one job for each enclosure, rather than trying to cram everything into one page. This separation of function allows more space to adequately develop the uniqueness of a novel. And, more author biography helps bring the writer alive, as if a character, and offers more ways for the query reader to relate to the person behind the story.

UNCONVENTIONAL QUERIES

By definition, unconventional queries break rules. Some writers create graphic formats that transform the query into something more like an advertisement or a newsletter than a letter. Some writers chance the use of colored, rather than standard white, or off-white, paper. Seattle-based agent Elizabeth Wales described her receipt of a query for a horror novel in a black envelope with red ink splattered on it to create the appearance of blood. Most agents would react in horror, all right. Elizabeth sent a rejection letter because she doesn't represent horror, but added a note telling the writer he had won her office's "unique package of the month" award.

Another agent told of receiving heavily perfumed paper, fabric-softener-like scented paper. She happened to have environmental allergies, so this thoughtless gesture on the part of the author gave the agent both a headache and a toxic-disposal problem.

Another break with convention is the inclusion of a long excerpt from your novel as part of a query package, not just a paragraph or two in the body. A talented friend of mine, Valerie Brooks, with a background in art and advertising, created an unconventional query package for her first novel, *Can You Hear Me Dreaming?* She used a legal-sized sheet of paper in a horizontal format. On the left two-thirds of the page, she typed the title in ¾" bold letters and, under the title, her byline in smaller type. The next line was a one-line synopsis, as it might appear in *Publishers Weekly.* Beneath that, she included a one-paragraph synopsis of the book. To the right, outlined to appear like a page from a published book, she included a climactic excerpt. She completed her package with a one-page author biography and a query letter on printed, letterhead stationery.

Her agents, Mary Alice Kier and Anna Cottle, who had also met Valerie at a weekend writer's workshop, responded positively, not only requesting her book and representing her, but telling her how impressed they were with her creative query.

However, an unconventional query can just as easily backfire. You may recall the foot-in-the-door story in chapter five of Charles Snellings. He had sent a query package (query, synopsis, photo, author biography, and excerpt) to an agent who subsequently represented him, but he took Charley to task for the excerpt. "It confused me," he said. "I didn't know what it was supposed to be and I didn't like the smaller font."

E-MAIL QUERIES

Don't. Don't send e-mail queries to agents or editors, except in two circumstances: they invite you to send e-mail, or, you live on a remote island off Madagascar with mail service from the mainland boat that comes once every three months. Or, in Sri Lanka, as was the case for an author who e-mailed Seattle-based agent, Elizabeth Wales.

Worldwide Internet service has created the capacity for anyone with a computer and modem to send mail to anyone with an electronic, i.e. e-mail, address. The reason that e-mail queries are not yet universal, despite their ease of transmission and elimination of paper consumption and postage expense, is because agents and editors must reserve their e-mail for business use—communication over contracts, deals, and details involving their published, or soon-to-be published, authors. For both agents and editors, "acquisitions" ranks far below serving the existing clients who are paying their bills. As more people shift to electronic mail, however, it's likely that agents will post one e-mail address for queries and another for business. As one, ahead-of-the-pack agent confided to me,

"E-mail response to queries is quicker, more expedient. Less paper and faster response time. I prefer e-mail queries."

ORAL QUERIES

Until now, we've been talking about queries that you the author makes. However, agents pre-sell books through telephone contact with editors. These are oral queries. Having secured interest from editors, agents follow up by sending manuscripts, often accompanied by synopses.

First-time novelists seeking to break in may also succeed via oral queries. For the most part, they have three avenues: via conferences, telephones, and arranged meetings. Actual strategies for marketing a novel in each of these three ways will be detailed in chapter ten on systematic marketing. However, the foundation of every oral query is a synopsis, be that one line, one paragraph, or one page.

Although composing the query, this "most important piece of paper you'll ever write," can be quite challenging, with practice and revision, you can make it look easy. As you know, anything done extraordinarily well looks, to the untrained eye, exceedingly simple.

To help train your eye, and provide models for queries from which you can pick and choose, the next chapter features and analyzes over a dozen successful queries for many different kinds of novels.

A FOOT IN THE DOOR

"Overcoming Marketing Block"

Patsy Hand, author of mystery, suspense, and mainstream novels

By her professional credentials, Patsy Hand is someone you'd select for your marketing team. Former director of a company with a program for schools and cities to combat drinking while driving, Patsy crisscrossed the country, marketing, selling, and administering the program, which now serves 600 cities. As a former real-estate agent in the "million-dollar club," she might just as well have been called Ms. Market. As a high-school English teacher, she made the toughest sale of all—making literature and creative writing come alive for teens.

"I worked at each job for three years," Patsy explains. "I got to the top and got bored. I kept getting drawn back to writing where I've never been bored and where I'll be challenged to learn for the rest of my life."

When it came to marketing her own writing—five completed novels and one in progress—Patsy floundered. "I'm a perfectionist," she admits, "and any feedback that my work 'wasn't right for us' meant in my mind that it was substandard. My tendency, after five, six, seven rejections, was to decide that a novel wasn't a very good work and to put it aside."

While her decision was an understandable reaction to form rejections, Patsy knows now that she completely missed the good news in the many long, personalized letters of rejection that she received over the years.

"The first time I sent my first novel, a contemporary mainstream, to an established New York agent, she sent back a fifteen-page letter indicating how I might rewrite the novel and telling me how she really loved the story. Being a complete novice, I put that novel on a shelf and never marketed it again."

Patsy then set her sights on mysteries. She sent her first to Jean Naggar Agency where two assistants and Jean read it and sent back a critique and encouraging rejection. "Among other things, I remember they said the ending was too predictable," Patsy recalls. "So I worked ten hours a day for two weeks and put a twist on the ending but never sent it back. I did market the book about fifteen more times and collected fifteen rejection letters. 'A great concept but the beginning is too slow,' they said. In hindsight, what I needed to do was revise it and mail it back, but I did neither."

When she completed her third novel, another mystery, Patsy sent it to an editor at St. Martin's. The rejection letter told Patsy that the story was "extremely interesting but somewhat episodic." And Patsy never rewrote it.

She recalls: "The comments about what didn't work in my stories always triggered the question, 'Does this rejection mean I should rewrite or start over?' I often missed the signals that my stories were worthy of revision."

She remembers well the day in her critique group when she proclaimed her marketing expertise and explained how easily she could market everyone else's work in the group. "I didn't realize until that moment that I had a marketing block when it came to my own work." Patsy says. When she began another novel, speculative suspense, her critique group and family hounded her to finish the novel and market relentlessly. They encouraged her to rewrite as recommended and, if rejected, not to cast the book aside and start another.

"Lots of agents requested it and responded with personal letters of rejection," Patsy comments. "Then I let weeks and months go by. On a brave day, I was looking through the agent directories and decided to call a New York agent who said she was interested in new writers. I pitched the book right on the telephone, and the agent requested the first 100 pages, telling me she didn't usually do this. I'm really good on the telephone. It's as if I'm selling to someone else, like I'm once removed." Despite her success on the phone, the book was again rejected.

But this time she kept on marketing.

She even captured the attention of a Pulitzer nominee, a novelist and writing teacher who is the cousin of a good friend. Tapping her public relations skills, Patsy suggested lunch and boldly asked the author if she would, for a fee, look at her work. She did.

Patsy remembers her comments: "I know her to be an abrupt, cuttingly honest person. She told me that I was overdue to get published, had a unique story and good characters."

While Patsy did as she has always done, moved on to write a next novel, this time mainstream/literary, she continued the momentum of marketing her former works. One member of her critique group had found representation with an agent who represents several bestselling mystery writers. Patsy followed up suggestions and queried the agent on three novels: her first mystery, a psychological suspense story, and her speculative suspense story. She sent a synopsis and first chapter on each, relying upon a letter of recommendation from me as her book editor.

Patsy recalls the day she had long awaited: "The agent called me, said she liked all three of my novels. All of them! She liked my style, my voice, the fact that each one was different. We agreed that my psychological suspense novel, *Windstalker*, should be our first focus."

After reading the entire manuscript, the agent asked for some minor revisions, adding, "If you can make these changes, you've got yourself an agent." In contrast to critical feedback by agents or editors on her first works, Patsy agreed with the assessment and knew exactly how to make the changes. No sweat.

Patsy also recognizes the irony that as a marketing expert, she found difficulty in selling her own work. "One of the most effective approaches to any sales is networking. If a writer knows someone who is published, who will write a note to an agent, that may do it. It did in my case."

In hindsight, despite her marketing block, Patsy has always known she would get published. With an agent helping her, she believes that day is close at hand. "I truly don't believe in odds. Someone has to succeed so it might as well be me. Writing is the only thing in my life that I haven't immediately succeeded at," Patsy reflects, "which has doubled the frustration. But I've always set high standards for myself and held to an inner dream. When a person or situation has touched me, I've wanted to create a story that in turn would touch the reader. Writing is the most joyous adventure I could go on, and ultimately the inner satisfaction is far greater than outer recognition."

CHAPTER SEVEN

Successful Queries

- Literary—Contemporary
- Literary—Generation X, Magical Realism
- Mainstream Historical, Biographical
- Mainstream Historical
- Mainstream Historical, Epic
- Mainstream Contemporary Christian
- Mainstream—Contemporary, Adventure
- Mainstream, Contemporary, Gay/Lesbian/Bisexual
- Mystery
- Suspense
- Speculative Fiction
- Fantasy
- Romance, Regency
- Romance, Western Historical
- Children's, 9–12s
- Breakthrough: "Don't Tell Me What I Can't Do" by D. Marion Wilkinson

When writers step into the world of marketing, they can shield themselves with one piece of knowledge: No matter how brilliant the sword of editorial judgment, it is always tempered by the personal tastes and preferences of its owner. I was once given a referral by another freelance editor to a writer with a novel set in Texas. Because the editor had suffered a bad experience related to that state, she would not edit any story set there. Put her in the shoes of an acquisitions editor at a publishing house. Two fine queries arrive at her desk and one describes a Texas historical epic. The other is set anywhere else. They may both get rejected, but based on what I've related here, which one is more likely to be rejected?

This chapter presents full-length queries of first-time authors whose books subsequently sold, of writers who are now agent represented, and queries of aspiring novelists who gained a high request rate for their manuscripts. I have provided so many examples because I believe that one of the most powerful ways we learn is through modeling, following a good pattern set by someone who has succeeded.

In the right-hand column of the page, you will find comments about structure, content, and style. Because this too is editorial opinion, compare my evaluations with your own. You may reach different conclusions, just as valid.

Last of all, you'll find a short biography of each query's author and the history of the author's efforts to break into publishing. At the end of the chapter, you'll find a more fully developed breakthrough story.

Note: You may want to return to this chapter when you are ready to study and write your own query letter.

QUERY LETTER

Literary—Contemporary

Where River Turns to Sky by Gregg Kleiner

Published in 1996 as an Avon Books Hardcover, this literary novel has been compared to *Fried Green Tomatoes at the Whistle Stop Cafe* and *A River Runs Through It.* One reviewer called the novel, "A heady mix of *Cocoon* and *One Flew Over the Cuckoo's Nest.*" This query connected the author to his agent. Gregg Kleiner's full breakthrough story is featured at the end of chapter twelve.

LETTER	COMMENTS
Dear Agent:	
I thank you in advance for taking the time to consider representing *Where River Turns to Sky*, my recently completed first novel.	A nice opening. You can't go wrong thanking someone in advance.

LETTER

Where River Turns to Sky is a novel about aging and dying, except the story—told from two alternating first-person points of view, one male and the other female—is a bizarre blend of magical realism, small-town farming, and Native American spirituality, all stirred together with a strong sense of place, the smell of earth and rain and fish, the sound of Canada geese flying over in the middle of the night.

As we baby boomers round the final corner, realize we're not immortal after all, and try to figure out how we're going to "do" old age, the timing for this novel is prime, because it tells a different story, an alternative approach to growing old.

Where River Turns to Sky is the story of a half-dozen strangers who wind up living together in a rundown mansion in a small Oregon town called Lookingglass. The twist is that all these people are over eighty years old. And what brings them together is George Castor's lifelong fear of his own death, his hatred of nursing homes, and a dash of magic by a half-Paiute woman named Grace.

As the novel opens, eighty-year-old George Castor has just discovered his last good friend Ralph has died in a local nursing home while George was away on a fishing trip. Driving home to his farm in the rain, George makes a promise to Ralph that changes every remaining day of George's life.

COMMENTS

No wasting time, we learn right away about the themes, who tells the story, and the category of writing, literary, magical realism.

A 'strong sense of place' is a selling hook—a promise, and then he writes an immediate sample into the query.

Back to theme and the timeliness of it.

Tells what adds uniqueness to his rendition of this theme.

Now we get the story synopsis.

We meet the protagonist and learn what his fear is and how it manifests.

Reveals inciting incident.

Establishes call to adventure and story goal.

LETTER

At his mailbox that same night, George learns he's just inherited his dead son Jason's fortune (Jason—a wealthy, fast-lane lawyer who was killed a year before in a car wreck on the Columbia River—was George's only living relative). So George uses the "death money" to buy a massive old house in a stately and affluent part of town. He moves in, paints the house lipstick-red, plows under the front yard to plant a vegetable garden, and then starts his struggle to find people who will move in and live with him. It's an odd assortment of souls George (and Grace) assemble:

Grace, a storyteller, fled a brutal childhood on the Warm Springs Reservation and later met a woman in the Arizona desert who changed her life, taught her about the circle and about spirits. Clara (the other first-person narrator of the book) has not talked or walked since a stroke years ago put her in a wheelchair, took her voice away, stilled half her body, and ended her career as a club singer/pianist in Las Vegas—but Clara hears and sees everything. Clara is plagued by guilt about what she did to her only daughter years and years ago.

There's a retired steel mill worker named Clayton Liu who does Tai Chi and chain-smokes Camel straights. There's Bert, a taxidermist, who moves into George's house with his dead wife's

COMMENTS

Seems potentially contrived through coincidence of timing.

Not clear how one has a car wreck on a river.

Elimination of expendable person makes possible the protagonist starting the journey.

Glad to see there will be struggle = conflict = suspense.

Seems like a strong main character with a backstory that promises character depth. Looks like she'll supply the rationale for the magical elements.

Fascinating choice in the other first-person narrator.

Shows substantial development of her as an empathetic character.

Supports author's promise of supplying an "odd assortment of souls."

LETTER

Siamese cat he stuffed twenty years ago. A tiny man named Fred is a former defense industry engineer, who drinks gin, wears bow ties, and cowers to his obese wife Emma, a woman who's done nothing in her life but wiped off their Formica dinette set, watched soap operas, and bossed her mousy husband around.

Then there's "the Rhino," the female administrator of Silver Gardens Nursing Home, from which George "takes" a few of his housemates. There's zany Mrs. Beasley who lives down the street with her wolfhound, her flowered pant suits, and her binoculars. And there are of course the neighbors, the City, the papergirl, the police, and others....

Where River Turns to Sky is a story of facing and sharing the End from a different angle. The story of people who try to celebrate (and escape) growing old by dancing on the edge of sanity, playing baseball at eighty, swimming with whales in the Pacific, burying bodies in their back yard, and skinny dipping in icy Oregon creeks. This is a story of passing blood, swallowing the fear of death we all share, and living around into the beginning. It's a story about rivers and candles and circles and salmon and music.

This is a book that takes a wild shot at a society that's forgotten how to value and respect old age, at a nation that shuns its greatest (and wisest) treasure: the old—a

COMMENTS

Here I'm worrying that the quirky characters might become comedic or forced and I hope not.

This extensive list and brief characterization emphasizes the importance of character diversity in this novel. By the query alone, it seems the quirkiness could be over the top, but then, as they say, "It's all in the execution."

Circles back to the book's theme and creates a strong emotional mood.

Strong demonstration of the author's ability to write. Lyrical. Inspiring.

Seems like this has already been said several times.

LETTER	COMMENTS
state in which most all of us will some-day find ourselves.	
Thank you again for your consideration. I look forward to hearing from you.	Succinct closing.
Sincerely,	
Gregg Kleiner	
P.S. The first sixty pages of this novel qualified me as a semifinalist for two years in a row in The Heekin Group Foundation's $10,000 Fellowship for the Novel-in-Progress (in conjunction with Graywolf Press and Soho Press). I'm also the recipient of the 1994 Summer Walden Residency (through Lewis & Clark College), a six-week writer's retreat at an isolated cabin in southern Oregon.	Left as last impression for query reader. I would probably have moved this up to the first paragraph. The thorough explanation, rather than short mention, of the prizes gives them context.

ANALYSIS

The most compelling quality of this letter is the author's voice. Within the task of telling the reader about his story, Gregg Kleiner manages to weave in the lyrical, poetic, original style that one hopes corresponds to his book. In addition, he clearly relates the particulars of the story and emphasizes two prominent features: theme and characterization.

Its major shortcoming is its length. I felt he could have accomplished all the tasks of the query in a third less length. While compelling enough in all respects to elicit a request to see the manuscript, I'm uncertain if the development given to describing quirky minor characters works for or against him. They seemed over the top, perhaps too wacky, but when we meet them in the novel, under the skillful direction of the author, it might be their individuality and how we relate to them emotionally that would come through strongest. Again, a shorter query would take care of this problem.

QUERY

Literary—Contemporary

The Stolen Child and *Eyes Like Mine* by Paul Cody

Published under a dual contract by Baskerville Publishers in Texas, both books by Paul Cody were glowingly reviewed. *The Stolen Child* was also excerpted in *Harper's Magazine*. A third novel, *So Far Gone*, was published by Picador USA. Paul's breakthrough story is featured at the end of chapter 3.

LETTER

Dear Editor:

I am a writer in Ithaca, New York, have an MFA from Cornell, and am associate editor of *Cornell Magazine*. I've received a grant in fiction writing from the New York State Foundation for the Arts, as well as a Stegner Fellowship from Stanford (which I declined). I was represented several years ago by Georges Borchardt when I wrote a first novel; Georges was unable to sell the book and we amicably parted ways.

I wrote a second novel called *Eyes Like Mine*, which is autobiographical, and is about coming of age in the 1960s in an Irish-Catholic, blue-collar family in Boston. Sections of three chapters appeared in *The Quarterly*, and another chapter appeared in the journal *Wind* and was nominated for a Pushcart Prize this spring. I was also awarded the Stegner Fellowship based on a chapter of *Eyes Like Mine*.

COMMENTS

Credentials this strong deserve to take the lead.

Most agents, if they represent literary works, would already be on the phone requesting material.

Mention of an agent would be peculiar in any other query. But, if your agent is known for Pulitzer winners and Nobel laureates, you bet you should mention he'd represented you.

Short synopsis and list of awards speak for themselves.

LETTER	COMMENTS
I have written another novel called *The Stolen Child*, which is about a boy who is abducted from a suburb of Boston in 1963, a month before the assassination of JFK. The book has multiple narrators, including the abducted boy (grown up), his mother, brother, and various people who met or knew the boy as a child and later as an adult. The book is about the abduction of this particular boy, but also about how he was stolen, in some way, from everyone who failed to rescue him, and how everyone who grows to adulthood has their childhood stolen from them, in one sense or another.	Normally a writer shouldn't query on two novels in the same letter. Paul Cody's credentials are so outstanding, he obviously can. Here he offers a synopsis of his third novel, which I find totally compelling. Notice how he tells what the theme is.
I'm wondering if you'd be willing to take a look at either book. I've enclosed a section from *Eyes Like Mine* that appeared in *The Quarterly* to give you a sense of my writing. Thanks for your consideration. I look forward to hearing from you.	Smart strategy to include a small sample of the writing, which should fulfill the promise of this strong query.
Best wishes,	Standard close.
Paul Cody	

ANALYSIS

This query letter shows a master at work. Succinct yet understated, the letter presents impressive author qualifications, profiles two novels, and engenders excitement in just one, short page. Shorter is invariably better than longer.

You should know, however, that it is generally unacceptable to query on two novels in one query, unless you have credentials equivalent to Paul's. You would also not want to mention former agent representation in a first query, unless that agent is of the stature of Georges Borchardt, or unless that agent has recommended that you contact the agent to whom you address the query. Former agent representation can immediately raise questions and assumptions for which the reader can only fill in the blanks, often erroneously. Do note, however, that Paul's query was sent to publishers, so the risk in mentioning an agent would have been lessened. He was not seeking representation; he was seeking publication.

QUERY

Literary—Generation-X, Magical Realism

Berlin Café by James D. Axtell

Querying on his fourth book, James Axtell piqued the interest of agent Jamie Forbes in the Jeff Herman Agency. Although considered literary, the book fits a sub-type referred to as Generation-X and uses elements of magical realism. James' excellent synopsis is located in chapter five and his foot-in-the-door story appears at the end of chapter four. Eventually, Forbes was unable to sell the novel.

LETTER	COMMENTS
Dear Agent:	
I am writing to see if you would be interested in a novel I have written that would fit into the category of offbeat mainstream. It is 50,000+ words long and is in completed form. It begins like this:	Lead needed editing: "I have completed a 50,000-word, offbeat mainstream novel that begins like this:"
I got the feeling that the world had come to an end and nobody'd noticed. So, we sped down a narrow strip of road lined with desert, sagebrush and crowded yogurt stands looking for signs of life....	I like the voice, the desolate mood.
This is *Berlin Café*. It is about love, death, and obsession. Three friends driving up	Clear statement.

LETTER	COMMENTS
the West Coast meet a strange hitch-hiker named Lola and an older sister who drinks coffee like a chihuahua on a three-day binge. The driver and narrator is Wiley. He is obsessed with dreams of a past lover in 1920s Berlin, a pilot. A vision of her lost plane puts a strain on his concept of reality. He must follow her, but his friends don't want any part of it. Rebecca, his well-armed girlfriend, wants nothing more than to keep up their aimless traveling day and night. To her, no bed is more comfortable than the front seat of a moving car going anywhere. In the back seat is Fritz, a real pain and small-time criminal, but also a best friend.	Needs lowercase on "west coast." This paragraph briefly describes the book's main characters and conveys the Generation-X style. The synopsis of the dreams and the title add an interesting dimension. Gives me a solid feel of the author's style, cadence.
It's funny, sad, and often irreverent, but it is never boring. *Berlin Café* is a meaningful book, but also an enjoyable read. I have enclosed an SASE for your convenient reply and look forward to hearing from you.	Solid confident summary of novel's strengths. Promises depth and entertainment. Typical business close.
Sincerely, James D. Axtell	

ANALYSIS

This query was one notch short of the highly skilled job James Axtell did for his synopsis of *Berlin Café*. It needed one more pass to make every word count, to correct several grammatical mistakes (the capitalization of "west coast"), and to add two line spaces between his last two paragraphs—something not visible in the printed example. Otherwise, the small excerpt did introduce me to the author's voice, although I would have preferred a longer paragraph. The short synopsis of the book promises interesting characters and an original plot idea. For an agent or editor who is interested in this category of fiction, this query should yield a request to see the manuscript. Also, when James Axtell used this query, he may not have felt certain how his book would be categorized in the eyes of others. "Offbeat mainstream" is one of those terms that casts a wide net and tends to include rather than exclude possibilities. It was a wise marketing choice.

QUERY

Mainstream—Historical & Biographical
Land of Thirst by Patricia Jean Hyatt

A placement winner in three contests, this first novel by Patty Hyatt was agent represented but did not sell. Her query was rewritten and polished a dozen times over a period of years and yielded about a one-third rate of request to see her book. Patty's excellent synopsis and foot-in-the-door story are given in chapter five.

LETTER

Dear Agent:

Love heals grief and makes us whole. What happens, then, when a young woman is denied love in the midst of grief? In *Land of Thirst*, she suppresses her pain with the thrill of adventure. But adventure is not love; nor is it a substitute for love. This is the theme of my 460-page mainstream historical novel based upon the true lives of English aviator Bill Lancaster and Australian aviatrix Jessie "Chubbie" Keith-Miller. Their lessons—that decisions have consequences bigger than ourselves, that we cannot

COMMENTS

While this lead proclaims the thoughtful nature of this book, it could make some agents stop and debate whether they agree with the premise.

The description of the theme and the biographical backdrop for the novel are complex and dense. The query

LETTER	COMMENTS
live outside society's rules, that grief and feelings of loss must be attended to or we become stuck in bad choices—these are lessons that transcend Bill and Chubbie's own colorful lives and historical period. This is not a romance novel.	might have read more easily with a new paragraph at "This is the theme" and a break up of compound sentences into simple ones.
Land of Thirst explores the choices made by these larger-than-life adventurers who, beginning in 1927, set open-cockpit aviation records throughout the British Empire and America. The pressures of the Great Depression magnify the flaws of their personalities, flaws which create events that lead to Bill's being charged in Miami with the murder of a writer who seduces Chubbie away from him. Bill is acquitted, but within a year, he, too, meets death. For the next twenty-nine years, the circumstances of Bill's death remain an aviation mystery. Chubbie becomes outcast, stamped with society's judgment that she is morally responsible for the deaths of both men, yet she does find her way back to a productive, contented life with love at its center.	No question but the novel is a mainstream study of character. Conveys an exciting time period and setting, as well as daring pursuit. Signals dramatic events that sound like fiction, making the story even more compelling that they are not. The mystery draws me in. Shows the deeper characterization promise. Glad it will have a happy, resolved ending.
The story unfolds from both Bill and Chubbie's point of view. The setting spans England, Australia, the United States, Indonesia, and exotic ports of call across the British Empire—Baghdad, Agra, Allahabad, Calcutta, Rangoon, and Singapore—places that shape and propel the characters. A Navy pilot has	This paragraph sings. It is comfortable, clear, and confident. The author shows the amazing range of locations covered in the book raising questions about how deeply she has researched. The use of experts offers assurance

LETTER	COMMENTS
authenticated my flying sequences and a medical examiner has corroborated analysis of the murder forensic evidence.	and makes me confident in the author's skills.
I began the full-time researching and writing of *Land of Thirst* in 1988; in 1993, it placed second in the Adult Mainstream Novel category of the Pacific Northwest Writers Contest. In 1995, it was a semifinalist for the Heekin Group Foundation $10,000 James Fellowship for the Novel-in-Progress. I finished the book in 1996 and am now working on a contemporary mainstream, *The Applejack Cafe.*	This tells me to expect high-quality research. The fact that the book has been distinguished signals that it succeeds as a novel, not just as biography. A second novel in progress signals a career novelist.
I enclose an author's bio, which you indicated in Jeff Herman's *Writer's Guide* you like to receive. May I send some or all of *Land of Thirst?*	Personalized to the agent also conveys an attentive author.
Sincerely,	
Patricia Jean Hyatt	A nice ending note relating to the agent's accomplishment.
enc: w/SASE	
P.S. Congratulations on *The Last Cowboy.*	

ANALYSIS

This is a well-done query for a complex book. Complex in terms of the real-life people and events upon which it is based and in terms of the emotions that the characters must reconcile. If Patty were to send this query again, I'd recommend simplifying the first paragraph. The two middle paragraphs do a fine job of summarizing the novel's content and painting the colorful and exciting backdrop of the times and settings of the novel. As much as writers should strive for the one-page ideal, I would have suggested that the author go into a second page, add full one-inch margins (not visible in the example), and possibly break the longer paragraphs in two.

The paragraph just before the closing one answers all the questions an agent would have about the thoroughness of the research and how successfully the author has novelized real life. Notice, too, how Patty has personalized the query.

QUERY

Mainstream—Historical

Allah's Amulet by Therese Engelmann

The author of this historical novel is revising it. However, when she sent out her first six queries, several agents responded to her fine query, which is a model of effective brevity. Agent Linn Prentis at the Virginia Kidd Agency saw enough promise in Therese's work to critique her sample chapters and a resubmitted entire manuscript.

LETTER	COMMENTS
Dear Agent:	
At her mother's grave site in a fictional 16th century European duchy, eight-year-old Ella swears to reach her mother's home in Persia so that she can live with her people. But sixteen years later, after a journey of about 90,000 words, Ella discovers that assassins have slaughtered her sister and all her relatives. The horror of this discovery threatens her sanity, but she accepts what she cannot change and realizes the oneness of all life.	Taking the direct approach, this query makes points for cutting to the chase.
	The author clearly establishes the historical period, the character's problem, and displays some of the dramatic conflict.
	Not clear how or why she would "realize the oneness of all life."
My strong vision of Ella's metamorphosis as well as my persistence in attempt-	

LETTER

ing to describe it make me uniquely qualified to write *Allah's Amulet*. For years, with the help of Elizabeth Lyon and one of her critique groups, I've researched, analyzed, refined, and revised the manuscript. I should finish its fourth revision this fall, and its fifth by the end of the year. Then, it should be ready to market.

My prior publications include a co-authored nonfiction book on parenting (Simon and Schuster, 1966) and several professional articles on the law. (I retired from the Oregon State Bar about ten years ago.)

Are you interested in *Allah's Amulet*? I enclose a SASE.

Sincerely,

Therese Engelmann

COMMENTS

In lieu of awards or prior fiction publications, the author still forcefully conveys her seriousness and tenacity.

Any agent would be happy to see her commitment to revision.

This paragraph conveys her professionalism and experience with writing, albeit nonfiction. It feels confident.

A pleasant way to close.

ANALYSIS

The fact that this author skips the lead and works information about her book's length into the query synopsis is very clever. She shows that it is historical from the plot summary. Because writers of historical fiction often err on the side of verbosity, Therese Engelmann's brevity would be a breath of fresh air. The only weakness that I see is in the leap from the protagonist's near loss of sanity to a realization of oneness with all life. Acceptance of what she cannot change seems logical, so when Therese resubmits, she might drop the last phrase or give the reader more to make this leap.

Therese also offers a good example of how to portray information about the author when one does not yet have accomplishments in fiction. Her two author paragraphs convey a strong sense of self and commitment that would add to the likelihood of securing a positive response to this query.

QUERY

Mainstream—Historical Epic

Not Between Brothers by D. Marion Wilkinson

David Wilkinson's unconventional (exceedingly long) query given below brought a high response rate from editors. He sent his queries with a letter of recommendation from a professor at the University of Texas at Austin and with copies of letters from the editors saved from querying on a former novel. *Not Between Brothers* was published in 1996 by Boaz Publishing. It sold out within three months and was a Spur award finalist by Western Writers of America. David's breakthrough story is featured at the end of this chapter.

LETTER	COMMENTS
Dear Editor:	
Not Between Brothers is a novel of the clash of cultures at the time of the Anglo colonization of the American Southwest, and the bloody wars that soon followed. Larry McMurtry's remarkable *Lonesome Dove* chronicled the end of this era; *Not Between Brothers* portrays how it began. Set in early Texas, it's not a "Texas" historical novel, but a solidly researched, gut-level examination into the events that shaped the desperate, brutalized cultures that competed hand-to-hand for western North America. It just happened that they confronted one another here, in Texas. At the core of the conflict, as always, was the land.	Strong and clear statement of the historic setting and conflict. Subtle, effective mention of McMurtry's work, which sets the standard against which all similar Texas novels are compared. Author presents argument for consideration of his work by large N.Y. publisher. Clear statement of book's focus.
The novel begins in 1816 as Remy Fuqua, a Scotch-Irish/French halfbreed,	Synopsis demonstrates knowledge of plot and char-

LETTER	COMMENTS
is suddenly and violently orphaned. Doubly damned, he bides his time in the loveless house of his strict, abusive uncle, who sells Remy's father's land—his only inheritance and lifelong dream—to save his own. In the stormy upheaval that follows, Remy, a boy of seventeen, learns that Mexican Texas has recently opened to American colonization. When the frontier calls, Remy answers out of desperation. It becomes his only hope to replace what's been lost. He wanders to the wilderness, and takes his place in Stephen Austin's original colony. He finds a hard, violent, and lonely life waiting for him. He struggles to adapt.	acter development of protagonist. Book begins with protagonist's wound. Call to adventure. Clear driving story goal.
In the hill country of Central Texas, a Comanche boy comes of age. After days of fasting and isolation, he meets his spirit guide and fights it for its name. But while his transformation to warrior appears successful beyond his wildest dreams, the vision that soon follows bodes darkly. War such as no Comanche has ever known is coming to his homeland, and Kills White Bear learns that he was born to lead his people through it. He accepts the challenge without truly understanding its cost. Tragedy strikes immediately in the destructive wake of European diseases, which claim his young wife and child. It is his first taste of the power of his	Introduces the book's second protagonist. Call to Adventure and The Challenge. Elimination of characters loved by protagonist deepen reader pathos and create more character motivation to face the challenge.

LETTER	COMMENTS
yet unseen enemy. In a self-mutilating rage, he vows a most vicious, lifelong revenge.	His story goal.
[Author's note: I have omitted the next three long paragraphs of story synopsis that fall within this query's body.]	
The balance of the novel is dedicated to the vicious and bloody Indian Wars of the 1840s and 50s. Many twists and turns ensue as each character deeply scars the other until their blood is tragically mixed. Both young men, representing their respective cultures, are firmly ingrained with the importance and power of their contested land. The Comanche worship it as it is and watch in horror as whites struggle at great personal cost to bend it to their collective and violent will. Social imperatives of each race, never completely understood by the other, guarantee that this patch of rocky, dry earth can never be shared; and both races nurture, understand, and honor war as the truest measure of the human spirit. The two young men— once friends, now bitter enemies—are hurled at each other in a struggle from which only one can survive. For one to succeed, the other must fail—and the stakes could not be higher. In the end, after the upheaval of fiery, all-consuming rage that has smoldered in each man's heart for forty-five years, Texas is lost to both on the eve of civil	Reveals the epic nature of the story, constant conflict in the wars of the times, made personal and gripping to the reader through the battle between the two protagonists.

Summarizes the central issues and themes of the novel.

Promises the highest of dramatic tension and to some degree a tragic ending since one protagonist must die. |

LETTER

war. The reader watches it all efficiently unfold within the pages of *Not Between Brothers.*

You may sense the manly odor of overbearing maleness in this query, but it is not so. At this story's core is the strongest portrayal of frontier women, and the male characters cling to their strength and wisdom for a lifetime. Women shape men in this novel, and rightly so. They did in Texas what they've done since time began, and *Not Between Brothers* pays them their due.

I come to you with this proposal unpublished, and "over the transom" to boot; and I understand and acknowledge the immediate sense of doubt that comes to any editor's mind with these last and most troubling details. Yet I tell you without the slightest waver that twelve years of struggle, perseverance, patience, unswerving belief in myself, blood and sweat provide credentials of their own to the keener eye. Let there be no doubt. I am a writer who was lucky enough to stumble across a timeless tale and then seize it. Entering into Fuqua and Kills White Bear's wilderness, I emerged from my own. Never have I been more focused and so sure, and never have I had a better story to tell. Three long years in the making, *Not Between Brothers* unfolds unconsciously like a dream—that of my ancestors, and yours—and like the best of dreams, it's vivid, real, and disturbing. Beneath all the

COMMENTS

Reveals the historical irony that steals the prize from both men.

Aware that today's fiction must not antagonize a female readership, the author assures the editor of his sensitivity to this issue and promises strong female characters.

Author appeals to editor in his own voice.

Query exudes such a commanding author presence, even though all of the rules would suggest greater restraint, the author's appeal is so entwined with his book's story that the personal *is* part of the sales' job.

Although the author dislikes the word "passion" applied to his writing, this part of the query is passionate and persuasive.

LETTER	COMMENTS
war, personal turmoil, and loss is the deepest, most sincere, and desperate sense of hope as both men cling to their fading futures. I know these people.	
As a child I sat at the knees of my pioneer family's elders (both men and women born in the 1870s), who as children talked to them (it's weird, but true). I marked my heritage well as a boy—and then, as a man, I used it. I heard my characters' voices whispering in my ear as clearly as I hear my own. And I told their story as they urged, stiffened with a staggering amount of subtle, unobtrusive research, in a way in which I know their real contemporaries would approve. The result, by some admitted miracle, is startling. I offer you an epic of young America before her bloody boundaries were drawn.	If a book moves people, stirs, and generates a strong emotion, it sells. David's query offers a convincing sample of what the book will do. Supplies his personal reasons for writing this epic. There is a certain eloquence and distinctly Southern diction that adds style to the author's expression.
I've said what I felt you must know. A letter of recommendation (of which I'm also very proud for it did not come easily), a bibliography of sources and SASE are enclosed for your convenience. I'll gladly forward a copy of the manuscript at your request. Call if you wish, and a FEDEX will soon follow. I sincerely apologize for the length of the query, and thank you for the gracious sacrifice of your time.	A highly dramatic close to his pitch. Somehow, I don't believe the apology....
Kindest regards, D. Marion Wilkinson	

ANALYSIS

The strengths of this query are the power and eloquence of the author's voice, the high conflict and drama of the historical era, and how the novel promises to play out the historical forces through two strong, developed, dramatically different characters. If a publisher handled long historical epics like this, this query would get a positive response.

The weakness is the query's length. Three pages single-spaced is excessive, although David Wilkinson incorporated what might be the equivalent of a five-page (if it were double-spaced) synopsis into the body of his query.

If the query were being revised, I would recommend pulling out the synopsis and making it a separate document. I would expect that the unbridled and strong author voice would be one feature that would either excite or distress an editor, whether the disclosures were less or the length shorter.

QUERY

Mainstream—Contemporary Christian

Thorn In My Flesh by DeLora N. Jenkins

The author's initial contact with Bethany House, a large, established Christian publisher, was made through a phone query. This query represents a follow-up to that conversation. Having passed this editor's scrutiny, the book gained review by the editorial committee. DeLora has previously written two juvenile novels, not yet published, for the secular market.

LETTER	COMMENTS
Dear Editor:	
As we discussed by phone, I'm sending the first three chapters of my contemporary novel, *Thorn In My Flesh*. I estimate the novel is nearly half finished. I'm enclosing a summary of the fourteen completed chapters and a synopsis of how I	Clear confirmation of details from phone conversation. Editor requested a chapter by chapter outline.

LETTER

plan to conclude the story. Thank you for considering this manuscript.

My characters, Amy and Paul Leighton, make decisions about court-related adoption risks, suicide, mercy killing, and abortion. Contemporary and believable, the story weaves their lives' darkest threads into a modern coat of many colors.

T. Davis Bunn's *Promise to Keep* and *The Quilt* are about relevant problems, but the issues examined in *Thorn In My Flesh* are different. I've found no other publishers' titles dealing with the social and moral problems my characters must wrestle with as they grow toward maturity.

EDUCATION AND WRITING EXPERIENCE: [her caps] B.A. with Distinction, English, University of Nevada, Las Vegas, 1980; additional writing classes; presently attending the writers' critique group of editor/author Elizabeth Lyon. PUBLISHED WORK: nonfiction how-to article, *Key* magazine, 1962; several nonfiction articles for *Christian Standard* 1970s, short fiction stories for Sunday School handouts, *Straight* and *Lookout,* 1970s; one paperback Christian Education book for college age, *What's That Mean?,* 1971 (all for Standard Publishing); four feature stories for the *Las Vegas Sun* newspaper; three features for the *Las Vegas Review Journal* newspaper, 1980s; stringer for two small-town newspapers, 1990.

COMMENTS

Although this story summary identifies the two main characters, it shows the emphasis on modern-day issues.

Nice demonstration of writing and allusion to story's symbolism.

This paragraph demonstrates that the author knows the literature and promises a unique contribution.

Unusual resume-style presentation of author bio. Although this does drive home the author's qualifications to write Christian fiction that deals with social issues, an attached resume might have been a better choice for presentation.

A resume listing can backfire and make the author seem insecure.

LETTER	COMMENTS
RELIGIOUS BACKGROUND: Accepted Christ in 1947; ten-year jail and prison teaching ministry in Nevada; presently teach, encourage and counsel women in my local church.	Appropriate to mention in a query to a religious market. Also adds a strong dimension to author qualifications for this book.
Sincerely,	
DeLora N. Jenkins	
Enc: Synopsis, Three Sample Chapters, SASE	Helpful addition.

ANALYSIS

Because the initial contact had been made by phone, this query is a good example of a cover letter combined with a query letter. It serves to remind the editor of the prior conversation, rather than to cover all of the ground a second time. This author did a good job of keeping the focus on how her story is unique, makes a contribution to the literature, and supports why she is qualified to write it—by writing skill and by personal and professional experience.

I would discourage writers from using a resume-type listing within a query. Instead, summarize the important highlights and enclose a resume or bio to fill in missing details.

QUERY

Mainstream—Contemporary, Adventure

Sweat of the Sun by Charles H. Snellings

This query sent to a senior editor at a New York house brought a request to see the entire manuscript, but was rejected with comments that led the author to rewrite. The next request came from an agent who lauded the writing but said this kind of adventure story simply was not being published and added that she'd had poor luck interesting New York editors in stories involving southwestern and Mexico settings. The author then marketed the book to a small publisher with marketing connections in Texas. Enthusiastic about the book, the editor has asked if he can hold it until he raises sufficient capital (agreeing to let the author continue marketing it) and in the meantime has forwarded it, with the author's permission, to a friend in a large movie production company.

LETTER	COMMENTS
Dear Editor or Agent:	
I have recently completed a 90,000-word mainstream adventure novel called *Sweat of the Sun*.	Clear statement that orients reader.
Two gold couriers, mistrustful of each other, are set up to be killed in Mexico City. A crime syndicate covers all the airports, train and bus stations, and major highways, so they are forced to make their way back to Dallas, Texas, by hitch-hiking or walking—sometimes through dangerous jungles, all the while being pursued by the cartel.	Synopsis begins. Reveals story problem and goal and settings. Lots of passive, to-be verbs. Promises danger and excitement.
Protagonist James Wardell, one of the couriers, loves Samantha Sullivan and wants to marry her. She refused his marriage proposal the day before the fateful trip to Mexico. She loves him but lives with the ghost of her mother telling her to marry only into wealth.	Introduces protagonist and a romantic subplot. Transition seems abrupt. Seems like too much space allocated to subplot character.
James and his partner, Mark Mendoza, work for a man named Sal Gonzales. James thinks his boss is a wonderful and fair man, despite his temper, but as a deep-cover agent for the Secret Service, Mark knows that Sal is anything but a nice guy. Mark knows Sal is a counterfeiter and a killer and eventually reveals this to James.	Seems like this paragraph might have worked better in place of former one. Good description of character flaw and further characterization. Thickens the plot.

LETTER

Through adversity, Mark and James become friends and learn to trust in each other. When they finally reach Dallas, James and Mark face another horrible discovery: Samantha has been kidnapped by Sal Gonzales. Because they didn't come back on time, Sal thinks James stole the briefcase filled with rare gold coins and something else hidden inside the cases. Something worth 500 times more than the gold: the world's most perfect nonconsecutive counterfeit plates. He uses Samantha as leverage on James.

James must face his greatest weakness—misplaced loyalty—and find a way to save Samantha from the man in whom he had placed that loyalty. Then he is faced with a final choice, one that could change the very nature of his being and gain him all the things he's never had: wealth, a home, and Samantha as his wife.

This is my fifth novel (none yet published). For the last four years I have been working with a professional editor and critique group. I look forward to hearing whether you'd be interested in reading the novel or a partial of it.

Thanks for your consideration.

Sincerely,

Charles H. Snellings

COMMENTS

Reveals some of the character dimension and reinforces the theme: trust.

Plot looks like constant conflict, a plus.

Why 500? Why not 100?

Good plot twist. Shows intertwining of subplot with plot.

Promises character development along lines of theme.

We know some of this; could be streamlined.

"Very nature of his being" clichéd.

May justify earlier subplot paragraph.

Shows persistence and practice. No dishonor in not yet having been published. Memberships show commitment.

Standard close.

ANALYSIS

This query reveals a strongly plotted novel with a clear theme—about loyalty and trust—and some promising symbolism about money, loyalty, and trust. The weakness of the query is in the expression of the ideas rather than in the ideas themselves. The author's writing style sometimes seems awkward, words or phrases repeated, a certain lack of artistry. On the other hand, the writing promises a direct, uncluttered style. I would recommend that the author polish the query, possibly relocate the paragraph with the romantic subplot or work the information in elsewhere, giving the subplot less space and therefore less emphasis. In the actual query, the author failed to double-space between single-spaced paragraphs. It's better to continue on a second page allowing for the visual relief of white space than to cram everything into one page for the sake of a one-page letter.

Note how Charles indicates that none of his five novels have yet been published. Sometimes writers wonder whether to admit they are unpublished, perhaps feeling embarrassed and worried that this will prejudice an agent or editor. Not only is there no dishonor in having a body of not-yet published works, it speaks well to a writer's commitment to succeed. The disclosure should be received with respect.

QUERY

Mainstream—Contemporary, Gay/Bisexual

Crooked Lines by James A. Hughes

It would be reasonable to expect less response to a more specialized category of writing, unless the author targets his marketing efforts very narrowly. Of the forty-one queries sent out by James, three agents requested all or part of his book, four did not respond at all, and the rest declined. One agent who declined re-directed him to a publisher who specializes in gay/bisexual and lesbian fiction, exactly the kind of "tip" James had been hoping someone would offer. He has also submitted to an agent who wrote an article for a handbook on gay and lesbian publishing.

LETTER

Dear Agent:

I am seeking representation for *Crooked Lines*, a mainstream novel. The manuscript runs to approximately 116,000 words.

Crooked Lines explores the struggle of Tom O'Dwyer, a Catholic priest, in Phoenix, confronted by stark, seemingly irreconcilable choices. Tom favors a married clergy and has been compared to Father Chisholm in Cronin's classic *Keys of the Kingdom*. But his otherworldliness can't keep him straight.

Deeply immersed in the gay subculture, he is tormented by guilt and a life at variance with cherished spiritual values. Desperate, he seeks professional help in California, but there, the gay ambiance, beckoning on all sides, proves to be his downfall. Appalled by his failure, he returns to the East Coast, where he undergoes hypnosis therapy and eventually marries.

With his family he settles in Tucson, but private married bliss doesn't obliterate the nagging shame about his past and his continued feelings of attraction to other men. Personal liberation is tied to his public support of a gay priest who, outraged by the Church's stance on homosexuality and the AIDS crisis, resigns his ministry.

COMMENTS

Clear but could be streamlined: "…a mainstream novel of 116,000 words."

Solid direct introduction of book's focus.

Why Phoenix?

Comparison to other book excellent, but it would have been better to say earlier that the protagonist is gay/bisexual: "…a bisexual Catholic priest…"

Shows a strong central conflict.

Why California? No good therapists in Phoenix?

Why the east coast (lower case is correct)?

Marries gay or marries straight?

Unclear why he settles in Tucson. Is the author tongue-in-cheek about "married bliss?"

Glad that the exterior plot is a means for character action and change.

LETTER

The National Catholic Reporter, a headline-making liberal newspaper, in a full-page article on November 1, 1996, examines facets of the burgeoning gay lifestyle among Catholic clergy. For sixteen years I was in the active ministry and my MS reflects significant portions of personal experience, with a special angle: forced to choose among celibacy, a gay lifestyle, or marriage, Tom chooses the latter, but his identification with gays and the pain they suffer only grows stronger.

Underscoring a wide interest are Andrew Greeley's many bestselling novels and other portrayals of priests, men apart, involved in a search for intimacy and personal growth.

As past president and board member of Western Washington Writers in Olympia, I have been active in tapping professional resources for fiction writers for several years. A former teacher, I hold a Master's degree in language and literature, with studies in creative writing.

Enclosed please find a synopsis, three chapters and SASE for reply. The completed manuscript is available at your request.

Very truly yours,

James A. Hughes

COMMENTS

At first I thought this was within the synopsis. Might start paragraph with date. Good introduction of author background, interest, and personal experience.

Avoid MS abbreviation.

Brings us back to the story and how character resolves his problem but pays a price.

Awkward phrasing of clause. Good referencing and expression in the rest of the paragraph.

Additional writer-related qualifications and educational background well stated.

Increases the promise of a well-written novel.

Solid query package—to be sent only to agents or editors who request sample chapters.

Standard close.

ANALYSIS

Overall, done well, this query promises a character-driven novel with great conflicts—both from within and from without. Especially noteworthy are the author's references to other books and authors. This signals that the author knows the field, *reads*, and it gives the agent or publisher a marketing handle, i.e. "similar to Cronin and Greeley's work, but unique in his...."

In revision, James should tighten some vague and awkward phrases, state earlier that his protagonist is gay, and explain or drop references to locations, since it doesn't appear from the query that setting is an important feature.

QUERY

Mystery

So Easy to Kill Her by Carolyn J. Rose

This well-written query for the author's first novel brought a high rate of requests to see the manuscript from the agents Carolyn queried, although the manuscript itself received only rejections. With the perspective of a second published novel and many short-story publications and contest wins, the author now sees the first novel as a "learner novel." Her long years in the news field have provided her with an uncommon ability to write effective short queries. (See the Model Query in chapter six, page 114, for a second excellent example of a mystery query.)

LETTER	COMMENTS
Dear Agent:	
The secrets of the residents of a small Catskill Mountain town, and their deadly efforts to conceal them, are the focus of my recently completed mystery-suspense novel, *So Easy to Kill Her.*	Strong lead expresses focus of novel—secrets—and offers setting.
The protagonist, Charlotte "Charlie" Rogers combines the curiosity and	Solid paragraph describing protagonist. Especially effec-

LETTER	COMMENTS
memory of Miss Marple with the youth and tenacity of more modern female sleuths. She's often overlooked while she sorts the mail, but from behind the counter of the Post Office she has a box seat for the daily dramas of the community. And although Charlie doesn't pass along gossip, she does collect it, matching up scraps of information to discover her neighbors' secrets.	tive to compare and contrast her to classic sleuths. Announces that author reads the genre. Mysteries need strong protagonists, so emphasis here helps establish that.
When Charlie's husband and alter-ego stumbles on a two-decades-old murder, however, it is the secret she is keeping herself that drives her to find the killer and get revenge for a childhood tragedy. Her relentless pursuit of the murderer jeopardizes her marriage, and her life, and forces her to decide whether the truth is balanced by the pain of revealing it.	Story synopsis keeps continuity with focus on secrets and deepens protagonist's characterization. Reveals secret and backstory and what is at stake. Demonstrates facility with language. Good expression.
The novel is set in a fictional version of my hometown, Bearsville, New York, where, as in most small towns, more than mail is sorted out at the post office.	Good transition and clever segue linking author experience to plot. A tease.
I am a television news producer and have been writing for that medium for nearly twenty years. Since 1990, while completing this novel and a number of short stories, I've been a member of a critique group. I have been published in *Seventeen, Dogwood Tales, Ellery Queen's Mystery Magazine* and *Murderous Intent.*	Strong author credentials. Critique group membership signals openness to criticism and revision. Short-story credits mean the author has paid dues and offers the likelihood of a well-written novel.

LETTER

COMMENTS

So Easy to Kill Her runs about 86,000 words. I am enclosing a synopsis and an envelope for your reply.

Sincerely,

Carolyn J. Rose

ANALYSIS

This query does nearly everything well. There is a quiet but confident artistry in how the author weaves the idea of "secrets" into four of the six paragraphs. The promise that the setting will be developed is reinforced by the author's mention of basing the setting on her home town. Carolyn devotes the most space to developing her protagonist, knowing that mystery sleuths must be strong enough to carry a series. Although the plot is sketchy, she ties every bit of it to deeper character elements.

One weakness of the query is in its vagueness about plot details, when so much in mystery hinges upon logical development of clues, suspects, motives, and twists. Even so, she substitutes a tease for details. Given the strength of the query and an enclosed synopsis, that may not be a problem.

QUERY

Suspense

Windstalker by Patsy Hand

This author, Patsy Hand, has written two mainstream novels, two mysteries, and two suspense novels. For every book she has written a sufficiently compelling query to gain a 25–50 percent rate of requests to see part or all of her manuscript. Furthermore, she receives more personal feedback and critique than any aspiring novelist I know. Her pattern is to receive from one to six rejections and then put the novel on the shelf. Her story about "marketing block" is a foot-in-the-door story at the end of chapter six. This query brought strong interest from several agents and enthusiasm over her sample chapters.

LETTER	COMMENTS
Dear Agent:	
I have recently completed a suspense novel, *Windstalker*. It is set in the Columbia Gorge in fictional Bailey Creek, Oregon, in the midst of an enclave of windsurfers. It is a novel of psychological suspense and discovery in the tradition of Jonathan Kellerman's stories involving the psychologist Alex Devereaux. In my novel, protagonist Merritt Walker is a forty-five-year-old woman who is a medical social worker.	Great suspense title. Promises exciting, unusual setting. Tells what genre it is and most effectively positions it in the marketplace. Clear introduction of protagonist.
Dealing with life changes and crisis as someone with a compulsive desire to control, Merritt Walker is forced to discover her own special courage. She must cope with problems of a manic-depressive sister whose severely asthmatic son has disappeared, and with Max, a grief-stricken murderer who has chosen Merritt as his target of revenge. When she discovers that her missing nephew Patrick witnessed a so-called accident, she is pulled into the local conflict that swirls around the death of a windsurfer by the captain of the tugboat, "Prometheus." As a search for the boy progresses, Max stalks her, alternately threatening and cajoling, and her greatest fear develops into the very real terror that somehow Max will find Patrick before she does. As she fights for her own survival and that of her nephew, Merritt begins to	Identifies the character traits and weaknesses and psychological goal. Promises fascinating characters appropriate to a "psychological suspense" novel. Introduces antagonist, stakes, and subplot. Promises more of the windsurfer culture. Shows intertwining of character with plot.

LETTER	COMMENTS
discover an inner strength she hadn't known existed.	Promises character growth out of adversity.
The climax of the novel brings together all the elements in a final scene of confrontation and horror on a bridge that spans the mighty Columbia River. Merritt, buffeted by high winds and the specter of death in the white-capped waves running beneath her, is forced to make an impossible decision. She is forced to choose between saving her nephew and herself by jumping into the waters below or facing certain death at the hands of Max, who has blocked the only logical means of escape.	A whole paragraph devoted to the climax is a mixed blessing; it is an effective tease—like a coming attraction. But, it also introduces an expectation of a similar level of drama throughout the story, which may or may not be present. Excellent Catch-22 dilemma.
I have been writing for eight years, have an M.S. degree in Health and Psychology and have published in the health field. I have enclosed a synopsis of *Windstalker*. The completed novel is about 90,000 words. I have also enclosed the first chapter.	Confident presentation of author qualifications, including ones relevant to portraying a medical social worker and the psychological aspects of the story.
I am looking forward to hearing from you at your earliest convenience.	
Sincerely,	Standard close.
Patsy Hutchinson Hand	

ANALYSIS

This well-written query selects the right details to "advertise" a psychological suspense novel. The author gives a psychological profile of each character. Patsy effectively draws the problems, fears, and neuroses of her protagonist and shows how the plot details will pressure the character to change.

The details of the plot are not entirely clear, except for the sense that the reader can expect a strong interaction between the subplot of the missing nephew and the main plot of the protagonist being stalked by the "grief-stricken murderer." There is a strong implication that windsurfing will be a part of the story throughout, a compelling and unique focus for a novel. However, based on the expressed disappointment from agents who expected more use of this setting, it would be better to either revise the book in that direction or to revise the query to omit the promise.

Worth mentioning is the clear way that Patsy outlines her protagonist's strengths, weakness, fear, and growth. In these elements of character, she models what any writer of a similar psychological work should include.

QUERY

Speculative Fiction

Frozen in Time by Patsy Hand

So taken was one agent by this query, she wrote back to Patsy saying "Although I've stopped reading new material because of my current workload, your letter did interest me enough to break my moratorium." The manuscript was subsequently rejected as not quite what the agent thought it might be. The agent who now represents Patsy likes her writing but believes the timing to sell this book will be stronger sometime later.

LETTER	COMMENTS
Dear Agent:	
Frozen in Time is a novel of speculative fiction set in Portland, Oregon. It is a story about a strong, humorous, gutsy woman's fight to regain her life and punish those who were responsible for almost taking it away. *Frozen in Time* features a successful, thirty-two-year-old, commer-	Straightforward business lead.
	Good characterization and statement of character goals.
	Describes protagonist and the inciting incident.

LETTER	COMMENTS
cial Realtor, Georgia Diehl, who is found on the streets of Portland with a gunshot wound in her gut. Four days later she disappears from Parker Memorial Hospital.	Pulls reader right into the story synopsis.
Georgia wakes up after three months only to discover she has been used in a cryogenic experiment by a physician who believes he has given her back her life. To Georgia, who has temporary amnesia, Dr. Kroll has taken her life away for she can't let anyone know what has happened or risk being seen as a scientific freak. Her intrepid attitude and fiery temper give fuel to her escape from his secluded clinic. Her goal is to reclaim her old life and punish those who have used her so badly. Three main obstacles drive her into hiding: 1) Who shot her and put her in the hospital in the first place, and why? 2) She must flee the demands of the physician who has based his reputation on her survival and now claims she is at risk of a deadly virus. 3) What is the terrible event reoccurring in her dreams that will end in multiple deaths if she does not remember in time?	Introduces story premise and speculative twist. Begins to outline character's dilemma and competing forces. Strong character traits promise a compelling character. Reiteration of story goal. Effective and clear list. Would be better with parallel construction, three questions. Promises ticking clock and lots at stake.
Georgia's quest takes her from an expensive condo filled with designer clothes into the lives of a streetwalking, homeless teenage girl, a bedraggled woman standing on the doorstep of a dirt poor farm on the outskirts of the city, and an elderly woman living in a high-rise in downtown Portland.	Shows another layer to add richness and complexity. This paragraph enumerates the variety of settings and characters in the novel, but I found it unnecessary.

LETTER

Georgia teams up with an investigative reporter, Alex McKenna, who must eventually make the most difficult decision of his life. Should he expose Georgia, sending her into scientific exile, and perhaps win what he wants most in life, the Pulitzer? Or should he honor his promise and their burgeoning relationship and not write her story?

Georgia discovers a prior self who was literally "frozen inside" long before the experiment. In the climactic scene, she must put her life at risk amidst flames, darkness, and fear, and make a decision diametrically opposed to what the "old" Georgia would have made.

I have in front of me a copy of *Publishers Weekly* of August 12th which features an article stating that Associate Publisher of Del Rey, Mr. Quo Yu Liang, is very excited about a speculative suspense novel Del Rey has purchased based on a cryogenic incident by author James Halperin. I also just saw a clip from the new Hugh Grant suspense movie that pivots around patients being abducted from a hospital by a physician and used for research. The new movie starring Geena Davis is about a female protagonist with amnesia trying to get back her life. I believe my novel would dovetail very nicely into this current trend in fiction.

COMMENTS

While this paragraph introduces a second point-of-view character, his goals and motives, and a promise of a romantic subplot, I felt it was unnecessary and introduced more questions than could be explained in the query.

This is a strong important paragraph that describes the symbolism and promises a satisfying ending.

This paragraph about synchronous real-life exploration of cryogenics and other books and movies similar to this book works against the query. It raises the idea that what might have been seen as the originality of the author's story has actually already been done or will at best catch the end of a trend.

It also belies a possible insecurity in the author, as if the story wouldn't be compelling enough on its own, when it is.

LETTER

COMMENTS

I have enclosed a synopsis and SASE. I
look forward to hearing from you soon.

Sincerely,

Standard close.

Patsy Hand

ANALYSIS

This query is as weak as it is strong. If the author would simply keep
the paragraphs that describe her protagonist, her unique situation and
goals, and the discovery of the symbolism of "frozen inside," she would
have an irresistible short query. As written, this query is evidence that
more is less. Most agents recommend that nonfiction events or newspaper
references not be introduced into a query for fiction. Fiction must stand
on its own. Labelling your work as timely can backfire too easily in the
industry's fickle preoccupation with fads.

I would have liked a new paragraph for the "three main obstacles"
listed in paragraph three. These would have more impact in a paragraph
of their own, particularly if construction of the three obstacles, or three
questions, is made parallel. Last of all, in the actual query, the writer did
not double space between single-spaced paragraphs. She should have.

QUERY

Fantasy

Three Faces of the Goddess by Candice C. Davis

Marketed to agents and editors, this query brought requests to see the
manuscript from both. When Candy's first chapter of this novel won first
place in the Pacific Northwest Writer's Conference, it opened the way for
her to meet the judge of the finalists, New Mexico-based literary agent
Irene Kraas, who became Candy's agent. Her second novel was also a
semifinalist in the former Heekin Group Foundation nationwide contest.
She has many short-story credits, a completed second historical fantasy
novel, and a produced screenplay, *Butterfly Man*.

LETTER

Dear Agent or Editor:

Three Faces of the Goddess is a historical fantasy set one thousand years before the common era on the western edge of what is now China.

The book begins with Harp's terrifying initiation into an elite sect of healers. If she lives, they will give her the name of a woman. If she dies, they will build a legend around her. She survives to earn the name Anjali and the elaborate throat tattoo of a healer of extraordinary power. Though she was abandoned in the jungle as an infant, by the close of the book she has managed to rise to a position of power at the court of her royal benefactor. She is brought face to face with a dreadful choice in which she must transcend her fear of death, and even her own pride, as she finally realizes that although her love for the ruler is the ultimate passion she has been seeking, she must help him die by her hand.

Her mark throughout is a desperate courage flawed with great pride. She boldly faces this first ordeal, illustrating the theme of the book: Risking everything in the face of terrible odds lends a transcendent passion to life.

Her main goal in the first section is to achieve the exalted title of Berh Sarajh healer, until she encounters the charismatic hero, who at the age of twenty has mistakenly been named successor to the

COMMENTS

Straightforward business lead makes clear what the book is and its period and setting.

Promises a dramatic opening.

Situation of high stakes and immediate suspense.

Call to Adventure begins her journey.

Brief mention of backstory trauma.

Classic story structure—having gained the prize, she must risk loss to gain true rebirth.

Guaranteed dramatic suspense.

Identifies character strength and weakness.

Elevates the query by the author stating the theme.

Also offers a refreshingly unique theme.

Synopsis of book begins.

Introduces main character and love interest, who para-

LETTER

throne against sorcery, civil war, clever assassins, and his own nearly overwhelming lusts.

Anjali falls in love with him but considers it hopeless, until one day she intentionally steps in front of an assassin's knife meant for him. From that moment, their lives weave a complex pattern of duty, love, and power that changes them from political allies to lovers ready to sacrifice themselves for each other in the final scene.

Writers such as Marion Zimmer-Bradley, Dorothy Dunnett, and Gary Jennings have toyed with the concept of the venefica, a woman nurtured from childhood on the juice of poisonous plants, but only in brief glimpses of less than fifty words. The heroine in *Three Faces of the Goddess* is of the same mysterious breed. Capable of love, but knowing that any physical union with a man would end in his death, Anjali is torn between her strong sexual desires and her honest love for the quixotic hero. Her dedication to her vows versus her passion for him is the very turning point of both her power and her self-denial throughout the quartet as she struggles to subjugate the demon of her pride.

I have been a paid freelance writer for *Yoga International* magazine, the *Oregon Writing Project* quarterly, and *The Observer* newspa-

COMMENTS

doxically is the antagonist to her character goals.

Identifies an emotional turning point.

Excellent references to other writers signal that author is reader of similar works. Good explanation of esoteric concept and uniqueness of this book.

Paradox creates high suspense out of impossible dilemma.

Shows deeper characterization.

Quartet implies four books involving same protagonist.

Gives writing credentials but omits short-story credits

LETTER

per. I am a submitting member of the Lane Literary Guild, as well as an active participant in a critique group led by a local professional editor and author. I lived in the back country of China in order to study Qigong, a subject central to the healing techniques described in this book. My research into the Eastern esoteric arts goes back many years to include Tai Chi, Zen, Buddhism, Shamanism, and metaphysics.

Please consider representing my work. At your request, I would be pleased to submit any number of chapters you would like.

Sincerely,

Candice C. Davis

COMMENTS

and contest wins—perhaps achieved after query was written.

Shows writer's commitment to a career as a novelist. Personal experience that adds veracity to research.

Variation on standard close.

ANALYSIS

The high level of language in this query combined with the complex theme promise a literary novel. This interesting and effective query includes two story synopses: one in the second paragraph that describes the dramatic arc of the book and its thematic meaning relative to the protagonist, and a second synopsis that covers more of the typical plot points of the story. The query is also strengthened by the inclusion of references to other fantasy writers and by explanation of the esoteric practice of "venefica." Had this explanation been given earlier, it would have delivered a clearer interpretation of the implication of the hero's "nearly overwhelming lusts" and of the risk of falling in love with Anjali. Also, it was a surprise to learn that this novel is the first part of a quartet, information that might better have been worked into the first paragraph. On the whole, however, this is a good model.

QUERY

Romance—Regency

Fire and Thorn by Melissa Jensen

Literary agent Denise Marcil saw enough potential in this query to request the first three chapters and a five-page synopsis. In fact, she offered to read Melissa's sample chapters in four weeks, one-third her usual time, writing a note to her assistant saying, "Because her letter is so good, I'm eager to read it." Denise did not represent this book, but she did encourage the author to rewrite it and then to write another Regency romance. The story of Melissa's publication of five novels in one year, all sold by Denise, is featured in the breakthrough story in chapter eleven.

LETTER	COMMENTS
Dear Ms. Marcil:	
Sometime in the late part of the eighteenth century, Sebastian Chamfort said, "Love, such as it is in Society, is only the exchange of fantasies, and the touch of two bodies." Among the *ton* [upper class] of Regency England, the sentiment holds just as true. Having read, reread, studied the works of Jane Austen, and greatly appreciating her wit and talent, I still find myself wondering what sparks might have flown had Darcy and Elizabeth Bennett *touched* in full view of the reader.	This "artistic" lead is so different—relaxed, literate, revealing the author's knowledge and appreciation of the period of her novel.

Her own unique perceptions come through and set a promise of potential for original voice. |
| Lucky for us, the romance novel has lost much of its modesty. The trick is to make sure it keeps its literary value. There is infinite possibility in the exchange of fantasies and a good deal of fun to be had in recognizing physical attraction. In my | For me, this seemed a bit too didactic and verbose. After the loquacious lead, I was ready to hear about her novel. |

LETTER	COMMENTS
novel, *Fire and Thorn*, the Earl of Greyburne falls in love when he gets an eye-level view of Aidan Brand's delightful posterior as she stands stuck on a library ladder. He simply doesn't recognize his feelings as love—not then. Instead, he responds to both her well-shaped figure and the fact that she, both back and front, does not remotely resemble the image he'd created of her based on previous, and less-than-flattering, description.	Introduces her characters and the situation in which they meet.
	Seems like too much development of the inconsequential.
	Stirs curiosity about the Earl's sources and why.
Aidan, on the other hand, dislikes him on the spot. He is not precisely what her fantasies are made of, arrogance and rudeness not being among her list of ideal mate characteristics. She is, however, affected by that first touch of their bodies. Fantasies have a way of changing, and the touches only improve with experience. In other words, it takes very little time for the Thorn to grow on her.	Reveals the typical romantic "go-away closer" dynamic.
	Pleasant reminder of the lead of the query.
Fire and Thorn is a heartfelt love story. Set in Norfolk and London in 1812, it is the tale of two people whose very different life experiences and characters make them a natural match, but also make it inevitable that they will hurt each other a bit along the way.	Having established the hero, heroine, and their attraction, this paragraph clarifies setting, period, and the typical love/hate, attraction/hurt stage of romance.
Aidan Brand is lovely, inherently caring, and a true Original. She maintains a rotating menagerie of injured animals and a pet hedgehog has a tendency to—as she says, "climb things," excels in several languages including Latin (always good	Solid paragraph of characterization about the heroine. Awkward wording makes the hedgehog excel in languages.

LETTER	COMMENTS
at a party when you want to make a discreet quip), and curses fluently when upset. When her sister-in-law all but banishes her from her home, she ends up in London on that traditional, frustrating search for a husband. Her sponsor, a warm, flighty woman who trails yards of gauzy fabric and good will, provides the necessary training. More importantly, she provides a nephew.	Presents an interesting heroine with lots of diverse traits and quirks. Offers the mood of the story—warm, lightly humorous.
Thornton Ashleigh, Earl of Greyburne, expects to be chronically disappointed. His youth was spent salvaging a familial estate ravaged by gambling, inept management, and theft. He is basically a good man, with a saving sense of humor and the soul of a poet, but he is also tough, unyielding, and quickly pushed to rage by anything he perceives as dishonest.	Solid paragraph of characterization about the hero. Interesting backstory. Shows strong, diverse character traits of a deeper nature than Aidan's.
When his aunt coaxes him into playing escort to her new charge, he expects, at the very least, to be bored. Instead, he is alternately infuriated, bewildered, and bewitched by Aidan. She feels precisely the same way. When Thorn eventually coerces her into marriage, using his payment of her brother's debts for persuasion, she fights him, but only briefly. Her life has been full of trust and love, and she cannot help but give him both.	Reveals the usual development of conflicting emotions. The first mention of her deeper positive traits. Feels like end of story.
For a marriage with such inauspicious beginnings, it progresses extremely well. Despite the fact that she fills his house with small animals, insists on quoting	This paragraph introduces a second story arc and comes across as episodic develop-

LETTER	COMMENTS
long-dead philosophers with amazing regularity, and charms his already-bumbling staff into happy chaos, Aidan gives Thorn's life a new foundation. In bed they are the perfect team; out of it, they are the perfect sparring partners.	ment. It makes me think the book has major structural problems.
	Good description of their lives and effect on each other.
The problem? (And what is a good romance without a good problem?) Threatening parcels begin to arrive, a tenant farm is vandalized, there is a vicious attack on the road (Aidan vanquishes one of the thugs with the carriage door), and precious possessions begin disappearing. Thorn, ever wary of deceit, soon determines that his wife and her "wastrel" brother are behind the whole scheme. Driven by dubious evidence and twisted logic, he makes her life a living hell by first condemning her outright and then sending her away.	Hard to regain interest after the romance has been consummated.
	Good use of character flaw to create plot obstacles.
Of course, love conquers all. (What is a good romance without a happy ending?) With the help of some investigation and Aidan's strained-but-unfailing trust, there is a Happily Ever After. There is also a collection of interfering relatives, an unpleasant former mistress, a few amusing and not-so-amusing members of Society (Regency England is awfully *fun* to write about), and a few surprises to keep the lovers and the reader guessing.	Good use of the heroine's strength to win out. Doesn't reveal how she changes and grows.
	Feels like too many details in query.
Fire and Thorn is my first foray into the romance genre, but it was a natural one. My university degree is in Romantic Literature	

LETTER	COMMENTS
(Austen, Byron, Sir Walter Scott, etc.), bringing with it a good deal of study in the customs, dress, and attitude of the times. I am a published poet, and am presently working on a piece for an anthology of women's writings on baseball. I am also a fan of such writers as Amanda Quick, Judith McNaught, and Julie Garwood. They have mastered the art of the Regency romance by creating sensual, amusing, *intelligent* love stories that appeal to a wide range of readers and are never boring (a little bit of history, psychology, etc. is great, but there's a fine line between engaging the reader's mind and making him/her feel like a beleaguered student). I try to give the reader the same pleasure—a true love story set in truly romantic times.	Author qualifications seem ideally qualified to write romance and Regency romance. She makes a good sales presentation of herself. Indicates she reads modern Regency writers too. For me, the author's verbosity gets distracting and feels insecure. I don't think the agent needs this lecture, but it also tells her what the author knows.
The manuscript is complete and is approximately 126,000 words. I have enclosed a SASE and look forward to hearing from you.	An incredibly long book.
Sincerely,	Standard business close.
Melissa Jensen	

ANALYSIS

I would characterize this query as too much of a good thing. The author goes overboard in convincing us that she is qualified to write Regency romances and probably didn't know that she accomplished that job many times over. She does portray interesting characters with flaws that form the basis of the romantic conflict. The long story synopsis raises red flags about the book's plotting, and the excessive length probably supports those suspicions. However, the author's voice and personality do ring through the query in as much warmth and good humor as her characters. I can see why Denise Marcil would respond with a request to see more, and I can also see why *Fire and Thorn* became a first novel permanently shelved.

One of the greatest strengths of this query is the focus by the author on her love for the category, on her qualifications, and on her knowledge of Regency romances. Who better to write them?

QUERY

Romance—Western Historical

Tempered With Love by Wendy J. Brown

As an aspiring romance writer, Wendy's query was strong enough to draw requests for her novel from two publishers. The personal rejection letters from both indicated a need for stronger conflict and deeper characterization, a common shortcoming of first romances, if not first novels. Wendy is committed to improvement and has written several additional novels, including several mainstream novels co-authored with her father.

LETTER	COMMENTS
Dear Editor:	
I am querying for your consideration of my western historical romance entitled *Tempered With Love*. It is 102,000 words in length and is set in a small town in northern California in the year 1878.	Feels a little awkward as a lead. Seems long, and "in length" is redundant. Clear statement of time and location.
Rebecca Ainsley is in big trouble. Through misfortune, she's turned to stealing cattle as a means of keeping her young brother and sisters fed. She's just been caught trying to rustle her third cow by rancher Forrester Essex, a formidable man who has avoided women since the death of his wife five years earlier.	Refreshing to have the heroine be the cattle rustler. Effective way to introduce hero and his problem.

LETTER

Now the cattle rustler and the rancher are forced to come to terms with each other. She's lying to him about something and he's got a secret agenda of his own. What ensues is the coming of age for our heroine and the hero's journey as he works through self-recrimination over his first wife's death and learns to love again.

I have been a member of RWA, Seattle Chapter, for four years. Also, I have taken many English classes and meet with a critique group twice monthly in order to sharpen my craft.

I would like to take this time to thank you in advance for considering the first three chapters and synopsis of *Tempered With Love* and would be pleased to mail you the complete manuscript.

Sincerely,

Wendy J. Brown

COMMENTS

Would have preferred a less vague description about her secret.
Gives more sense of characterization about hero than heroine.

Important to mention and carries weight. Tells editor she is serious and committed.

"in order…" redundant

A little unusual—"take this time" but sweet.

Good specifics.

ANALYSIS

Besides its brevity, the most compelling quality of this query is the role reversal of the heroine as the cattle rustler. The author has introduced just enough about the characters and her study of romance to explain why she got positive responses requesting the full manuscript. With some polishing of awkward phrasing and redundancies and some strengthening of the characterization and conflict, this query will sparkle.

QUERY

Children's 9–12

Ice Ax by Bill Lynch

Extensive marketing eventually led this author to agent representation of this juvenile novel but not to a sale. The query was praised by another agent for its directness and clarity. The author intends to shift from marketing among agents to marketing directly to publishers, especially ones located in the western part of the country. Bill also independently published a limited edition for family, friends, and personal satisfaction.

LETTER

Dear Agent:

Ice Ax is a 33,000-word adventure story for fifth- and sixth-grade readers. It won the 1994 Juvenile Fiction third-place award in the Pacific Northwest Writers Conference contest. I am seeking a publisher.

In the manner of Phyllis Naylor's *Shiloh*, this story teaches while gripping the young reader's attention. Aimed at youngsters living east of the Rocky Mountains who have never seen a large snow-capped peak, *Ice Ax* tells about volcanic mountains, living near them, and climbing their steep, icy slopes. In this story a mountain-climbing accident thrusts upon a boy the responsibility for taking lifesaving actions.

The mountain is Mount Hood. A brief educational addendum describes it as part of the Cascade Range, mountains which are unique to the degree that outside Alaska, these are the only snow-capped, living volcanoes in the United States.

COMMENTS

Straightforward business lead identifies reader age and tells about the book. Position of award effective in lead. Mention of seeking publisher extraneous.

Good positioning to another similar book.

"Youngsters" an old-fashioned term.
Not sure if targeting only kids in the East might dissuade agents.

Good explanation of educational value.
Introduces story conflict.

This paragraph felt like too much emphasis on explanation of instructional dimension over story. For me the prior paragraph was sufficient.

LETTER

Beyond the excitement of the mountain-climbing adventure for young readers, this story will appeal to teachers, librarians, and parents because of the lessons it offers in geography, geology, and about life.

A veteran newspaper reporter-feature writer, I have climbed the Cascade Mountains for many years. My climbs include some twenty-five to the summit of Mount Hood, most of them as climb leader, often taking youngsters on their first ascent.

Enclosed is a brief synopsis and chapters one, two, and thirteen, plus an SASE. I would be pleased to submit the entire manuscript. It is also available on a Mac floppy disc.

Sincerely,

Bill Lynch

COMMENTS

In lieu of more appeal to the adult reader, a story synopsis and characterization of the protagonist would be more effective.

Author bio.

Experience mountain-climbing adds promise of details and immediacy.
Repeat use of "youngster" may unintentionally elicit an ageism prejudice and rejection.
System and disc availability unnecessary.

ANALYSIS

The strength of this query is in its clarity and in the explanation of how the setting can be used educationally. The weakness is in the omission of a plot synopsis and compelling characterization to convince the reader there is a story that can stand on its own. The author's interest in explaining about the uniqueness of glaciers in the experience of most readers could be taken care of more briefly within the second and fifth paragraph, supplying a solid story/character paragraph instead.

Although the computer age is firmly entrenched at all levels of our culture, the only publishers interested in knowing about the computer system and disc would be small publishers, and then not until the manuscript has been accepted. In queries, this information should be omitted.

BREAKTHROUGH

"Don't Tell Me What I Can't Do."

D. Marion Wilkinson, author of an historical epic novel

Faced with the decision of heavily revising his first two novels, Texas writer D. "David" Marion Wilkinson decided instead to focus on his third novel, *Not Between Brothers*, more than half written and a work that had seized his soul. A sweeping epic involving Texas history, the novel had already absorbed a year of research.

"I had two false starts," David recalls. "At one time, I had about ten point-of-view characters drawn from real-life people. That just wasn't working, so I cut about half the scenes and focused on two characters—Remy and Kills White Bear."

The second false start came after David consulted me on the first 200 pages of the book. Among many suggestions, I recommended that he adopt Joseph Campbell's hero's journey for dramatic structure and replace omniscient point of view with the multiple, third-person point of view.

"I made the mistake of reading so many old books that were so stylistically different that I didn't think there was any kind of structural thing that could be taught." David explains. "In short, I was oblivious to structure."

Another obstacle for David was a reluctance to seek outside opinions of his work from freelance editors or fellow writers. "I have a deep distrust of the fringe industry," David explains. "I see ads in *PW*, people on the prowl for editorial dollars. Maybe they are good, but maybe not."

David is especially wary of agents who offer editorial services and charge big bucks. He took the bait once, "in a moment of madness," he says, "and the critique didn't make a lick of sense."

When he had most of his novel done and had polished his query, he started marketing *Not Between Brothers* while he worked to finish it. "It was a good nine months of hard pitching," David says. "At first I queried an agent who had looked at some of my other stuff, so when she rejected it, I panicked. I'd lost *three* months waiting." After that, David queried in batches.

"From that point on, I decided to market almost exclusively to editors. My experience has always been better with editors. They understood what I was shooting for and communication was better."

He'd send a copy of an old letter of correspondence from marketing a prior novel. "Something they'd written to me along with my new query. That way they'd see I'd been doing this for awhile, that I wasn't a complete novice." David adds, "And they'd see that we'd had some kind of previous author-editor relationship."

His strategy worked. About half of the fifty editors he queried gave him a personal response. "In some cases, they forwarded my query to someone in their house who might be a more appropriate editor for this work," David recalls. "In one case, I even got a phone call." However, no one wanted to buy his book.

Then David heard from a friend of a friend that editor Tom Southern might like his novel. At the time David queried him, Tom was working for Ten Speed Press and planning to publish fiction under a Boaz imprint of his own. By the time *Not Between Brothers* was released, Boaz had become independent of Ten Speed, and David's Texas epic was Boaz's first fiction release. In hardback, 680 pages long, with a first print run of 5500 copies selling at $27.95 each. A tremendous risk.

"In a way, I was furious," said Tom Southern describing his impression of the manuscript. "I kept having to turn pages; I stayed up all night reading it. I knew I had to publish it, and yet I hated that it was so long. But my gut told me it would sell."

Tom's instincts proved as accurate as David's. Within its first three months, the book had sold out its first print run and received rave reviews in *Publishers Weekly*, as well as in half a dozen daily newspapers across Texas.

David's first success represented the culmination of twelve years of hard work as a writer. One of the most important elements in his writing process involved volunteer readers.

"Readers are people who buy books, spend their money for books, spend their time on someone's books, and if you get good, sophisticated well-read readers, you're going to get some useful information. I've got a big group of readers, about fifteen people, men and women. They tell me what is working and what is not."

While David did not initially like offering his work to other writers or independent book editors, he's resigned to the inevitable. His publisher subcontracts with freelance editors. "It's a grueling process," David admits.

"I haven't made much money. I have family responsibilities. When I was writing books and everything was getting rejected and nothing was happening, I was terribly worried and I was getting loaded up with failure. I've still got a long way to go making a career out of this, but I don't worry about the writing any more. I think I've learned enough in the last couple of years to stay the course."

Boaz Publishing also published David's second novel based on his experiences working in oil rigs in Saudi Arabia. *The Empty Quarter* is full of strong-willed, obstinate individualists, not unlike the author. A second Texas epic about the Cherokee nation, *Oblivion's Altar*, is planned for publication in 2002 by Putnam.

In the meantime, *Not Between Brothers* has gained momentum. A finalist for a Spur award from the Western Writers of America, it also swept first place in the Austin Writer's League Violet Crown Awards. Fulfilling all of David's dreams, movie rights to his novel were optioned to NBC for a mini-series to be produced by Kevin Costner's production company.

"Did I have doubts?" David muses. "Almost every day. Did I think I was going to make it? Yeah. I really want to do this, so no matter how tough it gets, I'll just keep writing."

CHAPTER EIGHT

The Sample Chapter Tells All

- ◆ Which Sample Chapters?
- ◆ First Chapters—Expectations
- ◆ First Pages—Expectations
- ◆ To Prologue or Not to Prologue
- ◆ Mechanics of Format and Submission
- ◆ Breakthrough: "Every Minute Counts" by Marne Davis Kellogg

Not infrequently, a writer will hire me to edit a novel, but with the equivalent of a warning—either in an attached cover letter or over the phone. It goes like this: "I had some trouble with the beginning, but the story picks up after chapter six and by the climax, my friends tell me they couldn't put it down."

Sad to say, if you can't create a compelling beginning, you may not get the time of day from an agent or editor. So what if your novel takes off in chapter six if they never read that far? For all your careful work to create a compelling marketing package, everything depends on the judgment of your writing, and that rests first of all with the sample chapters.

Which Sample Chapters?

Any request for a sample chapter *always* means the first chapter. The reason for this is simple: You've got to grab the reader. Irene Kraas, New Mexico-based agent suggests that writers remember, "You have to think of the agent or editor as your first reader. If they are not going to be interested in the beginning, then no one else is going to get a chance to see it."

You may be wondering how the many famous books with boring beginnings got published. Two reasons might be: 1) The authors have such a name following, anything they write is guaranteed to sell (and they may not be edited at all); 2) Other elements—like style or characterization—are so outstanding, they make up for a slow beginning.

The point is, when you're on the seeking side of publication, you're held to higher expectations than when you have a cushion of a dozen books behind you. But after a dozen books, your writing, theoretically, should be stronger than ever.

If an agent or editor instructs you to send three sample chapters, this does not mean to send chapters one, eight, and twenty-three. It *always* means to send the consecutive chapters one, two, and three. Never send a potpourri from different parts of your novel. If their instruction doesn't prohibit sending more than three chapters, you may add a showcase chapter from later in the book, in addition to chapters one through three. If you do this, clearly label the later chapter so that the reader doesn't erroneously assume it is chapter four.

First Chapters—Expectations

According to California agent Anna Cottle, co-owner of Cine/Lit Representation, agents and publishers want to leave a legacy. As a result, they have three criteria for selecting a novel:

1. Do I like the writing voice?
2. Do I like the story?
3. Can I market it?

VOICE

The term "voice" refers to the style, diction, and even content that, when filtered through the author's personality, creates for the reader a sense of communicating with an individual unlike any other. The reader might experience that individual as the author or a character, but the overall effect is called "voice."

My experience is that more accurately, agents and editors seek voices that strike them as "fresh and original." This refers to individuality, a style all one's own. It has nothing to do with being youthful or with a story set in a specific era.

Rita Mae Brown, author of many novels and a book for writers called *Writing From Scratch*, tackles the problem of what underlies distinctive voice. Her book contains helpful insights, and you'll glean much about the interaction of language, social class, and voice.

Literary agent Irene Kraas sees voice as a reflection of the writer that springs from the unique combination of the many elements of craft. "What makes a voice of a writer stand out is the way that he has put the elements of a story together."

Is a fresh and original voice something you can acquire, or is it innate; you've got it or you ain't got it? Irene Kraas comments: "Part of voice is the unique gift of the writer and the other part is honing the craft of writing. Certainly, the two can work together." Although a writer can mimic the style, i.e. voice, of other authors, I doubt their writing will satisfy a reader for long. At least, not this reader. Authenticity of a character based on an author's honesty with himself, especially with deep and uncomfortable emotions, rings through a character and makes me want to read on. Perhaps the ability to mine one's emotions on behalf of a character, like learning how to balance while riding a bike, can be discovered but not taught.

STORY

A great learning exercise is to critically read the first chapters of several dozen of your favorite books. Most of my students discover all kinds of violations of rules I've been teaching them: extended narration versus action, dialogue without anything else, flashbacks, sloppy point-of-view shifts, characters who describe themselves in mirrors, or first chapters that open with a character in a car, bus, or plane en route to a location.

What these published and often famous novelists have is a command of narration, dialogue, plot, and characterization. Those who do break rules and thereby weaken their writing make up for any craft transgressions with originality—in voice or story concept or in some aspect of the craft. In fairness to the judgment of my students, a few of these authors are lousy writers and they got published anyway.

When agents or editors read your first chapter, whether or not they can articulate it, they will compare your writing with a story checkoff list. Irene

Kraas says that although she is definitely going by an intuitive gut feeling, she is always examining story, character, mood, and pacing. Successful first chapters by and large share certain features, as shown in Sidebar 8-1.

There are many fine books on how to write a novel that will fill in the gaps of these ten requirements. I especially like Nancy Kress's *Beginnings, Middles, and Ends* and Jack Bickham's *Writing and Selling Your Novel*. (See Resource Directory for information on these and other books on novel craft).

MARKET WORTHINESS

The livelihood of agents and publishers depends upon their being able to sell your book for a profit. When you query on a finished novel, it's a little late to be reining in the horses. If you have written well and believe in your work, continue marketing it. Be aware that agents usually develop specialties, and therefore reputations, in the sale of certain types of fiction, as do publishers. In later chapters on researching agents and publishers and on systematic marketing, you'll learn how to direct your work to those individuals who would be most receptive to it.

If you have not started your novel, you are in an excellent position to consider market worthiness before committing to your project. Read *Publishers Weekly, The New York Times Book Review,* and book sections of your local newspaper. Read writing magazines such as *The Writer* and *Writer's Digest*. Each of these print sources will report trends, what's selling and not selling. They regularly feature in-depth articles on specific types of fiction writing, such as mysteries, romances, gay/lesbian, or Christian.

Attend conferences and ask agents, editors, authors, and teachers about your type of writing. Most conferences have panels and workshops specific to different types of writing where experts cover the demands of craft and market considerations in depth.

Your best insurance of all for market worthiness is to read extensively books similar to the kind you wish to write.

First Pages—Expectations

An agent once told me a horrifying story. She had been on a sales trip to New York and had an appointment with a much-respected and influential editor. According to her, he apologized about the stacks of manuscripts

Sidebar 8-1

A STORY CHECKOFF LIST
EFFECTIVE FIRST-CHAPTER FEATURES

1. They clearly establish the setting and period by simple statement and by convincing details.

2. They introduce one or more main characters, often the protagonist, and offer a physical description and statement of exact or approximate age of these characters.

3. They contain at least one big scene where a conflict is present and often other lesser scenes of conflict, sometimes from another point of view.

4. They contain an inciting incident that sets up the protagonist's story goal or sets up the conditions that will lead to the call to adventure and story goal in chapter two.

5. They establish the book's viewpoint choice, first-person or third-person, limited or multiple, or omniscient.

6. They establish the kind of novel you are writing, in tone, style, and content.

7. They hook the reader's interest, leading to suspension of disbelief. They create empathy in the characters' situation and begin to involve the reader in the characters' deepest feelings and motives.

8. They limit exposition (backstory), narration, flashback, numbers of characters, and only include what is minimally necessary to introduce character, start the plot, and reveal theme.

9. They may initiate subplots, although some subplots must wait beyond the first chapter.

10. They end with a high point of tension, with conflict begun but not resolved.

everywhere as he moved some from a chair so that she could sit down. "He then told me that he rarely reads more than the first page of any manuscript," she relayed to me. "He said that he could absolutely tell from the first page of a manuscript whether a book would have any merit whatsoever."

One page. Not even one chapter. Certainly not six chapters deep where some authors believe their stories really take off. The late Jack Bickham, author of over one hundred novels and many books on writing craft, claimed you've got to hook the reader in the first twenty-five words.

Agent Irene Kraas, who prefers the first thirty pages and a cover letter (with SASE) and does not want a query or synopsis, is more lenient. "Sometimes a great first paragraph will stand out and is followed by nothing of interest whatsoever. I'd hate for writers to think that if they don't grab me in the first paragraph, they are dead and dying, because they are not."

Similar to the way ducklings become imprinted with attachment to the first animal they see—usually the mother duck, readers carry the imprint of a novel's first page, subconsciously if not consciously, until the last page. It's as if these words, perhaps the first line, are "original words," the first words and concepts that a reader has ever heard. They take on inordinate importance.

What you write on page one becomes the promise of the novel, and you spend the rest of the novel making good on that promise. You may have heard of Chekhov's dictum, referring to plays: If your setting includes a rifle over the mantle, that rifle had better go off before the story's end. It's part of your promise.

In addition to original voice and well-crafted story elements, agents and editors will look at your first page as a microcosm of the rest of the work. "Writing is not a process of putting discreet sentences together," says Irene Kraas. "Writing is a process of revealing a whole." Agents and editors will assess whether the promise for type of book, thematic statement, tone, and implied plot is in harmony with the other aspects of the writing. They'll decide whether it is their kind of work.

Work hard on your first line. Dean Koontz recommends a narrative hook, a first-line statement that engages the reader and delivers the promise of the novel. Granted, that's a tall order. Here are three outstanding narrative hooks to give you a sense of your mission:

- I'll make my report as if I told a story, for I was taught as a child on my homeworld that Truth is a matter of the imagination.
  The Left Hand of Darkness, Ursula Le Guin

- Many years later, as he faced the firing squad, Colonel Aureliano Buendia was to remember that distant afternoon when his father took him to discover ice.
  One Hundred Years of Solitude, Gabriel García Márquez

- "Listen to me. I will tell you the truth about a man's life. I will tell you the truth about his love for women. That he never hates them. Already you think I'm on the wrong track. Stay with me. Really—I'm the master of magic."

  Fools Die, Mario Puzo

On the other hand, "A book is a lot more than its first line," Irene Kraas states. "There are some stories that lend themselves to a narrative hook, but some stories are like onions that must be peeled away, layer by layer."

To Prologue or Not to Prologue

When an agent or editor instructs you to send only one sample chapter, the first, and your novel begins with a prologue, should you send the prologue or chapter one or both?

Prologues are a novelist's vexation. Some authors believe in them and others recommend against them. Some readers always read them; others always skip them. For the writer, the pressure is on to begin the book twice, to make two fine starts, not just one. That creates two opportunities for the reader to put down your book, two opportunities for rejection. Yet, a prologue can set up events in a story and foreshadow conflict in ways that beginning in medias res, in the middle of the action in chapter one, can never accomplish.

One convention about prologues is their length: short. While some may extend to half a dozen manuscript pages (and exceptions abound that are longer), many more prologues cover only one or two pages. Therefore, if your book includes a prologue, send it and your first chapter. Literary agent Irene Kraas comments: "If a prologue is an integral part of the book, then it is page one of your story, even though called a prologue, and you should both write it and make sure that it is as essential to your book as the first page of your book. I am leery of prologues," Irene adds. "They are often misused." If your prologue happens to be twenty or more pages, send it as your sample chapter. Chances are it *is* your book's beginning and may actually be chapter one misnamed as prologue.

Mechanics of Format and Submission

If you attend to the art and craft of your novel, but fail to attend to the requirements for format and submission, you're missing the point. It would be similar to a highly qualified job applicant arriving at a job interview in crumpled clothing. One requirement for submitting your manuscript has to do with creating a positive and professional impression. One has to do with making the reading task easier on agents and editors.

The requirements for format and submission have remained relatively constant over the years. However, use the following guidelines about paper and page format, packaging your submissions, and receipt replies.

PAPER AND PAGE FORMAT

More choices of paper exist than ever before, including types designed for the ink jet and laser printers that many people now use. In most cases, however, what you will be mailing is a photocopy. You should always retain an original, on computer disk or in hard copy. Make sure that the paper the agent or editor receives is white and 16- to 20-pound bond.

It's okay if you haven't joined the computer users of the world. Typewritten submissions are still acceptable, but the print must be in dark ink, from a nearly new ribbon. Or submit a photocopy of an original that has dark ink. If you are printing from your computer, make sure the type appears in clear, crisp, dark ink.

Acceptable font size is ten to twelve characters per inch (cpi). It's easy to confuse cpi with point size, but they are different. Twelve-point size will in some fonts create fifteen characters per inch. Small print and many words crammed on a page depress a reader, gives her bad thoughts about the inconsiderate writer.

In the old days, typewriter font was Courier and the size was pica—10 cpi, or elite—12 cpi. Now, computer technology puts all the choice of a print shop at a writer's fingertips. Select whatever font pleases you that is at the same time easy to read (serifs versus san serif), not italicized or in script, and measures out to 10 or 12 characters to the inch (Get out your ruler if need be and measure!). Another way to guarantee that you have the right type size is to count (or instruct your computer to count) the number of words on a single page. The standard manuscript page should average 250 words per page (with one-inch margins). Naturally, if your story features a lot of dialogue, your page will average less than 250 words per page. If it averages more, your font size is too small.

Create a title page for your submission. Think first impressions and marketing, not school reports. Select an attractive font and larger letter size—one-half to one inch if you want. Drop down about half way and center your title and/or subtitle. Underneath the titles, center your byline, providing the name you wish to appear in print. If it looks more visually attractive to have the byline in smaller print than the book's title, that's up to you.

In the lower right-hand corner of the title page, single space your legal name, address, phone number, fax, and e-mail address if you have one. Do not put your social security number as you might with a short story. Details of payment for a book are handled through the book contract.

Queries, cover letters, and short marketing synopses are single-spaced. In contrast, *always* double-space your sample chapters and any synopsis over one-page long. Indent five spaces (the typical tab indent) for your paragraphs, but do not triple or quadruple space between paragraphs.

Print or photocopy on one side of the paper. Leave one inch to one-and-a-quarter-inch margins on the sides and bottom. On the first page of each sample chapter, drop down about one-third of the page and center your chapter title or chapter number, double space, and begin your type.

Create a header for the top of every page by dropping down one inch (six line spaces). A header should include your name or pen name (last name only is okay), a word or two from your book's title, and the page number. Page numbers can be on the left, following the name and title or they can stand alone at the far right. Generally, the current preference runs against centering them at the bottom of each sheet. More important than location of page numbers is the fact that you have them, that the pagination is consecutive and consistent in location. If you offer more than one sample chapter, say a prologue plus your first three chapters, start paginating with page one of the prologue and continue consecutively through the last page of chapter three. Don't start over with page one for each new sample chapter.

PACKAGING YOUR SUBMISSIONS

An array of large envelopes exists for mailing sample chapters. Your main consideration should be selection of a size that does not bend or crimp your pages and a sturdiness that guarantees that your submission will look crisp and professional upon arrival.

If you send your entire manuscript, or several hundred pages, use a box rather than an envelope. While stationery stores or paper outlets may carry "manuscript boxes," it is perfectly acceptable to use an appropriately sized box that you have freed from another use. For instance, I sometimes use boxes in which I've received mail-order books, or boxes that once held a ream of stationery or 100 manila envelopes. Balance the use of a recycled box against the image it might have at arrival. Reusing the box that formerly held your imported Cuban cigarillos or your infant's disposable diapers might send the recipient in directions you don't really want him to go. Be professional.

Never clip, staple, or bind any portion of your sample chapters or full-length manuscript. It may give you an insecure feeling about all of those loose pages, but unbound manuscripts are the convention. That's also why you must use headers and pagination, in case pages get separated from the flock.

RETURN REPLIES

The bane of every agent and editorial assistant is the requested submission, or even query letter, that does not include a self-addressed stamped envelope (SASE) in the amount of postage sufficient to return the material. If you send a query, include an SASE with first-class postage. If you send a sample chapter in a 9x12" envelope, include a 9x12" envelope, self-addressed, with the necessary postage to return it to you, even at media postage rates.

If you have sent your manuscript in a box, enclose labels and postage for affixing to the same box for its return, or to an enclosed collapsible box, already labeled and stamped, this latter constituting the required self-addressed stamped mailer (SASM). Another alternative to the awkwardness and expense of an enclosed box is to provide a heavy-duty, large padded envelope for the return of your entire book. You probably won't be able to reuse the manuscript as another submission because the page edges may be bent. On the other hand, even with a boxed submission, if your manuscript is read, especially by more than one reader, it may not come back in reusable shape. This, however, should be the least of your concerns.

Many writers like to include with their manuscript an SASE that covers only a letter response, but not the return of the manuscript. Perhaps postage would cost more than the costs of photocopying the manuscript again. If you decide to do this, make it clear in your cover letter that, should the manuscript not be of interest, it may be recycled, but that you've included a SASE for reply status.

Some writers enclose a postcard for confirmation of a manuscript's safe arrival. Typically, you should write your own message, such as "Your manuscript (title) has been received by (agent or editor's name)." Then, the assistant need only drop the postcard into the outgoing mail.

A controversy continues among writers over whether you should include a checkoff rejection letter to substitute for the maddening form rejection. Some people take a checkoff form as a poor vote of confidence in the quality of the writing, believing that it signals an amateur writer and an inferior work.

The one way to guarantee you'll never hear back from an agent or editor is to fail to enclose *any* SASE. Most agents and editors do care about writers and also hate to see the wasted effort and opportunity that follows from throwing away manuscripts. But it's prohibitively expensive to pay return postage, given the high volume of queries and submissions that cross their desks. It is not their obligation. Don't forget your SASE.

Last of all, when you affix the outer address label on your package, if your manuscript has been requested in response to an initial query, do one more thing. To the left of the label, print: Requested Material. This may save you unnecessary waiting time, because most office assistants will pull material so designated out from the piles of unsolicited material and act on that sooner.

The final reality of sending sample chapters is that at last your writing will be judged on its merit. The query and synopsis, or your oral pitch, created the opportunity for consideration. The sample manuscript delivers on your promise. It's up to you to follow a terrific query with a terrific novel. Some agents, like Irene Kraas, ignore the query or synopsis and only read the actual novel. After all, this is what your writing is all about, being read and enjoyed for what it is, not for how it is described. Writers can have terrific queries but terrible novels, or terrific queries and terrific novels. This book promotes the latter.

The next two chapters lead you through the maze of research about agents and publishers to help you find the best match for your work, including creating a systematic marketing plan to achieve your goals.

BREAKTHROUGH

"Every Minute Counts"

Marne Davis Kellogg, author of mystery novels

"You have too strong a personality," Marne Davis Kellogg remembers being told by her professor in the Graduate Fiction Workshop at Old Dominion University in Virginia about her 700-page tome. He explained, "It's overwhelming all the characters in your novel. Try writing in first person."

Marne acknowledged that a strong personality expressed through the first-person voice might be an ideal match for a mystery sleuth. She abandoned her former book that, according to Marne, "never went anywhere," and drafted her first mystery, *Bad Manners*, featuring protagonist Lilly Bennett, whose strong personality has allowed Marne to make her into a sequel character.

After twenty agents rejected her query, only one asked to see the manuscript and recommended revision, then rejected her rewrite. "I was disappointed and decided to try a different route," Marne says. "I gave it to a friend in CBS. He knew the publisher of Warner Books. He sat in her office and read aloud my first three chapters. The publisher said, 'We'll buy it,' and then gave me a two-book contract.

"I've been told that *Bad Manners* was the first mystery Warner purchased without an agent," Marne says. "I was so grateful and excited at being published, I wouldn't have done anything to jeopardize that contract."

After the publication of *Bad Manners* and then *Curtsey*, both Mystery Guild alternate selections and recipients of rave reviews, an agent sought

Marne to represent her third book. "Actually, two or three agents called when they saw the galleys for *Bad Manners*," Marne recalls.

Although she believes she got a "very good deal" without an agent for the first book, Marne was happy to accept agent representation to negotiate better contracts on future books and to help her with her career.

What Marne quickly learned is that an agent can negotiate for a larger print run, which in turn determines the publisher's involvement in the book's promotion.

"A print run builds in a self-fulfilling prophecy and 10,000 is Warner's cut-off," Marne explains. "If they run less than 10,000, great reviews won't make up for the print run. Book promotion is left to the author, and you'll just never have a chance to make a big list."

While Marne has always believed that "if you love to write, then that's what you should be doing," that belief was forcefully driven home before her publication success. She was still laboring over her first long book when her husband had a brush with cancer. "My husband and I are very close. Although he is fine now, it really delivered a major message: You could die in fifteen minutes. Do you want to die having intentions of doing things or do you want to die with achievements?"

Living and striving to do her best are exactly what Marne Davis Kellogg is doing. Her achievements speak for themselves. Film rights to *Bad Manners* have been optioned to Norman Twain Productions. Her third Lilly Bennett mystery, *Tramp*, was published in 1997, and *Nothing But Gossip* followed in 1998, and since then, *Birthday Party* and *Insatiable*.

"I want to learn to be a good writer and improve," Marne reflects. "My husband's cancer changed our lives. Now we don't put off doing anything. I'm like the woman whose horse won the Kentucky Derby when she was 92—she never gave up. The idea of doing everything now and never giving up is how I live. It is so much a part of every single thought."

CHAPTER NINE

Researching Publishers and Agents

- ◆ Setting Up Your Own File
- ◆ Publishers' Specifications
- ◆ Directories
- ◆ Trade Journals
- ◆ Classification of Literary Agents
- ◆ Databases, Acknowledgments, & Word-of-Mouth Opinions
- ◆ Breakthrough: "Bring the Body and the Mind Will Follow" by Martha Lawrence

Your search for the best agents or editors to query about your novel will be most productive if you hang up your writer hat and don your consumer hat. Like any other profession, the publishing industry has good and bad houses, good and bad agents and editors. But a great agent or publisher for one person might be disastrous for you, your novel, and your goals. How can you tell?

Research.

While your main purpose is to find the right match for your book and personality, the more knowledge you gain, the better your overall understanding of the operations of this complex industry and the better your odds for success.

Chapter one included an overview of the publishing industry, highlighting the types and sizes of publishers of fiction—from small presses to entertainment conglomerates. From Calyx Press to Random House and everything in between—including the mid-sized publishers and the regional, niche, and university presses.

Now is the time to systematize and deepen your knowledge. Step one: Set up a system to collect your research.

Setting Up Your Own File

Assume that it may take you a year or more to place your novel with an agent or editor. That placement is as much a process of elimination for you as it is for the agent or editor. I've compared the process to a job search, especially that of a career change, but it is also similar to dating. Both parties are waiting for the match that lights that special fire.

Many novelists assume that they can volley off a couple of query letters and be done with marketing. As a result, they don't bother to systematize the process. Because anything is possible, you may become one of the lucky exceptions and immediately find the right agent or editor who not only requests your manuscript but represents or buys it. I have watched writers who have to play out this fantasy before they are ready to go the long haul. Most people don't meet with instant success; in fact, in writing as in life, success follows hard work. Therefore, this chapter explains how to gather and collect information for marketing your novel over time.

The system that works for you may be as complicated as setting up a computer database, or as simple as an alphabetical set of manila file folders. Recently, one of my critique groups decided to pool alphabetical, cross-referenced information in a shared notebook.

CATEGORIES OF INFORMATION

Some headings that I have found useful include: Publishers, Agents, Authors, Trends, Marketing Plan, and Results/Re-direction.

Publishers

In this file section, collect names of your most promising publishers. Add to the listing as you find detailed descriptions of their acquisitions, changes in editors, or as you gather word-of-mouth opinion. Even if you decide to seek an agent, it's a good idea to know which publishers handle your kind of book. Since many agents are generalists representing several different kinds of fiction, you may find yourself in the position to make recommendations to your agent based on your research.

Agents

Begin a list of agents most likely to represent your kind of work. Collect profiles of their agencies from conference bulletins, directory listings, and brochures sent when you query. Keep diary notes from your personal impressions, experiences of other authors, and your own and others' rejection letters.

Authors

As you read in newspapers and magazines about the success and life experiences of other authors of books like your own, clip the articles and store in a file. Mark, highlight, or make notes about the contents relevant to your writing or marketing.

Trends

Magazines such as *Publishers Weekly*, *Writer's Digest*, and *The Writer*, and newspapers such as *The New York Times* or *The Wall Street Journal* forecast trends and acquisitions. They offer feature articles that zero in on particular types of writing, such as the romance or thriller or literary novel and the related trends in writing and publishing. They also report which agents have sold what to whom. Clip, mark, make notations, and collect these articles.

Marketing Plan

In this folder, plan to map out a strategy for each of your novels, deciding whether you will query agents or editors or both. Build lists of names and the order in which you will approach them. Create a vision that defines a Plan A, Plan B, and so on, according to the best of all results, down to the most modest of all results. Later in chapter ten, I'll introduce more specifics on implementing a marketing plan.

Results/Re-direction

Here's where you'll store communications from agents and editors, track editorial comments, and file requests for your manuscript. Include a calendar and establish a "tickler" system that alerts you when you should send a reminder note because you should have had a response. Develop a log or diary to explore directions different from those originally planned, based on input from editors and agents.

Publishers' Specifications

By publishers' specifications, I am referring to what you, the novelist, must supply to gain a publisher's request to see more of your work. To understand the ever-changing preferences, standards, and specifications of the publishing industry, writers need not throw darts in the dark. A great number and variety of writers' organizations constantly inform their members about all types of writing. In directories like *Writer's Market*, you'll find contact information for groups such as Society of Children's Book Writers and Illustrators, Sisters in Crime, Mystery Writers of America, Horror Writers of America, Romance Writers Association, International Women Writer's Guild, and National Writers Association.

Publishers list their preferences and needs in annually updated directories. Many also have detailed guidelines available at a writer's request for the inclusion of a SASE. More and more publishers are posting these details on their web sites, saving one and all time and money.

What about writing *for* a trend, a wave? That's a dangerous business I would never recommend. It takes so much time to write and market and print a novel, today's hot tip is tomorrow's glutted market.

Directories

A visit to your library's reference shelves will acquaint you with a broad range of directories for the publishing industry, most of which are updated annually. While you can get to know some of the publishers of your kind of novel by reading books and browsing bookstores, it's all but impossible to get a comprehensive picture except through directories and trade journals.

For those writers who have joined the electronic information stream, thousands of publishers maintain web sites where more than the usual details available at libraries are displayed, including complete catalogs.

Later, I'll discuss whether to market to publishers directly or through literary agents, or both. For now, here is a description of the most common directories available on publishers, editors, and agents.

Literary Market Place is the industry "bible" and gives the most comprehensive listings of large and small publishers, literary agents, and freelance editorial services. To page through the *LMP*, as it is called, is an education in itself. The publisher and agent listings provide the most current addresses and personnel, and sketch what kinds of books they seek.

Writer's Market is a wish-book of publishers' specifications; it lists what they want and don't want from writers. *Writer's Market* (including the CD-ROM version) provides a limited number of agent listings. Over 600 agent listings can be found in *Guide to Literary Agents*, a separate directory.

A Writer's Digest publication dedicated to fiction is their annually updated, paperback *Novel & Short Story Writer's Market*. This directory supplies the specifications for commercial publishers, small presses, agents, as well as magazines that buy short fiction.

Children's writers can substitute *The Children's Writer's and Illustrator's Market* for *Writer's Market*. It's also published by Writer's Digest Books but eliminates the distraction of all the adult-only houses.

LMP and *Writer's Market* tend to focus on mainstream publishing. However, that means that as many small publishers are excluded as included. For a comprehensive directory to all but the large, commercial houses, consult *The International Directory of Little Magazines and Small Presses* (Dustbooks). Most libraries carry it and its address is listed in this book's Resource Directory.

Another type of directory is a regional writer's market. For instance, in the Northwest, we are served by the *Writers Northwest Handbook*, listing virtually all regional publishers, editors, and writer's organizations. California, Ohio, Hawaii, and other states also have directories serving their regions. Check with your local bookstores and libraries.

A unique directory written by an agent, not a publisher, is Jeff Herman's *Writer's Guide to Book Editors, Publishers, and Literary Agents*. This is a writer-friendly directory, a favorite among most writers I know. Jeff provides a brief history of each of about 300 publishers and 1000 editors. It is valuable to know, for instance, the particular editor in charge of women's fiction within a publishing house with 50 editors. This directory also includes about 80 agent listings, providing far more detail than available in other agent directories. Jeff's unique guide gives quotes from each agent about: the percentage of fiction writers represented, the percentage of submissions (queries and manuscripts) that are rejected, how many writers they represent, how many previously unpublished writers they've take on in the past year, and how many titles they have sold during the past year. I would like to see Jeff ask agents to report how many novels they sell each year.

Photocopy the listings of your favorite publishers, or create a form into which you can put their specifications and tuck this into your folder on publishers. Do the same for agents, drawing from some of the following agent resources.

If your main desire is to secure an agent to represent your novel, consult the *LMP*, *Novel & Short Story Writer's Market*, Jeff Herman's *Writer's Guide*, or Writer's Digest agent directory, *Guide to Literary Agents*. This directory distinguishes fee-charging agents from non-fee charging. The fee paid by the writer typically covers reading the manuscript, and perhaps evaluating or editing it. The issue of whether to seek a fee-charging agent will be discussed later, but you should know that the professional organization for agents, the Association of Authors' Representatives (AAR), prohibits agent members from charging fees and the majority of agents do not charge reading fees. The AAR provides a list of member agents at their website or for $5 plus a self-addressed envelope with two first-class stamps. (See Resource Directory for address.)

Literary Agents: A Writer's Guide is published by Penguin Books in association with Poets & Writers, Inc., an organization that publishes a magazine by the same name. While the guide is a good basic listing of over 200 agents, the information is not updated annually; nor does the guide list membership in the AAR or other writers' organizations.

Remember that the listings in directories are as much an aid to agents and publishers as they are to you. It provides them with a way of narrowing the information they receive and allows you to select a best match from your point of view.

If you write category novels—genre fiction, such as romance, science fiction, mystery, or horror—research may help you find directories dedicated to your type of writing. For instance, the *Romance Writer's Pink Pages* is a comprehensive directory of publishers' guidelines, literary agents and acquisitions editors, articles, writers' organizations and magazines for the romance writer.

Science fiction and fantasy writers should consider investing in a copy of the *Science Fiction Writer's Market Place and Sourcebook*, a Writer's Digest publication. In addition to the expected listings of agents and publishers (of novels and short stories), this directory includes some foreign markets, the anthology and gaming market, on-line services, conventions, clubs, organizations and workshops, and must-read lists.

No matter what directories you review, make sure you look at their appendices, bibliographies, and side articles.

Trade Journals

Writing and publishing is a trade with its own journal, *Publishers Weekly*. It covers all aspects of the industry, from talking books and electronic publishing to celebrity biographies, publishing's lawsuits, trends in commercial publishing, and distribution systems. In effect, you could take the table of contents of *Literary Market Place* and use that as the agenda for *PW*. *PW* costs a tidy sum if you subscribe, but most libraries carry it. Or, find several writer friends and share the subscription.

PW provides an invaluable sense of trends. Whether you write for children or for Generation-X, this magazine will eventually feature interviews with editors, agents, authors, and booksellers of your kind of novel. *PW* articles belong in your TRENDS, PUBLISHERS, AGENTS, and AUTHORS files! After reading it steadily, you'll become savvy or cynical, or both, and you'll have an accurate sense of the major players and an increased ability to make an informed marketing plan.

An additional feature of *Publishers Weekly* is its reviews of new hardback and paperback fiction. Not only is this another way to take the pulse of trends, but these reviews offer superb models of synopsis writing.

Other writers' magazines and writer-organization websites include sections on marketing trends, reviews, interviews, convention and conference data, and articles on craft.

Among newspapers, *The New York Times Book Review* is practically legendary in its coverage of authors, publishing deals, and the industry. Most large bookstores carry the *Times* and the *Times Book Review*. Children's writers should also become acquainted with *Horn Book* and *School Library Journal*, which review children's literature. Read these resources regularly for marketing help and also for models of synopses.

You should not overlook your local newspaper's coverage of books, authors, and the publishing industry. Often this will be part of a weekly section of the newspaper.

Classification of Literary Agents

Book publishing is a big-money industry, and agents stand at the pivotal point between the money-maker—the author—and the money-giver—the publisher. Obviously, the agent holds a position of great power and great responsibility. I've come to classify agents in terms of "teams," the A-team through the F-team, from the best to the worst. As you research agents, you may find it helpful to also categorize them in other ways that will facilitate making an informed list of the best agents for your book.

The A-Team

The A-team agent is a superagent or celebrity agent. This agent cuts big deals with big names. Through a combination of knowing the "right" insiders with power and control over the purse strings, of attracting the "right" authors, and of wielding lots of personal power, charisma, or chits due, these agents get to fly first class. Generally speaking, most not-yet-published novelists will rarely gain consideration by these agents. The A-team agents typically no longer attend conferences. Their agencies run at capacity, and they rely upon recommendations from bestselling authors or editors to acquire new clients. A-team agents easily meet the ethical, financial, and longevity criteria for belonging to the Association of Authors' Representatives, the AAR.

The B-Team

B-team agents are hardworking, overworking agents. They are well known by editors and authors, well-respected, and make occasional big sales that get mentioned in *Publishers Weekly*. These agents make up the larger part of the bell-shaped curve. They often attend conferences and encourage queries from unpublished authors, but they can afford to be extremely selective about the new authors they represent. They've already built their reputations and their agencies, and they make decisions based on what they personally like as much as on what they believe will sell. They may or may not ever join the A-team, and many do not aspire to that club. They may be content to fly coach, having values other than money or fame propelling their work and their relationships with authors. B-team agents sell enough works to belong to the AAR if they choose to, and they adhere to that organization's ethical and business standards whether or not they belong.

The C-Team

Just because an agent is on the C-team doesn't mean that agent is C quality. It all depends…. C-team agents are most likely newer agents starting a business and building a reputation in a highly competitive industry. They may have been sub-agents or associates in another agency, or readers, editorial assistants, or even senior editors who have made career changes. The C-team agent may have no background in publishing beyond a love for books. The good news for an unpublished novelist is that the C-team agent is hungry for clients. Not just any clients. C-team agents know they'll need to find stars to establish a good impression and future business with the editors they court. Even so, they are likely to have broader parameters than B-team agents. They may also roll up their sleeves and offer more editorial work with promising authors than would B-team agents. The bad news is that C-team agents might have good intentions that never pan out. Under the pressure of competition, many C-team agents go under—without having sold many, or any, works. Inclined to conserve their resources, C-team agents take the bus. C-team agents are eager to qualify by sales for admittance in the AAR, but may not yet succeed, though they may already follow the AAR's standards for ethical and business practices.

The D-Team

D-team agents may be part-timers or editorial services masquerading as agents. Part-timers may rely upon some other source of income because, though their active clients may number a dozen, their yearly sales are few. If they have a passion for your book, and you have exhausted all other avenues (or have written such a quirky novel that few people would take the risk or see its merit), then D-team agents may be exactly right for you. However, be warned that the D-team also includes operators who pose as agents but who make their money primarily charging for evaluations of manuscripts. They are not freelance editors, or independent book editors, or legitimate "book doctors" whose specialty is editorial criticism (and who do not pose as agents). D-team editorial services may give you some valuable suggestions, but they usually come at an unjustifiable price. Their carrot on the stick is that once you make adequate changes in your book, they will represent you and make that sale. Rarely do these agents make a sale. They couldn't qualify to belong the AAR on any grounds, even if they wanted to.

The F-Team

The last of the agents is the problem agent, the unethical person. Usually the underlying agenda of this shyster's conduct involves separating you from your money. These so-called agents may say they charge no fees, but deeper into your commitment, you find that they really do. These F-team agents may get kickbacks from "selling" your book to a vanity publisher, or from referring you to a so-called editorial service. Getting caught in these agents' webs costs you in trust, time, and money. It may even cost you a respectful and respectable publisher. None of the F-team agents belong to the AAR; nor could they qualify.

When you reach the point of feeling ready to see your work published, it is a natural desire to want a bestseller, be represented by a superagent, and rake in the dough. For an exceptional few new novelists, this is viable and their marketing efforts will soon bear this out. However, I pass on to you the best advice given me: Never seek to be the exception, because exception means not very often. Instead, follow the path established by countless other novelists who have broken in; then be graciously surprised if life selects you to be an exception.

As you sort out who you want to represent your book, many factors beyond money are worth considering. Many agents talk about wanting to sign on only novelists who have more than one book in them. Everyone knows that first books may not make a profit. But writers improve. Readers discover writers. Perhaps a writer's fifth book will make enough profit to cover the losses of the first four. Some agents, however, don't look that far down the road. If you anticipate a career as a novelist and plan on seeing more than one novel published, you certainly would not want to commit to an agent whose philosophy is "Take the money and run."

Several years ago, one of my friends finished her first novel and got her foot in the door with an agency. But, while publishers raved about my friend's voice and her potential, they said that her story, which involved a protagonist with a past that involved incest, "had been done." The market was saturated, they said, with novels focused on child abuse of all kinds. My friend was naturally disappointed but was already well under way writing her second novel. And what of her agent? I expected that her agent would have said adieu and good luck. Instead, her literary agent made it clear that she had committed to my friend as a person and a writer and would wait for that second book. My friend did not lose the agent because the agent could not add to her bank account. True to her word, the agent has called my friend throughout the two years that it has now taken her to write and polish this second work.

Other differences for you to consider are whether an agent's forte is in selling first book rights or in selling reprints, foreign translation, or other subsidiary rights. Agents develop specialties. You must decide what potential exists for your book and find an agent who possesses those skills.

If a writer has already garnered enough rejection letters to paper the proverbial bathroom wall, he has a tendency to shine the shoes of any agent who wants him. This can be a terrible mistake. It pays to ask questions *based on your needs* and determine if this person is the best match in the long run.

You may recall Patricia Hyatt, whose query, synopsis, and foot-in-the-door story were featured in earlier chapters. *Land of Thirst* had been rejected by over sixty agents by the time Patty reached one who said, "I love it." Being coolheaded, Patty squelched her elation long enough to inquire about the agent's background (Patty had found her name on an Internet agent listing and not in the usual directories). The agent was new but that was okay by Patty. She'd already been rejected by A-team and B-team agents. She was ready to accept the possibility of growing with a C-team agent. However, when Patty asked the agent questions of an editing nature, based upon comments from prior agent rejections, this new agent swept them all aside, unable to respond to technicalities. All the agent knew was that she liked the book, and was a fan of open-cockpit aviation history. A further disclosure revealed that the agent had no prior experience in agenting or editing.

It was a most difficult decision, because Patty had been marketing her book for about three years, had suffered several near-miss representations from agents she liked, and because she felt a warm reciprocal relationship with this new agent. After consulting her mentors and sleeping on it, Patty knew what she had to do; she declined. Representation from a C-team agent with less understanding about novel craft than Patty's and virtually no editorial connections or sales did not seem in Patty's best interests. Six months later, Patty connected with a New York–based, established agent who guided her through a last revision and sent *Land of Thirst* out to specific editors based on a strategy born of experience that takes into account Patty's second novel in progress.

Because the market is tight, novelists too often compromise their own vision and begin to see themselves as beggars willing to take whatever crumbs an agent or editor of any ilk throws their way. Think again. You have a whole career in front of you.

Databases, Acknowledgments, & Word-of-Mouth Opinions

Your primary marketing job is to find the best agent or publisher for your individual needs. Directories and trade journals provide some of the objective data. It's nearly impossible and not very relevant to find out about individual editors at publishing houses. The best you can do is read *Publishers Weekly* and go to events where editors speak. Editors do seem to jump ship and change houses often. It would be time better spent learning which publishers produce your kind of book than to focus on the editors within the houses. Directories and trade journals are best for that. However, how do you find subjective data on agents?

A great way to select an agent is locating his name acknowledged in books you admire. Use objective data from the directories to make your final decision, but the fact that he represented an author's work you admire is a powerful endorsement, one you should mention in your query letter. Ask a librarian to run a search on the Internet for any agent, and you'll get back a list of publications where that agent's name appeared in print. Request a printout of the articles, because often an article will include an agent's personal or business history, thus providing you with more clues about his preferences and performance.

Some writer's organizations maintain databases of their members' subjective opinions about agent performance. National Writer's Union, for instance, offers a frequently updated agents' database to any of its members. The Authors' Guild (for member published authors) provides a similar service. Other organizations print uncodified information and reported problems in newsletters and "writer beware" bulletins. Over the last year alone, these notices have alerted me to possible vanity publishers posing as legitimate publishers and to a possible kickback scheme involving editorial services between a publisher and agent.

Because you can never assess whether a rap on an agent or publisher comes from sour grapes and is undeserved, it's up to you to file the information away in your notes and make up your own mind. I've heard both sides of a rift that soured one writer on an agent. Their two versions were as far apart as men are from Mars and women are from Venus. The agent's story sounded more credible, but if you had only heard and believed this one author's side, you might have reached an unfair or erroneous conclusion.

Even so, "talking drums" opinion is a powerful and accessible source. Take advantage of it by going out of your way to ask writers about agents—their own, those you are considering, or agents other authors have liked. Go to book signings by authors promoting their books and ask frank questions. Attend meetings of writing organizations and events in your community and hang around for the social mixers. Talk. Ask questions. Take notes. Listen to the experiences of others in your critique group. Cruise the Internet for writer "chat rooms" for writers and pay attention to the gossip. Start your own database.

Writers' conferences are great places for word-of-mouth opinion. Replace "talking drums" with "grass fire" and you'll get a picture of the speed with which information, gossip, and rumors fly. At conferences you have the uncommon opportunity to rub elbows at the punch bowl with everyone from vice-presidents of New York publishing houses, to agents, to famous and unfamous published authors, to aspiring novelists like yourself. You'll be amazed how freely people give their opinions when asked. You'll reach your own first impressions of those you meet, but don't forget, they'll be assessing you too.

To balance things out, word-of-mouth opinion will also help you connect with extraordinary human beings, the agents and editors who give generously of their time and energy, never using their greater experience or positions to judge writers or make them feel anything but equal and worthy of polite response. They are the real superagents or supereditors, and for reasons other than the bottom line. They have the richness of respect for and by human beings. I've met many agents and editors who fall into this category as well, including my first publishers, Dennis and Linny Stovall.

By the time you venture into the jungles of research, you'll realize a need for a map. In chapter ten, you'll learn how to create one in the form of systematic marketing.

BREAKTHROUGH

"Bring the Body and the Mind Will Follow"

Martha Lawrence, author of mystery novels

When Martha Lawrence worked as an editor, first at Simon and Schuster and then at Harcourt Brace, she assumed that other editors held the same secret wish that she did: to become a writer.

"Not so," Martha recalls. "One day I asked around and no one wanted to be a writer. They were perfectly content with being editors. That's when I knew that someday soon, I needed to quit and fulfill my lifelong desire.

"I always knew I wanted to be a writer. In fact, I felt tortured because I identified so strongly with writers. I couldn't be hard-hearted. I was co-dependent with authors," Martha jokes.

Martha wrote from the time she was a young girl and pursued writing jobs when she was older. In college, she majored in American Studies and American Literature, writing her thesis on *The New Yorker* magazine. However, when she took a fiction writing course at The New School for Social Research in New York City, the teacher was hard. "I was crushed by her criticism of my short story," Martha says. "I lost the courage to write for many years."

Instead she got into book publishing, landing her first job with Simon & Schuster in 1982. "Writers often don't realize what editors do each day. It's a grueling job. They are busy all day long with business, marketing strategies, meetings." Martha adds, "I took home a briefcase full of work every evening."

From her editorial training, Martha knew that one of the most impor-tant things a writer can do is read, read, read. "So many writers simply don't have a grasp of what else is in print or how their book will be posi-tioned."

While Martha waited for the right timing to make her break from work as an editor, she nurtured an idea for a book. "I was pretty typical," Martha recalls. "I'd had an idea knocking around for years. I've always loved Sherlock Holmes and I wondered if I could create a character who could do for the right brain what Sherlock Holmes did for the left brain."

Martha gave birth to the idea of a psychic detective. She left Harcourt in the late eighties after a seven-year stint as an editor and faced the scary reality—being a writer—she had dreamed about for so long.

"Sitting down, forcing the muse, it's the hardest thing to do," Martha says. "A lot of people waver. My philosophy is to sit down and write. Bring the body and the mind will follow."

In three months, Martha had finished the first draft of *Murder in Scorpio*, featuring her psychic detective Dr. Elizabeth Chase. Then she faced the task of marketing.

"I sent a query with three sample chapters to three agents," Martha explains. "I'd worked with two while at Harcourt. I had kept the business card of the third, the one I favored. In the query letter, I reminded her of our connections."

Martha got her wish and was signed on by the third agent who, in turn, asked Martha to do some revisions. It took about a year to revise the book to their mutual satisfaction. After that, the agent sent it out to eight publishers, received six rejections, and had the remaining two publishers vying for it. *Murder in Scorpio* was sold to St. Martin's and, after a few more editorial revisions, was published in 1995. At last Martha was a published author.

Meanwhile, she had already turned her energies to writing the second book, which did not come as easily as the first. "My second book was like a breech birth," Martha recalls. "I wanted to use the same characters as in the first, for a series, but I was drawing on a very emotionally difficult experience I'd had ten years ago. It took me two years to write the book, and then my editor gave me four pages of criticism. I cut 100 pages and aced the revision."

The effort was more than worth it. Published in 1997, *The Cold Heart of Capricorn* has been critically acclaimed.

One might think that this former editor, now published mystery writer, would have had none of the insecurities that beset writers without backgrounds in publishing. But that is not the case.

"For awhile after *Murder in Scorpio* came out, I wondered if it was really any good or if it had been published because I had inside connections," Martha admits. "It was only after it had been nominated for the Edgar, Agatha, and Anthony awards, and my agent had sold foreign rights, and it was optioned for a movie that I finally owned that I know how to write. I am a writer."

With this recognition as a foundation, Martha charged ahead and saw the publication of *Aquarium Descending, Pisces Rising,* and *Arhes of Aries.*

Helpful in her growth as a writer has been joining a critique group of published writers and the mystery-writing organization called Sisters in Crime. "Writing is scary," Martha says. "You just have to keep trying." In moments of doubt, Martha also turns to such inspirational writers as Ralph Keyes (*Courage to Write*), Anne Lamott (*Bird by Bird*), and Natalie Goldberg, including *Writing Down the Bones* and *Wild Mind.*

Having been on the purchasing side of publishing, Martha passes on this advice: "Look at every 'no' as one step closer to getting a 'yes.'"

CHAPTER TEN

Systematic Marketing

- ◆ Your Marketing Target
- ◆ Executing Your Marketing Plan
    - Marketing Monday
    - Telephone Queries
    - Meeting Agents and Editors in Person
    - Follow-up
- ◆ Taking Stock
- ◆ Breakthrough: "The Power of Persistence"
  by Micah Perks

"The publishing industry has little to do with luck. I'm afraid it has little to do with writing. It has everything to do with marketing." So began a keynote speech by former corporate marketing consultant Michael Vidor, now one-half of the Hardy Agency, a literary agency located in San Luis Obispo, California. Speaking at a writer's conference sponsored by Cuesta Community College in San Luis Obispo, Michael briefed us on the kind of skills that marketing consultants know so well. And which novelists desiring publication must also learn.

Marketing is a large and amorphous concept in the same way that writing a novel is. Just as you gave attention to characterization, dialogue, setting, plot, marketing too must be broken down—the big concept into smaller, identifiable and achievable steps. I call the process "Systematic Marketing" in contrast to the scatter-shot approach of most writers.

Comparing the task of marketing to aiming at a target, Michael Vidor recommends that writers visualize six concentric rings, each narrowing down their focus and bringing them closer to a successful bull's eye—publication of a novel. Familiar to anyone in business, the six are mission statement, goals, objectives, strategies, tactics, and execution.

Of the six steps in marketing outlined by Michael, five are preparatory to the sixth, execution. By aiming to include everything you need to know about marketing your novel, this book has also been preparatory to taking action. For this reason, most of the rest of this chapter and the next lead you into what exactly to do to implement a marketing plan. First, however, let's go over the five preparatory steps. If you take the time to write down each of the steps and your answers, you'll see an integrated, systematic marketing plan unfold before your eyes.

Your Marketing Target

1. Mission Statement

A mission statement is a clear statement of your deeply held values and intentions translated into the area of life about which you are concerned. Think about your deepest reasons for writing. To entertain? To enlighten? To educate? To leave a legacy? Writing a mission statement will help you evaluate your later successes in terms of what you value most. You may not have thought about this prior to writing. However, it is important to think about it prior to marketing. A mission statement will give you a center of gravity, a core of meaning from which to know yourself as you interact with others who will question you about your writing and your life.

A mission is not static; it is an active journey. You should come back to your mission statement over weeks, months, and years and refine it as you chart your course. Here is an example of a simple mission statement: *I would like Planet Earth to be a better place for my having lived here.* Yours might be quite different or much longer.

As you can see, this mission statement doesn't directly address writing, but it does describe a core set of values that can be applied to writing. Once you've got a semblance of a mission statement, the next step is also preparatory to action.

2. Goals

Writing down your specific goals relative to your mission is another conceptual exercise. For instance, one of my goals for writing fiction is to convey the importance of communication and of developing a support network, a community. My goals for writing nonfiction are to support the missions of other writers. To my way of thinking, this makes the planet a better place. Are your goals as a writer consistent with your mission statement? Different writing projects may have different goals, but they are each in harmony with the mission statement.

As a reader, you can sometimes identify writers' goals from reading their novels. I would bet that at least one goal of mystery writer Carl Hiaasen is to save the Florida Everglades. What is his mission? No one can know another's mission statement unless he or she shares it.

3. Objectives

Even the clearest of goals congruent with a mission needs to be broken down into objectives. In the previous chapter, for instance, the goal of learning about your options for getting published was supported by the objective of researching potential agents and editors. Each objective is an *action step* which increases the chances of your goals being achieved. Closer to the mark.

4. Strategies

Strategies support implementing objectives. Because the nuances defining these preparatory steps can get confusing, here's how they stack up at this point in one example: Mission: leave the Planet a better place. Goal: support other writers' missions. Objective: research potential agents and publishers. Strategy: borrow friend's latest *Writer's Guide*, look at *Literary Market Place* at the library, and send off for publishers' guidelines and catalogs.

Strategies should be down-to-earth and practical. Of course, many strategies will serve more than one objective and goal. In that way, you can identify actions that do double-duty, are efficient several times over.

5. Tactics

Tactics are ways to implement your strategies on a daily or weekly basis. It may help you to hold tactical sessions where you share your plans with others, clarify fuzzy areas, reduce overcommitments, and develop tactics that are practical and within your reach. Your tactics' committee will hold you accountable and give you credit for each step. If you use an appointment book, tactics mean assigning a day and time during which you'll implement your strategies. When are you going to the library? How much time can you allow? What will you do with the information you write down? Tactics make strategies real by establishing a commitment within your daily activities.

6. Execute

At last you are ready to implement your marketing plan and you know by all your preparatory steps which actions come first. I think of this moment in marketing as the firewalk, similar to committing the first words to paper when you began writing your novel. As a writer on the path, you know that writing your novel was only the first step. You took the next step and rewrote it, then sought criticism for it, and rewrote it again, and again. That's execution. Marketing is every bit as much of a journey as writing. But hold in mind, you will not implement "Marketing" with a capital M anymore than you would sit down one day to write a Novel. Instead, you will execute the *tactics* that support the *strategies* that you outlined for the *objectives* that will help you reach your *goals* and fulfill your *mission*. You can breathe now.

The rest of the chapter outlines how to execute different aspects of your marketing plan.

Executing Your Plan

Every step on your writer's journey has led you to this point. You've completed your novel, written and polished your query and synopsis, and researched publishers and agents. Many writers get this far only to stumble. Why? Because, this is where writing ends. This is the point where a writer begins to sell himself and not just his work.

MARKETING MONDAYS

You may recall Patty Hyatt's foot-in-the-door story (see chapter five) and how she set up Mondays as her day to market. You may select Monday or Sunday, but choose one day that will allow you to systematize your marketing efforts. As you receive response mail or rejections during the week, wait to respond until your designated day, and you'll be more efficient, less depressed, and you'll lose less time. Keep writing as your highest priority.

One of the first things to do in preparation for mailing is to evaluate the results of your research on agents and editors. By now, you will have decided whether your goals will be better served through marketing to agents or publishers or both, and to what level of agent (remember the A–F teams?) and to what size of publisher. It's time to make lists ranking contact names, noting addresses and any other pertinent details extracted from directories and other sources.

I recommend sending out queries in batches of six to ten. That way, you will always be working to contact the remaining choices from your research in order of preference. Besides, you'll have a chance to assimilate results and make any changes that come from these communications. Sending in batches also allows you to pace your contacts and put more time between you and your creation, which always brings new insights and possible revisions.

Typing and sending six to ten queries or query packages (including synopses and possibly sample chapters) can take the better part of a Marketing Monday. You may need to run photocopies or buy postage, type address labels and set up the SASEs. Last of all, record your efforts in your computer log or other file. At the very least, note who you contacted, what you sent them, the date mailed, and the estimated date at which you should be hearing back. Perhaps you'll want to add a "miscellaneous" column in which to track other pieces of information about the source and status.

What else will you do on Marketing Monday? Log in rejection letters, send thank-you's for feedback on personalized rejection letters, and send sample chapters or full manuscripts (with a cover letter and SASE) to those agents or editors who have responded positively to your query.

If you end up with time left over on Marketing Monday, consult your directories or research notes for the next six to ten names. Be ready! Let no moss gather on this stone! Then, reward yourself with some creature comfort. A hot bath. Dinner at a five-star restaurant. A massage.

Not only is systematic marketing efficient for your time and energy, it is also designed to help you avoid marketing malaise. You know, the malaise that comes when a rejection letter saps your energy and weeks go by and somehow you have yet to send out another query. Remember your mission; remember your goals. Executing a marketing system is a tactical response to getting published sooner rather than later. By getting the process systematized, you remove it from the arena of emotional response.

You don't market when you feel like it, or when you're emotionally "up." You market because this is the day you have designated for marketing. It is your job and the shortest means to the most positive end.

TELEPHONE QUERIES

You may wonder whether you may call an agent or editor to describe your novel on the phone instead of sending a written query. The first answer is "No, *never*," and the second one is "It depends." Universally, the irritation agents and editors express most often is toward phone queries. Hardly any find this acceptable. Those who are receptive indicate their approachability by phone in the directories. But most are adamant that you make contact by mail, with a query.

However, I know writers who, as salespeople, television personalities, or communications consultants, have developed the gift of making acceptable the unacceptable. They know how to "cold call," present their need and create interest, and, at the same time show respect to the agent or editor. They may go one step further and plant seeds that eventually sprout into friendship. You know if you are a member of this club. If you are not, stick with the rules: don't phone.

Despite this advice, I will share one successful strategy I've used with surprising results and requests to see manuscripts. It involves calling publishers. Although queries should always be addressed to a name, to the editor in charge of reading your kind of novel, it is sometimes hard to get that information from a directory. I recommend calling the publishing company. Assuming you get through the maze of voice mail, ask to speak with an editor in charge of your type of book. Invariably, the operator will put you through to someone's office where you'll either find yourself speaking to an editorial assistant or to the editor.

State your purpose in calling—that you have written a such-and-such novel and wish to address your query to the correct editor. Besides receiving the correct name, you will often pique the interest of the assistant or editor enough that you'll be asked to further describe your book. Be ready! Have your one-line, one-paragraph synopsis handy. Although the editorial day is filled with concerns other than acquisitions, everyone is always on the lookout for the next great book. Editors are readers. Once a book lover, always a book lover. Telephone queries may work for you!

MEETING AGENTS AND EDITORS IN PERSON

On the surface, the publishing industry may seem to be a paper business not a people business. Not true. Books are sold from one person to another, and one of your marketing strategies should be to meet as many agents and editors in person as you can. Making contacts so that your work will be read by as many people as possible hastens the achievement of your goals.

A writer with superb verbal selling skills can make a pitch and follow it up with a meeting. If you know yourself to be such a person, you don't need my help. The rest of us can rely upon a system by which agents and editors are willing to meet unpublished writers in person in a way acceptable to all parties concerned. That system is the writer's conference.

Conferences

Writers' conferences, workshops, retreats, and other forums have grown in popularity and meet in nearly every state of the union and Canada. Although I live in the relatively less-populated Pacific Northwest, I would exhaust myself if I tried to go to every one of several dozen annual conferences in my region. Once you start looking around, you'll find more conferences than you have time or money to attend.

Conferences vary in size, in emphasis, and in number and availability of literary agents or editors with whom you can meet. In conferences oriented toward marketing, like Seattle's big and busy Pacific Northwest Writers Conference with as many as 800 writers in attendance and several dozen guest editors and agents, everyone's time is precious.

Prepare a pitch, an oral query, before you go. Review chapter four for guidelines on writing a synopsis that you can use as an oral pitch. Having this prepared ahead of time offers you the flexibility to read it aloud or hand it to an agent or editor.

In preparation for a conference, develop a handle for your book, as mentioned in chapter six. For instance, my ex-husband describes his first novel, *The Hidebehind*, as a horror novel in which *Deliverance* meets *Predator*. A handle is easy to remember under the pressure of a conference, and it can open a conversation.

If a marketing handle seems too crass for your sense and sensibilities, then develop the one-line synopsis of your book, like the one developed by Patricia Hyatt for *Land of Thirst*. It reads: "A fictionalization of the true adventure, romance, and journeys of self-discovery of an open-cockpit aviatrix and aviator of the 1920s." A complete example of an oral pitch, in the form of a prepared script or synopsis, is set out in chapter four (page 81) for Sarah Vail's mystery, *Fresh Powder*.

If you have strong communication skills and feel comfortable in a marketing and interviewing atmosphere, you may be able to speak extemporaneously, pick up on another's verbal and nonverbal cues, and generate an aura of confidence, even charisma. You, not your work (not yet), have made an impression that creates a curiosity in agents and editors to "see what you've got." Another level of their interest involves your promotability. The fact that you speak well and handle yourself well bodes positively for author promotion. These public relations skills can't substitute for excellence in writing, but they can help get your foot in the door with an agent or editor.

If you don't feel as if you can swim in marketing waters with the elan of a dolphin, should you bother to attend conferences and flounder among the expert swimmers and try to make an oral pitch? By all means yes. Most authors, published and aspiring, are ordinary folks—more like the extras on a Hollywood set than like the stars. In a delightful moment of disclosure at a workshop, Northwest literary agent Elizabeth Wales said of her clients, "Some of my authors are pugnacious, some shy, others merely possessed. After all, they're writers." Notice in her statement the two words, *my authors*. Represented. Works sold. Published.

A big reason to "work the conferences," rather than to mail queries, is because nothing can replace first impressions, visual data, and perhaps interpersonal chemistry. And it goes both ways. You can eliminate, often within seconds, someone who looked good in their directory listing or qualify someone you might have overlooked.

Rainer Rey, whose breakthrough story appears in chapter one, said he believes writers should learn business and marketing skills. I put Rainer on the spot by asking him how much of his success in securing the interest of his agent could be attributed to meeting her in person and establishing a warm rapport. "I believe my book had to stand on its own merit," Rainer said, "but meeting Diane face-to-face and developing a friendship was significant. Had we not met, I am not certain that things would have turned out as well as they have."

How often have I heard writers comment after a conference, "I would never ever want her to represent me," or "I loved her—I felt she really understood my story. She asked me to send the entire manuscript."

In the Resource Directory, I've listed books on conferences and organizations that host conferences. Keep your eye on your local newspaper's arts calendars. Bookmark shawguides.com, the most comprehensive Internet listing of conferences and workshops. *Writer's Digest* magazine and *The Writer* devote part of the May issue each year to listing conferences in all fifty states.

Arranged Meetings

One of the most successful ways to meet anyone is through a third party. It's easier for a friend or associate to talk about you and your book to his friend, the literary agent or editor, and suggest a three-way meeting than it is for you to do the same. Several of the authors featured in breakthrough and foot-in-the-door stories said they had met their agents through recommendations of faculty members or published authors. You may remember the breakthrough story in chapter eight describing how Marne Davis Kellogg's friend read her manuscript aloud to an editor who in turn gave her a contract.

One step better than the third-party recommendation is a three-way meeting. While no agent or editor whom I know would respond positively to a call by an unknown writer saying "let's do lunch," most will respond positively if the suggestion comes from someone they know. Patsy, a writer in one of my critique groups, learned that a nominee for the Pulitzer prize in literature had a speaking engagement in town and that this famous author was the cousin to a friend of Patsy's. She immediately asked her friend if the three of them might go to lunch after the speaking engagement. During lunch, Patsy shared her writing process and problems with the famous writer who in turn offered to take a look at one of Patsy's works, for a fee. The feedback was extremely helpful and her words of encouragement and praise like rainfall after a drought. In addition, she offered to refer Patsy to her agent when Patsy finishes her next book.

If you can spark any similar three-way meeting with an agent, editor, or published author, do everything you can to facilitate it. This is no time to be shy. You are implementing your marketing plan in order to reach your goals and fulfill your mission!

FOLLOW-UP

You executed your marketing plan, attended a conference, talked with agents and editors and now you're home. Mission accomplished, right?

Not quite yet. When you return from a conference or any other situation in which you have discussed your novel with an agent, editor, or author, smart marketing requires immediate follow-up. The nature of this follow-up will depend upon the contact. Effective follow-up involves handling seven execution details:

1. Thank-you notes
2. Exclusive submissions
3. Simultaneous submissions
4. Mailing strategies and time limits
5. Crafty cover letters
6. Follow-up fallacies
7. Full-circle follow-up

Thank-you Notes

If someone has been nice enough to chat, offer you ideas, problem-solve, or network, send a thank-you note. You can never go wrong saying thank you, and it's becoming a rusty art in today's culture. If anything comes of the leads from this conversation, follow up again with a report. Stay in touch—if there is a reason to do so.

Exclusive Submissions

Many writers return from conferences where they have met agents and editors with requests to send sample chapters, synopses, or entire manuscripts. Normally, the protocol for sending out your entire manuscript is to offer exclusive consideration to one agent at a time. If you had received a request from a query letter for your entire manuscript, this would be expected of you, unless otherwise indicated by the agent. The reason for this rule is that you are asking a substantial commitment in time and skill for someone to read your entire book and make comments. It would be terribly insulting and disrespectful if one agent got back to you, interested in representing you, only to find out that you had simultaneously submitted your manuscript to another agent and signed on there.

Simultaneous Submissions

Conferences involve different rules. The agents understand that they are competing for the first crack at a book and, in all truth, they give more go-aheads to see manuscripts than they would have had the same writers queried by mail. In this situation, as a follow-up to conferences, send your full manuscript to more than one agent who has requested it, simultaneously, but in a cover letter accompanying the book, explicitly state that you have sent the full manuscript to fulfill another request as well. That way, everyone knows what is going on aboveboard.

What if the request to send your entire book comes from several editors, or, one agent and one or more editors? There is no conflict in having one or several editors consider a full manuscript simultaneously with an agent's consideration. After all, if an editor reads it first and offers you a contract, you can get on the phone and tell the agent about it. You've already pre-sold it, and you won't have any trouble finding an agent to represent you.

If more than one editor asks to read your manuscript, as a courtesy, it is respectful to indicate in the cover letter that several publishers expressed interest and will be reading the manuscript at the same time. That also creates a sense of competition, and that can only be good for you. It may even create a push to read your book sooner rather than later.

Most of the writers I work with feel no need to announce simultaneous submissions of *sample chapters*. After all, an agent or editor is not likely to offer a contract until they have read the entire book, so reading sample chapters at the same time as someone else is still a preliminary step that won't inconvenience anyone. If more than one agent reads your sample chapters and requests the entire manuscript, you are in the best position for engendering competition. Now if you choose to send it out to many at once, you must tell each agent that you have interest from one or many others, who will be reading it at the same time.

Also, to expedite the recipient getting to your submission sooner than later, on the outside of your mailing envelope or box, write "Requested Material." It could save you weeks or months.

Mailing Strategies & Time Limits

A different strategy at this juncture is to check your list that ranks agents in order of priority. Send the entire manuscript to your first choice but give this agent a time limit, letting her know that you are offering an exclusive reading but that other agents have indicated interest. A reasonable time limit for responding to an entire book might be four to eight weeks. If the first choice agent rejects you, then send out to the next agent who requested the entire manuscript. Don't worry about how long the second (or other) agent has waited. It's not as if anyone is sitting around counting how many days have elapsed since requesting your book.

This system has several advantages over sending out all submissions at once to everyone who has shown interest. When you submit exclusively to one reader at a time, you derive the benefit of feedback on your manuscript. Correct the deficiencies before using up your next request. Each time your book improves. The only disadvantage is the passage of time.

Crafty Cover Letters

Take as much care in crafting your cover letter to accompany sample chapters or a manuscript as you would for a query. Never send a manuscript without a cover letter. You may vividly recall the agents or editors you met at a conference and be able to repeat every word they said to you. However, you're probably only one of fifty writers they met in appointments. These agents and editors may also have been guests at several other conferences before they return to their offices where your manuscript will reach them. Assume, therefore, that they do not remember you or your book.

Begin your letter by refreshing their memory. First refer to your meeting. Next, thank the editor or agent for his or her time and reiterate the conversation. Then, use the heart of the cover letter to provide a synopsis of your book and any outstanding author credentials or credits. This is an excellent opportunity to market your story and market yourself.

Follow-up Fallacies

If you do not hear back in a reasonable time, say eight weeks, follow up again. If you've sent the entire manuscript, you've gone to a great deal of effort and expense at their request. Therefore, after eight weeks, call, don't write. They requested your book. You have every right to ask for a status report.

Many writers are reluctant to follow up, as if so doing will jinx the response of the agent or editor. Or, worse yet, they imagine their request for a progress report will act as an irritant that so enrages the recipient that as punishment, the manuscript will be rejected, no matter its original potential.

These thoughts reflect imaginations gone wild; understandable, but irrational. Here is a story that reveals an entirely different way to look at what can happen when a writer leaves all of the decisions and action in the hands of the editor or agent. One of my students queried an editor with a New York publisher over the transom and received a positive request to send her entire manuscript, a suspense novel. *Six months later*, responding to the urging of her friends, the writer contacted the editor. He apologized for the passage of time, complimented the writing, and said he was not the right editor for the book, but could he pass it on to another in-house editor? Of course, the writer agreed. Another *six months* passed. Again, at the urging of her friends, she contacted the first editor, who thought she needed agent representation. He asked permission to give it to a prestigious literary agency. More months passed. The outcome? Three agents agreed that it falls between the usual cracks. One asked to see the next two books that the author had finished in the meantime. Despite the waiting and lost time, the writer said, "Yes. But I'm submitting it elsewhere simultaneously, and I'd like to call you for a response in a couple of weeks."

I can only wonder whether this wonderful novel, having received positive response by a host of highly placed New York readers, would have been in print by this time had the writer proceeded with greater marketing savvy. Part of the learning curve for this writer has been to regard herself as a professional. Professional follow-up demands regular follow-up with the expectation of a courteous but timely response.

Full-circle Follow-up

If you are rejected, but the agent or editor has gone to the trouble to critique your work, even if they make but a few comments, follow up with a thank-you note. Complete the circle of interaction. Don't throw away their letters to you. If you rewrite, make corrections, query again enclosing the former correspondence, and explain that you have made the recommended changes and ask if you may resubmit. Even if the answer is no, keep the letter to use when querying on your second book to this same person. Think in terms of building long-term relationships.

As you can see, follow-up often means making many contacts with an agent or editor over time, even if you eventually find representation and your book is sold to another publisher. You can never have too many friends or business contacts.

Taking Stock

It is one thing to track your results; it is another thing to take stock. Taking stock means that you consider what you are doing and how, assess your progress, and make decisions accordingly. In the next chapter, I'll specifically address how to take stock of rejections and how to proceed from there.

Taking stock also means to update your support community with whom you discuss your marketing mission, goals, objectives, strategies and tactics. Maybe that person is your mate, your mentor, or a critique group. The elapse of time between a writer's desire to write and sell a novel to the fulfillment of that desire is usually measured in years, sometimes in a decade. Within that time, you will make many adjustments to your course, perhaps using different navigational devices as you learn, grow, and make new contacts. Don't get overly attached and believe that one marketing plan will carry you all the way home. Be flexible. Be alert. Be ever open to new ideas and contacts.

By this point in the process, your tool kit should be filled with the know-how to write queries, synopses, sample chapters; with knowledge about the industry, its players and specifications; and with a systematic marketing plan. There is but one tool left, and it is the most important one of all, the subject of the next chapter: how to handle rejection.

BREAKTHROUGH

"The Power of Persistence"

Micah Perks, author of literary novel nominated for a Pushcart Prize

"I was out of college for a few years, waitressing during the day and writing at night. I didn't have any support," Micah recalls. Her first break came when she sent two short stories with her application to Cornell University's Masters in Fine Arts program. "It's a small program," Micah says. "They only accept four fiction writers each year." In 1991 Micah became one of them. "They paid for everything. I got a scholarship and a stipend. Everything," Micah explains.

Here she was given the support she needed from other writers and teachers. Her thesis was a number of linked short stories, which her teacher recommended marketing as a book. The teacher also recommended an agent, first one agent who couldn't sell it and then a second.

Micah explains: "The pattern of rejection letters was, 'lovely writing, no plot.' It was hard to shift to an audience of editors from the supportive teachers in grad school. The teachers cared about language, character, and meaning. The editors seemed focused on 'a good story.' Or maybe it seemed that way because that's what my book was missing." The book didn't sell.

"My impression is that small presses publish most of the new literary novels. A lot of my friends are getting published by small presses. Most in fact," Micah says.

She got busy writing a second book. "I had shared the idea with the agent before writing it, and she was skeptical," Micah recalls. "She knew I would be writing about something I didn't know much about: nineteenth-century Adirondacks. But I loved doing the research." When Micah gave the agent her final draft, the agent said she sounded too much like a teacher. The authorial voice was too dominant. "She said it needed a lot of work. Her long list of corrections took me another year."

By the time her agent sold *We Are Gathered Here,* published by St. Martin's Press, three and a half years had passed since the book's inception.

When her book didn't readily sell, she grew discouraged. "I had a sense of powerlessness and I didn't know how to gain power," she recalls. "It did block my writing. I believe writers need a combination of three qualities: luck, perseverance, and talent. And connections really help." Micah also found help from reading Raymond Carver's essays on writing and works by Flannery O'Connor and John Gardner.

She recommends that writers assume they will get a lot of rejections and do as one woman she knows: Always have an envelope ready to send out in the next mail.

"It's slow and depressing," Micah admits. "But, writers need to listen to the advice in rejection letters and look to see if there are any patterns. It's best to put the rejections away and return to them when you can be more objective. You have to balance out how you feel about the criticism and think seriously about rewriting and changing your novel." She adds, "Talented writers who persevere will publish in the end."

CHAPTER ELEVEN

Goodbye Rejection: Hello Re-direction

- ◆ The Re-direction Process Defined
- ◆ Consciousness Raising 101
- ◆ Dreamcrushers
- ◆ Four Types of Rejection Letters
- ◆ Personal Re-direction
- ◆ Breakthrough: "The Ideal Writer-Agent Partnership" by Melissa Jensen

"If it entertains, it enlightens; if it enlightens, then it empowers," say literary agents Mary Alice Kier and Anna Cottle. Speaking to a small group at a writers' conference, they shared the three E's that form part of the criteria by which they select new writers, and the foundation philosophy of their agency, Cine/Lit Representation, located in Santa Clarita, California. To my delight, Mary Alice and Anna also introduced a new concept that replaces rejection. They set me dreaming about a new model of communication. The concept is such a simple one: Not rejection. Re-direction.

The Re-direction Process Defined

In our present culture, fiction writers face the highest rate of rejection of all writers, simply because fewer opportunities for publication exist in the fiction market. As novelists begin marketing their works, all but the supernaturally blessed will face rejection. How they cope—or whether they cope—becomes the most critical skill in the tool kit, because only those writers who effectively cope with rejection will survive and thrive.

Rejection is nasty. The word has a final sound. The problem stems from the negative associations that spin off from it: bad goods, lacking value, unworthy, unfit, done-for, hopeless. The greatest problem with rejection comes not from rejection itself but from feeling rejected as a writer or as a person, how we set ourselves up for a fall. The core of the problem lies in what we say to ourselves.

Reaction to the receipt of a rejection letter makes some writers stop writing, as it did when a critique group lambasted my first novel and well-meaning friends added, "Your *non*fiction is really good. Why don't you just keep writing that?" Fifteen years elapsed before I finished the next novel. Some writers stop marketing when the impact of the first rejection letters hits home. I once received a call from a writer considering suicide because his novel had not advanced to the semifinals in a literary contest when he had imagined it would take first place.

In contrast, imagine if the word "rejection" and all the negative associations underlying it were replaced with the word "re-direction," as applied by Mary Alice and Anna. One obvious difference is that rejection indicates a static state of being, the dead-letter file, while re-direction implies movement, a process, a new destination. A new life!

Out of habit and apparent necessity, most agents and editors think in terms of "rejection," meaning, eliminating in a permanent way all unwanted queries or manuscripts. "Thank you for submitting to our agency. However, your submission is not right for our list." Period. The typical form letter, often badly photocopied, probably unsigned.

If I could spearhead The Re-direction Foundation, I'd advocate reeducation of writers, agents, and editors. In my ideal world, writers would constantly do their homework so that they query the appropriate agents or editors for their works. They'd constantly seek to improve their craft, taking responsibility for every step of their career. No victims here.

By the same token, agents and editors would not reject a requested manuscript (not query) without adding some vital piece of information re-directing each writer toward success, such as recommending a more suitable publisher or agent or suggesting further study of the techniques of writing a novel. With this philosophy, agents or editors would keep writers growing toward professionalism, help works find the right home, and elevate literacy and literature with every small action.

Redirection may sound like just a clever word replacement for rejection, but there are deeper, more positive consequences.

Many writers, agents, and editors already maintain this attitude at least some of the time. I remember the surprise expressed by one of the writers in my critique group when she received a rejection letter from Denise Marcil with a suggestion that she try agent Meredith Bernstein instead. Denise won eternal respect for that one small act of consideration. And Meredith Bernstein won a query letter tailored to her specific needs.

As a writer, two practical actions will help you assert this affirming philosophy for yourself. First, you can reinforce re-direction efforts by agents and editors by writing back and thanking them for their suggestions. Remember the power of words. Second, you certainly shouldn't wait around for the publishing industry to change. Change begins at home and, no matter how any other writer, agent, or editor acts, you'll further your own sanity and success by adopting a re-direction philosophy for yourself.

Consciousness Raising 101

Cine/Lit agent Anna Cottle distinguishes between two kinds of re-direction: the cosmic and the personal. The cosmic re-direction is out of the hands of the individual. The publisher just bought a similar book or did badly with a similar book in the past. Or, a company merges with a larger publisher, laying off its editorial staff and leaving as orphans many of its authors. Like refugees, some writers lose their publishers, editors, and even agents by forces that are entirely out of their control. Your only practical response to cosmic re-direction is to make the best of a bad situation. You begin marketing again and find another agent and publisher for your work.

Personal re-direction is another matter. Here's an example: Three agents tell you that your antagonist is overdrawn, too thoroughly evil to be convincing. What do you do? When my student Trish Bradbury got this response to one of her novels from three different agents, she stopped marketing and pondered the criticism. Agreeing with the agents, she rewrote the story and is much happier with it. She accepted the responsibility of making changes as a positive response to re-direction.

It's natural to feel disappointed when rejected. One of my writer friends responds to a rejection letter by getting out the vacuum cleaner. "I'm always less angry when the house is clean," she says.

The more swiftly you can re-direct rejection, the better off you'll be. You'll eventually become as adept at switching on re-direction as flicking on a light switch. It's up to you to stay true to your own course. That's why a pre-planned marketing strategy can bail you out by telling you, at your lowest moments, what the next step is—whether that is rewrite, mail elsewhere, or try another one of the eight ways that novels get sold.

Dreamcrushers

I believe that writers need to be particularly careful about getting caught in traps set by Dreamcrushers. I use this term to describe agents, editors, writers, family, and friends who, while being reasonable, caring people in other respects, maintain a belief in what I've dubbed the W gene or the S gene: the born writer—with the W gene, or the born storyteller—with the S gene. Usually adherents of the traditional rejection philosophy, Dreamcrushers hold a more fundamental belief system: If you never had it, you never will. They undermine the success of aspiring novelists, and you can't afford to let them.

The W and S are not genes that anyone can find under a high-powered microscope. However, they are just as real to those who believe in the existence of born writers or born storytellers. Some people think that like Mozart composing music at age five, a W-gene writer's first scribbles will evidence literary talent, original expression, and unique voice. By the time this writer begins to market novels, the W gene is in such evidence that the writer's work can easily be differentiated from the masses of writers not fortunate enough to be born with the W gene. Conversely, a writer with the W gene is virtually guaranteed publication, assuming he knows how to put stamps on queries and manuscript packages. A W-gene writer is someone like Anne Tyler, Barbara Kingsolver, Pat Conroy, to name a few. Those who believe in this genetic mythology would assume that Pulitzer-prize winners are exclusively W-gene people.

The other group of genetically blessed writers are born with the S gene. The Storytellers. What they lack in the W-gene ability to turn a phrase or render a poetic image, they make up for in charm, charisma, and plotting. In fact, storytellers often get the label "plot monsters." I hear this, for instance, used to describe some of the books written by the likes of Michael Crichton, John Grisham, and Tom Clancy.

Are some people born with talent? With the gift of literary genius or storytelling acumen? Of course. Dreamcrushers, however, believe that *everyone else* who is not as talented and gifted should stop clogging the channels of publishing and get jobs doing something else. Furthermore, some Dreamcrushers maintain they are entrusted by their superior ability to pass judgement on a writer's potential. (Perhaps they believe in a J gene.) They act as if they have a moral imperative to discourage any writer who doesn't show literary or storytelling genius. You can't let them.

In fact, one person in the position to judge and reject queries and manuscripts told me that he considers it his duty to "save trees" by discouraging aspiring writers in whom he sees no talent.

An agent's and editor's survival in business depends upon developing a critical eye that separates wheat from chaff. That's not the problem about which I am speaking. I'm talking about the sheer arrogance of discouraging someone on a misplaced belief in that person's lack of talent. History has proven the folly of such arrogance. Determined writers—amateurs, chaff—can learn how to write novels. This requires development of skill, not a brain transplant. Motivated writers must learn the rules of novel craft, develop technique, practice correct skills, and they *will* improve over time. Nothing magical. Nothing genetic. In the process, who is to say that such a novelist won't "find her voice," discover a storytelling ability that had been there, undeveloped, all the time, or one day experience the emotional freedom and courage to express the inexpressible and become commercially publishable or even literary and award-winning writers?

By definition, genius is rare; such blessed individuals represent only a minority of published writers. The problem with Dreamcrushers is that they inflict a lot of damage when they sit behind the agent's or editor's desk or, even closer to home, share dinner at your table. Knowing ahead of time that they exist, often as wolves in sheep's clothing, my hope is that you can discard their comments, even at your most vulnerable moments.

Let's face it, most of us fall between two extremes—genius and idiot— no matter what the Dreamcrushers say. Perhaps this is why Colonyhouse, my favorite writer's haven on the northern Oregon coast, features a wooden sign over the hearth, the words burned into the wood: "Illegitimi Non Carborundum." Lacking a Latin background, I asked one of the founders what it meant. With a wry smile, Marlene Howard answered, "Don't let the bastards grind you down."

Whether or not the new paradigm of re-direction ever becomes the industry standard, it's up to you, the writer, to re-direct rejection, block Dreamcrushers, and keep your own efforts based on a vision and marketing strategy.

Four Types of Rejection Letters

Virtually every rejection letter from an agent or editor to your query or manuscript will fall into four categories:

- a form letter
- a "bad" letter
- a personal, discouraging letter
- a personal, encouraging letter

A FORM LETTER

As mentioned before, receipt of form rejections in response to sending a requested manuscript is one of the most frustrating types of responses that writers receive. They say nothing. Some writers further classify form rejection letters into ones that are polite and ones that are impolite. The polite ones use phraseology similar to what I mentioned earlier; they describe the limitations of the agency, the subjectivity of opinion, and they wish the writer success elsewhere. If words hold power, and I believe they do, at least these carefully worded rejection letters affirm the writer while declining the manuscript. What they don't do is say why the work was really declined.

In contrast, impolite form letters run the gamut from a scrawled note on the writer's own query letter saying "Not for us" to tiny half-sheet or quarter-sheet forms with a simple one-line sentence saying something like, "Thank you for your submission. However, we are not considering manuscripts at this time," even though they may have requested them. While agents or publishers see the smaller-sized note as conserving paper and cutting costs, writers may feel slighted. After all, they are repeatedly told to carefully prepare their submissions. Directories like *Writer's Market* advise sending query or cover letters on quality bond. Others recommend using printed, letterhead stationery. The teeny form or scrawled message feels like the agent or publisher has not shown the same respect asked of writers.

From the agent's or editor's perspective, 99 percent of queries and submissions are sent to the wrong market. Therefore, the quality of a writer's presentation is immediately subverted. The agent or editor justifiably feels neither respect nor care. If the query or submitted manuscript is appropriate, it deserves and should get respect and response.

If you get a lot of form rejections, consider that you may be sending your query and/or manuscript to the wrong markets. Perhaps you need to better research regarding which publishers and agents would be most interested.

It can't hurt to revise your letter or sample chapters once again, and run these past your critique group. Many writers accept only half-a-dozen form rejections before they rewrite their queries, assuming that they must not have done their job well enough if they aren't getting requests to see their manuscripts. That's re-direction in action.

A "BAD" LETTER

Every industry harbors unstable, neurotic, and self-serving individuals. I would like to think that these individuals are as much in the minority within the publishing industry as in any other business. You may spot one of these miscreants if you are the unfortunate recipient of a "bad" rejection letter. I have received only two such letters in nearly twenty years of correspondence as a writer. You don't forget them. Their most identifying characteristic is that they attack you, the writer, and are laden with truly inappropriate insults. The two that I received were from editors in powerful positions. The insidious message of the rejector is that you are a horrible person, horrible writer, and should drop off the face of the earth.

How should you react to such a letter? After all, you can't let anyone get away with such abuse. Your first inclination may be similar to mine; you want to fire off a return letter so blistering that the editor or agent is pulverized into purple powder. I actually entertained a guerilla warfare-type strategy cleverly suggested by a friend: Send back the bad letter with a note written on it from you that says, "I thought you should know that some crazy person is sending out letters like this with your signature."

In reality, the best response is to rid yourself of the venom as quickly as possible, which means to stop thinking about what was said and any thoughts of revenge. If my experience is any measure, you're only likely to run into a bad letter about once every ten years. If it's any comfort, agents get "bad" query letters from writers, and probably in greater numbers. True example: "You'd be crazy not to publish my book." Or worse yet, threats: "If you don't represent me, I'll get back at you...."

If you feel strongly that it would be wrong not to do something, give yourself a week to cool off, then report your experience to the Association of Authors' Representatives, to the Author's Guild, to the National Writers Association, to the National Writers Union, and to any other organization to which you belong. See this book's Resource Directory for contact information. Then, re-direct your efforts in positive directions by consulting your marketing plan. Move on.

A PERSONAL, DISCOURAGING LETTER

Whenever an agent, editor, or assistant writes you a personal letter detailing the reasons why they had to pass on your work, you should take heart (and thank the sender). At first, you may feel discouraged; after all, it's a rejection, isn't it? Not really. With the stacks of manuscripts on every agent's and editor's desk, only promising writers receive personal letters.

Therese Engelmann, whose succinct query letter for her historical novel *Allah's Amulet* was given in chapter six, received a request for her first chapter from an established agent. The agent responded with a personal rejection letter in which she complimented Therese's writing but offered criticism of the first chapter and the synopsis of the book.

Therese re-directed her energies and revised based on this criticism—which echoed suggestions made by members of her critique group. Then, she contacted the agent again by letter, informed her that she had made the recommended changes, and asked if she could resubmit and send the entire novel. The agent agreed.

Once again, Therese received a personal rejection letter. Actually, it was a re-direct letter, because the agent wrote several pages' worth of incisive critique, an uncommon and generous gift. An action that also meant that the agent saw promise in Therese's writing. While Therese doesn't agree with all of the criticism, the feedback provided her with a perspective of the work that led her to see it in new light. Knowing that she has learned how to write a novel from this first book, Therese is not at all discouraged. She is now re-directing her energy into a second novel based on the same 16th-century duchy and characters, while jotting notes related to the revision of the first novel.

There couldn't be a better example of what you should do if you get a personal and discouraging rejection letter. Recognize the compliment in getting a personal letter. Seriously consider the critical comments. Decide what you should do next—rewrite or market anew. And, respond to the courtesy of the personal letter by sending that agent or editor a personal thank-you note. This completes the circle and encourages re-direction-oriented agents and editors to continue their practice of re-direction.

A Personal, Encouraging Letter

Once upon a time, a writer joined one of my critique groups. Her first readings seemed devoid of evidence of either the W gene or the S gene. After awhile, she put aside her first novel and applied new-found knowledge and skill on a second one, a mystery written primarily from the viewpoints of two police officers. She wrote and rewrote. She took a sabbatical from her critique group to take classes in criminology and police procedures. She rewrote again and again, incorporating the suggestions of her critique group and me, her independent book editor. Five years after she first entered the group, she began to market this mystery.

She attended two, large, regional writing conferences where she met with many agents and editors. Half a dozen asked her to send sample chapters and a brief synopsis. The first agent sent back a personal, "encouraging" rejection letter. The letter said that he'd almost decided to represent her on this book, but ultimately decided that the story didn't have a well-developed enough protagonist to carry a series, which is what he was looking for.

A second agent also sent a personal, encouraging letter, saying, "I really like this story, but I feel that your male police detective needs more character depth. If you would be willing to work on this, I'd like to see it again."

The magic words are: *I'd like to see it again.* If you get any letter that says this, please know that the agent or editor was captivated by your writing, and she sincerely hopes that you will rewrite per her suggestions. Open the champagne! This is worth celebrating. You have just received external professional feedback—as opposed to compliments from friends and family—that your writing has tickled someone else's imagination. Someone with the power to help you get published, who likes your work and may decide to help you with it. This is no small hint that you are on the right path. If you agree with her request, don't hesitate. While you are a fresh memory to the agent, rewrite and resubmit.

What you don't want to do is what this writer in my group actually did, although her story has a happy ending. She rewrote to deepen the characterization and gained the blessing of her critique group and editor. Then, she sat on the manuscript. Things were busy at her office. The holidays came and went. Months rolled by. She could have lost the opportunity. Fortunately, her phone rang one day and it was the agent, asking, "Are you going to send us that rewrite?"

Of course, as the writer's mentor, I was beside myself. I know her to be a perfectionist, which is one of the strengths that carried her from those first weak efforts at writing a novel to success at writing a salable one. However, perfectionism is double-edged, and I feared she might not ever stop rewriting. As she talked with the agent, she gained permission to send 100 pages, not just her rewrite of the first chapter. Within a few weeks, she sent the revision and in a short time later, got another call from the agent. "Now, would you please send us the entire novel," wisely adding, "within two weeks."

In general, when you receive either a personal, discouraging or a personal, encouraging re-direction letter, you'll further your cause by taking whichever of these actions apply:

1. Send thank-you notes acknowledging the time and energy that went into writing a personal letter with suggestions for rewrite.

2. Phone the agent or editor if you have genuine questions or confusion about the feedback. This is not breaking a rule. You have the thread of a relationship now. Organize your thoughts and be respectful of the agent's or editor's time.

3. Like the example set by Therese Engelmann, consider resubmitting your manuscript after you have made revisions by first contacting the agent or editor—by letter or phone—and asking if you may do so. Or, move this person's name to the top of your list to query on a subsequent novel. After all, something in your first work resonated positively enough for a personal response. Your next book might ring the right bell.

4. Move on. Don't lose time over a rejection letter, even a re-direction letter. Make decisions based on your marketing strategy and on the

growth in your skill in writing and in marketing. Re-direct your own energies.

5. Last of all, no matter what kind of rejection letter you have received, share your experience and your process with your writing friends. Whether you have a single writing buddy or belong to several writers' groups, use peers to support your marketing efforts, to help you interpret the results, to choose a next strategy, and to gain perspective.

In summary:

- Transcend the rejection.
- Decode the feedback.
- Discard the negative or unhelpful.
- Act according to your marketing plan.
- Share your results.

Personal Re-direction

Learning how to recognize the golden gift in feedback is one all-important skill in your tool kit. However, one of the most difficult judgments to make involves three different types of personal re-direction decisions:

- Deciding When to Stop Marketing
- Assessing the Impact of Culture and Timing
- Ending First-Novel Fixations

DECIDING WHEN TO STOP MARKETING

Upon hearing about the re-direction philosophy, Laine Stambaugh, a writer of romantic comedy, quipped, "It's not a rejection until you've run out of re-direction." So, what if you reach the end of the line? How many rejection letters should one accept before reaching the decision to stop marketing? Famous rejection stories inject caution: The Newberry Medal winner *A Wrinkle in Time* by Madeleine L'Engle was published after twenty-six rejections; the Pulitzer Prize winner *Ironweed* by William Kennedy chalked up thirteen rejections; other equally famous books and authors claimed this many and more rejections before publication.

Ultimately, the decision whether to stop marketing a particular novel rests with the author. Only you can decide whether you agree with feedback from your critique group, freelance editors, agents, and editors. Only you know whether twenty rejection letters or two hundred define a stopping point. I will say this: Substantially more people fail for lack of persistence than for persisting too long. At the same time, I have also watched writers cling to fantasy ignoring the feedback that should tell them they are marketing prematurely or incorrectly. My best advice is to measure your inner knowing against the opinions of those in whom you place trust, and then decide.

Assessing the Impact of Culture and Timing

What if your writing style is unpopular—anachronistic, too experimental, taking place in a time period or place unsupported by the current publishing interest? What if you are visionary or artistic in a way that places you ahead of your time? What if the political and cultural climate of your country discourages your kind of writing, or worse yet, punishes or imprisons writers?

In the summer of 1996, I attended the "Getting It Write" conference in Klamath Falls, Oregon. The keynote speaker was Peter Sears, a successful author of poetry and nonfiction. In his dual capacity as director of the Oregon Literary Coalition (a statewide advocacy group dedicated to protecting Oregon writing and publishing organizations) and as consultant to Writers Conferences and Festivals (a national advocacy group), Peter had much to say about writing for writing's sake versus writing for publication and profit, as follows:

The desire to be successful with one's writing and the desire to create art do not necessarily get along well. They may at first, just as the better you write, the better are your chances of getting published. But beyond that, things may no longer remain simple. So you are better off deciding up front which master you serve, which muse you follow. Then, if you happen to get lucky and get both, the artistic success and the financial success, you can celebrate your very good fortune.

If political or cultural forces run contrary to your passion as a writer, you have a perfect description of what the agents at Cine/Lit Representation referred to as "cosmic re-direction." Peter Sears went on to point out that writers could be immune to these outer forces as long as they like to write and derive personal meaning from both writing and marketing. Peter adds: "If your success or failure *out there* starts determining whether or not you can get yourself back in your writing, then you had better take another look at your priorities.... Things you love are worth protecting."

Sometimes it seems as if writers must wait for the proper alignment of the stars in heaven before they find the outer success they seek. Some writers "wait for Godot," but Godot never comes. For the writer who persists both in craft and in marketing, the diversity in our times of worldwide publishing opportunities offers a fertile, nourishing bed for nearly all kinds of writing. But the other watchdogs of our times predict a downward spiral toward commercialism and entertainment that history will regard as The Age of Mediocrity that muzzled the most artistic and creative authors of the times. Peter Sears says:

> Freedom of thinking and expression is a measure of a culture. It signals the willingness and capacity of the culture to change, to grow. Writing conferences [for instance] contribute to a culture in which there is a bullish commerce of ideas. Books are sold. Performances flourish. Art is everywhere. People talk freely, through their art work, of what is taking place. They re-examine, for themselves, what truth and virtue mean. In such a climate, great art may emerge. To participate in that possibility is exciting. Writing, however private, is a witnessing of the times.

Where does that leave you, if you are the writer of the unpopular or untimely? In all truth, it may leave you writing for yourself in this lifetime, or cultivating one body of your work for the marketplace and the other for your soul.

ENDING FIRST-NOVEL FIXATIONS

A common disease among new writers is obsession with a first novel. Like prisoners of a virtual reality, some writers get stuck revising their first three or six chapters, unable to cut loose, and enter the frightening uncharted region of the rest of the book. At least as common are those writers who "finish" a first novel and then rewrite it ad nauseam, sometimes until they do finally get it correct. Technically correct. They may query and be unfazed by over 100 rejections. It could be that the progress they have made in learning how to write has been so hard won, it doesn't seem right to put the novel aside without recognition or reward. Most of the time that is exactly what would be in their best interests.

I am sure others who are privy to the growth of writers have observed the ineffable phenomenon that so often takes place in a writer's second, third, or fifth novel. I'm talking about the quantum leap in growth of craft and style. Control, coherence, characterization, and creativity seem to combine in ways that were simply not possible within the confines of the first book. Magic happens. But, in some cases, it can only happen when you say adios to that first novel. In some seemingly universal principle, you've to let go in order to receive greater bounty.

BREAKTHROUGH

"The Ideal Writer-Agent Partnership"

Melissa Jensen, author of Regency romance novels

"There is not an agent in 1000 who would do what Denise Marcil did for me," says Melissa Jensen, author of four Regency romances, all published in 1996, of a historical novel published November 1997, and of five more Regencys as of 2001.

When Melissa queried New York agent Denise Marcil in 1993, it was about her 125,000-word "historical extravaganza," as she calls it. "I'd included a page or two excerpt, and Denise wrote back requesting the first three chapters, then later, the entire manuscript." In her rejection letter, Denise recommended cutting the book down to Regency size (70,000-75,000 words), saying, "You have promise here, but I can't sell this book." She also recommended that Melissa begin a second Regency romance.

"I pouted and scuffed my feet," Melissa remembers. "The first book is your baby. You don't want to be told that your baby is ugly."

She took the advice and started a second novel, still checking with Denise from time to time. "She was very patient and stuck by me," Melissa says. A year after she'd queried Denise on her first novel, she sent her the manuscript for the second novel and Denise accepted it, selling it twelve weeks later. Fawcett-Ballantine published it under the title of *Choice Deceptions* and under Melissa's pen name, Emma Jensen.

The next step in her career is amazing; she found the groove, although she ultimately shelved the first novel as a learning experience. By the end of 1996, she could claim four Regency romances in print, *Vivid Notions, Coup de Grace, What Chloe Wants,* in addition to her first published Regency, *Choice Deceptions.* Her first Regency-era historical novel *Entwined* was released in 1997.

"I consider my success a matter of timing, talent, and luck, and," Melissa adds, "it would not have happened without Denise Marcil. If I'd simply received a form rejection, I might still be shopping that first novel."

She recognizes that agents and editors need writers as much as writers need them. "There are more of us than them," Melissa comments. "Many writers look in reverence, awe, and fear at agents and editors. They are people and they have a job to do. They have a responsibility to writers as a whole, and no writer should be afraid to get on the phone and call her agent. It's nice if they give a reason why they reject a manuscript, but we must respect their time."

I'm certain that Denise would say that Melissa had a great deal to do with her own success. Although she has a degree in English literature from the University of Pennsylvania, Melissa considers herself self-taught. "I never took any writing classes," she says. "I just read. I devoured books, and I have a great mother who read to me as a child."

Melissa believes that you can't teach someone how to write. "It simply takes practice, practice, practice," she insists, "and a certain amount of ability." She also believes that writers must know what is selling and why. "You must read," she says, "and you must be patient. You must finish your manuscript, and it may take a long time to sell, especially," she adds from experience, "if your first book isn't 'The One.'"

"I also think that romance writers should be willing to do a more traditional romance before taking on the cutting edge, such as time travel or paranormals, which are very hard to do. It's not easy for agents to help a new writer break in." Melissa notes, "Tradition sells."

"You must read and write," she says. And, if you are fortunate, you'll find an agent like Denise Marcil with whom to form a winning partnership.

CHAPTER TWELVE

Choosing the Right Agent for You

- ◆ 30 Questions to Ask the Agent You May Hire
- ◆ Red Flags in the Author/Agent Relationship
- ◆ Breakthrough: "Writing From Soul" by Gregg Kleiner

You've probably heard the Catch-22 cliche about getting a bank loan: You need credit to get a loan, and you need a loan to establish credit. Much the same has been said about gaining agent representation for a first novel: You need an agent to sell your book, but you need a published book to get an agent.

As difficult as finding an agent seems, an even more difficult decision may be whether to accept an offer of representation. Many first-time authors don't realize this is a decision they must make. One literary agent told me that first-time novelists are so desperate to secure an agent, they rarely ask questions. "The questions come later," the agent said, "after they experience first contracts, the sale of subsidiary rights, and other money matters."

While this may be the norm, you will stand a better chance at a happy relationship with fewer disappointments if you are fully informed. That happens only after asking vital questions. Most important of all, you must realize that the partnership is a two-way street. Not only must the agent choose a writer she believes will be successful, but you must choose the agent who will be best for your book and a match for your individual needs.

The questions you should avoid asking an agent are those that you can answer from the many agent directories and books on publishing. In this chapter I have listed only those questions a writer should ask *after* the manuscript has passed muster and the agent offers representation. Your agent may be your single-most important and enduring literary partner, so ideally, you want to meet and exchange information face-to-face. Second best, make a special telephone appointment in which to talk and ask important questions.

Often, agents will pick up the phone and tell writers they want to represent them. Perhaps you have already been through a round of revisions, or perhaps the representation an agent offers is contingent upon revisions, but the moment is here! This is it! In either case, express something like the following and you will create the kind of opening you need to ask more questions later:

> I'm pleased and excited that you like my novel and are willing to be my agent. As you may remember, I'm serious about building a career as a novelist, and I've been looking for the right agent to help me reach those goals. Your call has taken me by surprise, and I am elated. I'd like to arrange a time when you can set aside about half an hour to answer the many questions I know I'll have.

30 Questions to Ask the Agent You May Hire

I've organized these following thirty questions into four categories: the work, competency and experience, money, and career. While it would be ideal to ask all of these questions before signing with an agency, you should know that you can ask questions any time. The author-agent relationship is an ever-changing one and, like every other relationship in life, needs periodic adjustments and assessment. Plan to ask these and other questions throughout your association with an agent. Open communication clears the air of misunderstandings and maintains a climate of mutual trust and cooperation.

THE WORK

1. What do you think of the book and its potential?

Measure how the agent feels about the work itself and its potential in the marketplace. If you hear hesitations about your writing or a lot of doom and gloom about how hard it is to sell first novels, the agent may not feel sufficient championship to continue marketing in the face of even a few rejections.

2. Do you see any areas that need improvement?

Recognizing that most novels require polishing before they are deemed ready to sell, this question flushes out agents with editorial skill, which may also correspond to their reputations for having works ready for sale. If an agent has no comments, or none similar to those you have received from several other sources, the agent may be too inexperienced to help you.

3. How would you describe my novel to an editor?

Editors are busy people approached by many agents. This question gives you an idea of an agent's skill in distilling the essence of your work and forming a sales pitch. A strong pitch means your work is more likely to be requested by editors.

4. When and how often can I expect to hear from you during the period when you are trying to sell my book?

One author may be unperturbed by three months between contacts with an agent while another would be a wreck without phone calls. Needs vary. What would you be comfortable with? How closely matched are you both in expectations concerning author-agent communication?

5. How often may I call you?

Communication must flow two ways. Say your agent calls you once a month. You know you need more frequent contact. It's possible your agent might not object if you call her once a week. However, if you get the sense that your prospective agent would be annoyed by contacts you initiate, think again about the long-term ramifications.

6. Will you send me copies of my rejection letters, and if so, how soon after you receive them?

Copies of rejection letters from publishers are one of the few means by which you can track your agent and hold her accountable to work on your behalf. Office policies vary: One agent may send the originals within twenty-four hours of receipt; another may never send copies. Still another may send monthly summaries of marketing efforts. What would you prefer?

7. Will you involve me in all particulars of a book contract, including the final decision to accept or reject an offer?

In the beginning of your partnership with an agent, I would think you would want to be consulted on every contract issue that is going to have bearing on your writing, royalties, or future career. If the agent doesn't want to go to all that "trouble" (it does lengthen negotiations to explain matters), then are you willing to turn over all control and accept whatever terms have been arrived at on your behalf?

COMPETENCY AND EXPERIENCE

8. Are you a member of AAR?

If you can answer this from directories, don't ask this question. However, if the agent listing does not show membership in this sole professional organization for agents, then by all means, ask why not? Lack of sales and the charging of fees are two reasons that preclude AAR membership and should make you question this agent's skill.

9. When did you start your agency (if independent), and how long have you been an agent?

Time doing a job does yield experience, connections in the industry, and most often, greater skill at a job. A new agent may become a great agent, one who can grow with you, but beware; there is a risk as well. A new agent might flounder or fail, might have limited or no editorial connections, and might not correctly assess your book's readiness or the timing of your career moves.

10. What books of the same type as mine have you sold?

Agents specialize; agents have preferences. Even a superagent operating outside her specialty might not prove as wise a choice as an agent of average skill with a strong track record with your type of book.

11. What is your plan for marketing my book?

You want to hear a plan, a strategy for selling your book. If an agent cannot report any, you have to wonder if she has a publisher in mind or is a totally disorganized, perhaps ineffective, sales person.

12. What range of publishers do you sell to?

Don't let the answer stop with, "Oh, a wide range." Get names. The fewer the names, the narrower the range of contacts. Are the contacts large publishers, small presses, or a mixture? Listen for names that match your type of novel.

13. How many clients do you currently represent?

Does the agent's answer jibe with the numbers listed in a directory? If the number is small, follow up with a comment about the agency being new or ask why such a small clientele. If the number is large—over 50, then ask if you can expect personal attention. Does the agent have hired assistants, readers, or sub-agents? Will the agent give up on you if a sale isn't instantaneous, knowing there are more authors waiting in the wings? How does the agent manage whatever the clientele she has?

14. How many novels do you sell, on the average, per year?

Put the agent's answer in perspective according to the percentage of her clientele that write nonfiction versus fiction. Also ask how many of those novels sold represent new writers. If an agency primarily represents nonfiction, you could face the heartbreak of having your novel returned to you a year or two down the road—if the initial representation is made from enthusiasm rather than experience or connections. On the other hand, most agencies add few new novelists, perhaps fewer than half a dozen or as few as one per year. But, more important than that is how much of the agency is devoted to selling fiction.

MONEY

15. What fees should I expect to be charged?

Some agencies list themselves as non-fee-charging, then charge exorbitant representation fees, sometimes as much as several hundred dollars per year, a questionable policy if not outrageous. If these fees aren't printed in a directory or made clear by the agent, I see this practice as a form of sleight-of-hand or bait-and-switch; meaning, once they offer representation, they've gotcha, because you're inclined to pay the fee rather than lose what you've sought for so long. The same technique may be used by agencies advertising editorial fees to critique manuscripts, where the implied carrot on the stick is that they also sell their edited books to publishers. A writer can be lured into paying high editorial fees that may or may not be comparable in value to what independent book editors charge, but the writer will naturally hope, perhaps expect, that eventually the manuscript will be good enough to sell—by this editor-turned-agent. If you are in doubt about the fees charged by an agent, join National Writers Union and ask their consultants, other agents in the business, or published authors.

16. What commission do you charge?

The answer should be a simple 15 percent. That is the industry standard, although you may encounter a few agents from the ice age who still charge a commission rate of 10 percent. In fact, be wary of agents who offer you "a deal," only 10-percent commission, but also a "small" representation or reading fee of "only" a few hundred dollars. One of my clients almost succumbed to this appeal. She received an acceptance letter and a contract from a new agent who offered her a bargain—only 10 percent commission on one hand—but a representation fee of $150 on the other hand. Looking closer, she saw that the contract was for a six-month period. It would be as likely as lightning striking the author for this so-called new agent to sell a historical novel by a new writer in just six months. In my opinion, my client had stumbled upon an F-team agent.

17. Are you incorporated or a limited liability company?

In general, incorporation or formation of an LLC, of any business offers greater legal protection against lawsuit than a sole proprietorship.

18. How quickly do you pay authors after receipt of monies on their books, and how do you handle author monies?

The answer you receive will indicate an efficient office with good business and management practices, or a chaotic one. Obviously, whoever holds the money accumulates the interest. Ethical agents following standard business practices should, in fact, have a non-interest bearing "holding" account for client monies that is entirely separate from the agency account. Only after deducting the 15-percent agent commission and agreed-upon author expenses are you forwarded the rest.

19. What subsidiary rights do you commonly sell for authors, and what potential subsidiary sales do you see for my book?

When an agent is competent in a number of subsidiary rights sales—foreign, book clubs, movies and tv, audio and CD ROM—you'll stand a greater chance of seeing more money, greater sales, and a greater boost to your career than if an agent does not have these skills. Some agents subcontract to other agents with strong subsidiary-rights abilities. If your agent tells you that she typically lets the publisher retain the subsidiary rights, you might discuss whether this will serve your long-term interests. Some publishers have subsidiary rights divisions that exceed the skills or connections of agents. However, retention of subsidiary rights by agents is more often to the author's benefit, because they can sell these rights and earn money for the author that cannot be deducted by the publisher against the advance.

20. How do you feel about auctions and do you ever hold them?

Not only does this question let you know whether your agent has experience with this most complex of book-selling strategies, it may also tell you whether the agent is comfortable with high-stakes negotiating. Not all novels are auction material, but if an agent sees your book as having auction potential, that means your agent is enthused, and enthusiasm sells books.

21. How would the editors you know rate you at the negotiation table?

This may be a more difficult question to ask, but the answer will tell you much about your agent's confidence and selling skills, as opposed to editorial skills. While an agent is unlikely to tell you if she is a pushover, an answer of "okay" or "average" might not bode well for the assertiveness required in tough negotiations that could occur at an important turning point in your career.

22. Will you issue an IRS 1099 form at year's end?

This is the legal tax form required of a business by the Internal Revenue Service when it has paid money to an individual who is not its employee and for whom it is not responsible for social security and other tax withholding. If an agent is not up to speed with this IRS requirement, how does she handle other accounting practices?

23. What happens if you die or become disabled?

It's as important for you to know what happens to your book and royalties in the event of your agent's death as it is in the event of your own. The book contract should specify what happens to your royalties. But how accessible are your book earnings in your agent's account at the time of her death? What happens to negotiations or half-completed deals? If she becomes disabled, unable to perform her job to your satisfaction, how can you exit gracefully? Make sure your author-agent contract addresses all forms of exit.

CAREER

24. Are you a specialist or a generalist?

Your first novel might be women's fiction, but what if you shift to literary or Novels of the West? If it is important to you to have an agent who can accommodate your choices as a novelist, this could be a telling question.

25. What kinds of novels do you not feel comfortable representing?

This is a different way to get at some of the same information. Ideally, you want an agent who feels comfortable and has connections to sell everything you might write.

26. If you don't sell my first novel, will you drop me as a client?

You need an honest, upfront answer to this question. Some agents make a commitment to a book, one book at a time, and others commit to the writer and a career. Flipping the coin, do you want the freedom to sever the relationship with one agent in order to try another, assuming the first agent is unable to sell your first novel, or would you wish to stay with the first agent and turn your efforts to writing a second book?

27. If the editorial consensus on my book is that it needs more work, can I count on you to help me editorially?

Some agents have the editorial skills to help direct a revision and others do not. Some have the skills but would rather sell books than work through revision with an unpublished writer. It is best to find out ahead of time.

28. Do you have contacts with reputable independent book editors, i.e. book doctors?

If an agent can produce a list of several independent book editors (also called "book doctors" or "freelance editors"), this can give you confidence that she maintains a separation between selling books and correcting them. No conflict of interest or the potential of sleight-of-hand mixing of editorial and critique fees with her work as an agent. A referral list can also indicate an agent who cares about writers enough to re-direct them to help.

29. At some future date, would you sit down with me and discuss how I can build a successful career as a novelist over the next five to ten years?

This question flushes out people-oriented agents versus profit-only agents. It also speaks to a commitment greater than selling your first book.

30. Do you have an author-agent contract?

Agents who readily provide author-agent written contracts project more professionalism and feeling of standard business practices than those who operate on a handshake. No matter what the reputation of an agent, I recommend that you insist on a written contract and be willing to provide one if necessary. Many agents prefer handshake agreements, no written contracts. After all, they say, nothing is important or real until the work is sold. But, that may take months, even years, and the book may be returned to the writer. Why bother with a contract? It sets goals and limits in a legal and business partnership involving large sums of money. Your money. Ask published friends to see their contracts, or contact National Writers Union for explanation of its "Preferred Literary Agent Agreement," or see the sample contract reprinted in this book's appendices.

Another important aspect of the author-agent agreement is any clause about the agreed-upon period of time of representation and how either party may terminate the agreement. Most agents ask you to agree to twelve to fifteen months as the term of the agreement. They are as hopeful as you are of a quick sale, but this is a profession of waiting—waiting for each key person in the chain from submission to sale to read your work. Likewise, you need an escape clause—and so does the agent. A reasonable clause will state that either party can terminate the agreement with thirty days notice—or less. *Never* sign a contract that doesn't have a reasonable escape clause.

Red Flags in the Author-Agent Relationship

The author-agent relationship is sometimes compared to that of the home-owner and real-estate agent. If it takes awhile to sell your home, you may get to know your Realtor quite well, and if you buy and sell a number of homes, you will have a chance to build a shared history.

But it's not the same. As an author, your novel has sprung from your imagination, your heart, and perhaps from a deep well of needs and moti-vations you can't even articulate. You've entrusted your literary agent to sell this extension of yourself, not only so that you can gain financial reward, but also to share your work with the world. You may be building a career and someday hope to quit your day job. Your agent holds a great deal more responsibility than a Realtor.

The thirty questions offered earlier in this chapter suggest a way to begin well and forestall later problems. These questions also suggest places where a relationship can sour or not meet your expectations. In general, be aware of the following six problem areas.

1. Communication problems.

Every relationship is bound to run into rough spots. Ask questions and express your needs and preferences. Don't expect mind reading and don't be afraid to pick up the phone to clear the air. If you've followed this advice and can't establish the kind of communication you need to stay sane, it may be time to shop for a new agent.

2. Integrity problems.

You may remember the situation faced by Charles Snellings whose agent repeatedly agreed to send him copies of his rejection letters but never did. Charley had also secured requests for his novel from querying publish-ers prior to having an agent. Although he forwarded these requests to his agent, he later found out that no copies of his manuscript had been logged in with the publishers—even though his agent claimed he had sent them. These might involve miscommunication, but they also certainly reflect problems with integrity. Other authors have encountered difficulties with fees, payment of funds, or kickback schemes with editorial services. These are integrity problems and not the norm in the industry. Seek legal recourse if you must, but terminate such relationships as quickly as possible.

3. Procedure Problems.

Your agent sends out a quarterly progress report of her efforts to sell your book. Rather than provide copies of rejection letters, she summarizes the comments from editors. She prefers to let an assistant handle all of your questions and concerns. These are procedure problems—her office procedures versus your preferences. Time to communicate. If she is not willing to change the way she does business, and you can't accept her way, it's time to change agents.

4. Enthusiasm problems.

You love your agent's philosophy of life. Her business practices are totally professional. She stays in close contact with you, and you couldn't be happier about her goodwill. In one year, however, she's only sent your book out three times, and the last action on it was four months ago when she said she made a phone call to an editor. This is clearly not an agent fired up to sell your book. It's time for a heart-to-heart.

5. Author expectation problems.

You've struggled for years to learn how to write and then to find an agent. It's understandable that you would hold high, possibly unreasonable, expectations. However, expectations can undermine the very success you seek. Expectations that your agent call you the very second he has heard anything, even say-nothing rejections. Expectations that lead you to call a publisher to check up on your agent. Expectations that your agent sell your book in six months or else. The only antidote to author-expectation problems is communication with your agent to find out what might be reasonable. *You* must change. Otherwise you risk losing a good agent because you're a bad client.

6. Graceful exits.

It's hard to duplicate the elation you felt when you finally secured agent representation. Almost as satisfying is parting on amicable terms. You may part ways because she cannot sell your work, or can no longer offer an objective perspective for your next revision. You may part ways because you have irreconcilable differences, or because your career is taking off and you want an agent with stronger ties to the movie industry. A graceful parting is one in which both parties affirm each other's value and wish each other well. No belittling, undercutting, or judgments. If the relationship stops being a win-win for all involved, don't continue it. That doesn't mean that you shouldn't stay in touch, support each other along your separate paths, or network, and build a new, but separate professional association. In this business as in most, it pays to be a bridge-builder not a bridge-burner.

You've done everything to find and choose the right agent, or you've decided to directly approach a publisher. You've done your job. Do you sit by the phone and wait? No. Turn your attention to writing your next novel. That way you'll be pleasantly surprised when the long-awaited phone call comes....

BREAKTHROUGH

"Writing from Soul"

Gregg Kleiner, author of a literary novel

"When I was sixteen years old, I spent a year in the mountains of northern Thailand as an AFS exchange student," Gregg says. "During that year, I lived with a poor Thai family that had extended family members who shared the same house or lived right next door. What struck me was how the elders were revered as sources of wisdom and knowledge simply because they had lived so long—they knew secrets about life and living that the young did not yet possess."

When Gregg returned to the United States, he was shocked by our culture's way of shuffling older people off to nursing homes, so different from his experiences in Thailand. He went on to graduate in journalism and in 1989, thirteen years after his exchange-student experience in Thailand, Gregg began to write a novel. He won a Walden Residency (through Lewis & Clark College in Portland, Oregon), where he completed the book.

His novel, "a quiet book, a story I wrote to tell, not to sell," is a tale about aging and dying, about how a ragtag bunch of strangers all over the age of eighty ended up living together in a rundown mansion in a small Oregon town where they decide to make their last days on earth an incredible adventure.

As Gregg was completing *Where River Turns to Sky*, his mother suggested he send it to the daughter of a friend of hers who she thought "had something to do with publishing in New York." When the book was finished, and after several agents had declined to represent it, Gregg decided to at last call his mother's friend and ask what type of work the daughter did.

"She told me that yes, indeed, her daughter was a literary agent in New York, and that she'd just sold Sam Walton's autobiography for $4.5 million," Gregg says. "As they say, 'Oftentimes, Mother knows best.'"

So he sent off a query, and the agent asked to see his manuscript. "Which I think she did only as a favor to both of our mothers," Gregg says. "But when the agent read the manuscript, she liked it so much she wanted to represent me. I am eternally grateful to my mother for her incredible intuition. She was killed by a drunk driver three weeks after I found out the novel had been accepted for publication."

Over the next year, the agent sent the manuscript out to twelve different publishing houses. "It came close at St. Martin's and Algonquin Books of Chapel Hill," Gregg recalls. "And finally, number thirteen, Avon Books, picked it up as part of their fall list for the new hardcover division they were launching that year."

Twenty-one years after the seed for his novel was planted in Thailand, Gregg Kleiner experienced the joy of holding his first novel in his hands. Published in hardcover by Avon Books, *Where River Turns to Sky* fulfills the promise made in his query letter: "This is a book that takes a wild shot at a society that's forgotten how to value and respect old age, at a nation that shuns its greatest (and wisest) treasure: the old—a state in which most all of us will someday find ourselves."

Gregg is philosophical about being a writer. "It's a long-term process," he says. "You can't give up, but you must be prepared for a long wait. Even so, you should follow your heart." Gregg adds, "Do what you need to do for your soul and things will work out. Focus on the work. Write every day. Tell the story you need to tell."

CHAPTER THIRTEEN

The First Sale and Beyond

- ◆ Negotiating Your Own Book Contract
- ◆ Agent or Lawyer for Hire
- ◆ Agent-represented Negotiation
- ◆ Shaping Your Career
- ◆ Second-book Queries
- ◆ Managing Success

The phone rings. Engrossed in plotting your second novel, your thoughts are a million miles from the message you are about to hear. An editor or your agent is on the other end of the line. "We'd like to do your book," says the voice. "They've made an offer." For most authors, that moment, that first book sale, is one filled with indescribable and complex emotions. Elation. A sense of unreality. Irritation that it took so long to get to this point. Apprehension about the future. Joy. Caution. What should you say?

Express your happiness, appreciation, thankfulness—whatever spontaneously comes to you in the moment. But, under no circumstances should you commit to any terms, contracts, or promises, even if you are agent-represented and have previously talked over the possibilities. Do say that you need to savor this moment and sort out what's in your best interest. Do say that you must think about all that has been offered, and you'll get back. Why? Because there is too much at stake in the terms of a contract not to give everything careful thought.

Many of us have built up a certain fear of the law, of how fine print in contracts can entrap us in unpleasant financial realities. Publishing contracts, too, are full of legalese and binding agreements, whether you have understood what you signed to or not. However, they can be rendered less formidable; for some, even fascinating.

You are likely to find yourself in one of three situations, each of which will be explained fully:

1. The offer to publish your book comes to you directly from a publisher. You intend to negotiate your own contract. This option requires the most knowledge on your part.
2. The offer comes directly from a publisher, and you intend to hire an agent or lawyer to negotiate this contract only. This option requires the second-most knowledge on your part.
3. The offer comes from the publisher to your agent, who will represent you and negotiate the contract terms. This option requires the least knowledge on your part.

You can handle each of these three situations well with equal aplomb—if you educate yourself properly.

Negotiating Your Own Book Contract

Knowledge is power. Self-education is a must if you intend to negotiate your own contract. The publisher is the experienced party, has selected a publishing contract that is the "boilerplate" they use for all authors. The publisher has managed negotiations in the past. You're the novice. Obviously, a publisher uses contracts that benefit its interest. That doesn't mean it seeks to give you less than you deserve. However, an inexperienced author who negotiates his own contract risks getting the short end.

Like the children's book writer who called me one day for names of agents he might contact—several years after he'd signed with a publisher and supplied the first two of a four-book contract. His first book became a bestseller among children's books. He was happy to promote it and eagerly wrote the second book as contracted. Then he got a bill. He'd expected a fat royalty check, so he was sure there was a mix-up, some terrible mistake. When the dust settled, there was no mistake. In signing the contract, he had agreed to pay the costs for art work, which in a children's work can be considerable. Now he was locked in for four books. Bestseller or not, he wasn't going to see a dime. He was going to see red in more ways than one.

You may recall that royalty rates are typically set on the retail, or list price, of your book. Occasionally, publishers, especially big educational houses, will stipulate in the contract that the royalty be based on the wholesale price of the book. I've also seen contracts without any provision for the author to have first dibs at buying back his own book when it goes out of print. These are just two of the points that could make a big difference to you.

The publishing contract is exceedingly complex. But, it's in English and, once you've translated some legal words, you can decipher it. Prepare, however, to study contracts. Several books will help you, including *A Writer's Guide to Contract Negotiations* by Richard Balkin and *Be Your Own Literary Agent* by Martin Levin. Others are listed in the Resource Directory.

Most of all, be aware that the typical publishing contract is a standard contract. Certain clauses are fixed and nonnegotiable. Others can be changed but only if you know the legal landscape and understand the nature of the publishing field. In addition to reading books about publishing contracts, you should know that National Writers Union has a model publishing contract available to members and a booklet that explains what parts of the boilerplate contract can be altered to the author's advantage. The Union also provides members with free access to contract consultants.

If you are considering handling the sale of your book rights, you must inform yourself about more than the contract. It's not as if a publisher manufactures terms out of thin air. Your future publisher is working from facts—statistics that estimate your book's production and promotion costs. It has in-house forms for these calculations. You need to operate from the same figures. Fill in this part of your education by reading *Book Publishing* by John Dessauer.

Yet another consideration in negotiating your own contract is the sale of subsidiary rights. Sub rights, as they are called, consist of rights for the publication of paperbacks (or hardbacks if your book first comes out in paperback), for sale to book clubs, for excerpts in magazines, for use in audio, video, and electronic media, for foreign purchase or translation, and for movies. The publisher usually retains the option to sell these rights for the author when there is no literary agent. Contracting away those rights has grave financial implications, because any monies derived from sale of rights must first be applied against the sum you are advanced— unless otherwise stipulated. Until the publisher recoups that advance, you won't see any sub-rights' income.

If you fight to retain subsidiary rights, as most agents would, then you must ask yourself whether you are equipped to arrange their sale. Each sub right involves different protocols, contacts, and bodies of knowledge. You might be better off if your publisher does manage the subsidiary rights.

Agent or Lawyer for Hire

The idea behind hiring an agent or a lawyer for one-time involvement is that you'll benefit from the best expertise, for a fee, but remain unencumbered thereafter. There is no 15-percent commission on all income that your book makes for all time, no go-between separating you from your publisher. You pay once. After the contract has been signed, you're left with a direct, theoretically simple, relationship with your editor.

For a first novel without blockbuster potential, an agent or lawyer for hire might be a prayer answered. To find agents who are willing to work on a for-hire basis, ask friends, contact writers' organizations, or contact the Association of Authors' Representatives, the AAR. The fee will vary, but expect to pay several hundred dollars.

There are disadvantages to hiring a one-time agent. The agent has no vested interest in you. Without the emotional interest in a long-term relationship, will the agent sweat to drive a hard bargain on your behalf? You may avoid being fleeced, but you may not otherwise reap extra benefit. Unless the agent you select comes highly recommended by a source you trust, you have no way of knowing how sharp or experienced she is.

If an agent or lawyer negotiates the sale of your book rights, what do you intend to do about the problem of subsidiary rights? You face the same dilemma as if you had negotiated your own contract. You're probably better off letting your publisher retain the subsidiary rights.

I used an agent for hire for my first book contract. As she would have for permanent clients, she retained all subsidiary rights for me, the author. This fact eluded me *and* my publisher. Only when I sold an excerpt of the book to *Writer's Digest Magazine* did I happen to look at my contract and realize that I owned the right to sell the subsidiary rights. Alerting my publisher, they in turn stopped the agents they use from pursuing the sale of foreign rights on my book. Further checking on my part told me I was not in a position to sell my book's foreign rights or any subsidiary rights. At first opportunity, I appended my contract relinquishing subsidiary rights to my publisher.

On the other hand, not every book deal benefits from full agent representation or is worth the agent's time. Many genre writers and children's writers receive no different contract terms for paying an agent's 15 percent commission than they would by negotiating their own. The reason for this is that a long precedence exists for a small print run and set terms for first-time authors. Sub rights may not be a concern. In addition, many agents would refuse to represent a genre mystery, for instance, or a first children's book, because the agent can't alter the terms of the contract and the publisher's small print run generally means a commission smaller than the agent's break-even point. They would lose money on these negotiations. They may, however, be very helpful with improving the terms for the same author on the second or third book.

A second contract expert that some writers prefer is an attorney. After all, business attorneys know contracts up one side and down the other. But does your attorney know *publishing* contracts? Agents understand publishing's idiosyncracies and so do publishers. Attorneys who are otherwise contract experts may not. Unless an attorney is a specialist in publishing law—and has negotiated a number of book contracts—he is not likely to be effective or creative in changing a book contract to an author's advantage. Furthermore, an attorney with experience and expertise in nonfiction publishing contracts may never have negotiated a contract for a novel. Subsidiary-rights sales for novels, especially adaptations for screenplays, TV series, and other movie rights are typically far more critical than for nonfiction books.

There are attorneys who are as competent as agents in all aspects of publishing law; in fact, some agents *are* attorneys. Check your yellow pages or your state's lawyer referral service. Or, contact the Volunteer Lawyers for the Arts (See Resource Directory). Expect to pay the going hourly rate for consultation with an attorney, probably more than you would pay an agent. It's up to you to grill the attorney or agent you would hire for this all-important job.

Agent-represented Negotiations

I have heard estimates that 90 percent of all published books are agent-represented. Many publishers, especially large houses and conglomerates, won't accept manuscripts from or waste time negotiating with anyone except an agent. In contrast, most small publishers are more accustomed to dealing directly with authors, simply because small advances, or no advances, mean small or nonexistent commissions for agents.

If a novel is suitable for larger publishers, an agent has everything to gain by representing you and your future works. The better royalty percentage, the more money the agent makes. The same holds true for negotiating a higher advance, selling subsidiary rights, and holding auctions. The agent is your ally, and a win for you is a win for your agent. Some publishers admit to having one contract they use when negotiating with authors directly—the publisher-friendly contract, and one they use when negotiating with agents—the author-friend*lier* contract. Publishers expect to pay more money when dealing with an agent.

Agents are sales people. As your representative, an agent can describe you as a rising star in the literary world in a way that you can't without sounding arrogant and self-serving. Based on an agent's say-so alone, a huge advance and superb contract can be wrangled—if that agent has chits to call in, a great reputation, and sufficient editorial respect. A strong agent can make all the difference in selling a first book and launching a career. In other words, far more than contract terms are involved in the sale of your book. Your agent is a key player.

Even if you choose to have an agent negotiate your first and future contracts, it's still wise to read the contract-negotiation books mentioned in the prior section. Being well-informed makes you a participant not a dependent. Your questions will be intelligent ones and may offer angles overlooked by your agent. No one, not even your agent, has as much at stake or as much interest in your book's future or your career's direction as you do.

As one agent told me, authors often become overly focused on advances and royalties. Money is important, but a good agent has broader concerns. A good agent wants to match you with a publisher known for treating authors well, for making positive efforts at book promotion, and for longevity, so it's still in business for your fifth book. If your agent recommends against taking the highest bidder for your book, certainly ask why, but trust in your agent's experience and wisdom.

Shaping Your Career

Sooner or later, as you market your first novel, the realization will hit: *You have begun your career as a novelist.* The impact may affect you like a letter bomb or a gift from heaven. Whichever it is, it's time to have a talk with yourself, your mate, your mentors, or with your Higher Power. Where are you headed? Do you have a second book or a drawer full of novels? Are they worthy of publication? Is your second book a sequel to your first? In an entirely different style or category? What do you plan to write in the future? Then have a talk with your agent or your publisher. Where do you want your writing career to be in one year, in two, in five, in a decade?

A novelist's career can soar or fizzle. Sometimes it depends upon management. Sometimes it's blind luck. Literary agent Donald Maass devotes an entire book, *The Career Novelist,* to the subject. Before an agent, publisher, or any other mentor can help you, you must be clear with yourself and stay true to your own vision. Patty Hyatt knows she wants to write literary novels, even though her first novel was biographical mainstream. Rainer Rey seeks to write bestselling thrillers that will be made into movies. James Axtell wants to explore the art of writing wherever it leads.

It would be helpful at this juncture to review the conceptual work you did for the systematic marketing process. Review or rewrite your mission. Rethink your goals and objectives. Define the interim steps that will achieve your goals. Include your agent or publisher in this process. It's vitally important that you and your literary partners be headed down the same highway. Until this point in your journey, you have probably been making all of the decisions by yourself—from what to write to how to market. Clearly, you've amassed the requisite skills in craft and marketing to join the prestigious One-Percent Club. You have succeeded. But only, as Paul Cody mentioned in his breakthrough story, in getting one book published. From this success forward, your decisions must be joint decisions. Tap the wealth of experience of your agent and publisher.

Second-book Queries

So what happens when you've finished your second book? Must you go through the same laborious process involved in selling your first? Usually not. For one thing, your author-agent contract and your book contract probably have a clause reserving the right of first refusal for your next work. You represent an investment to your agent and your publisher. They've given time and money and perhaps friendship, too, in initiating your literary partnership. While they have no doubt received a financial return on that investment, money, is rarely the only reason for the relationship. Agents and editors love books. They love being midwives to literature they believe in. As much as you might hear about decisions driven by the bottom-line, the people who work in this industry are far more than robototrons to a conglomerate's greed. They still carry their higher personal values into their work.

Most of the time, a novelist simply sends a good sales tool—a synopsis—and the finished manuscript of a second novel to the agent. Or if there is no agent, to the publisher. No query!

In other words, the second time around, you're already on the inside track. True, you are still a new author, but now you've got a track record based on the performance of your first book. That record will influence the reception of your future works, the size of your advances, and the direction of your career. Neither you nor your agent may have a great deal of clout when negotiating your second-book contract, but you're no longer outside the stadium looking in.

A second-time novelist may also be able to sell a book based solely on an outline. You may remember from the chapter on the synopsis that the word "outline" is often interchanged with the word "synopsis." A true book outline is a chapter-by-chapter summary of substantial length—perhaps fifty to seventy pages. It may even become more of a "treatment," meaning that it may read like the condensed version of a novel rather than a synopsis.

Eventually, you may sell other works based on outlines alone, and those outlines may become shorter and shorter until you sign contracts for books based on a phone call, a concept, or on your name alone.

If, however, your first publisher declines interest in your second book—for any one of a host of reasons—then, if you are not agent-represented, you will be forced to query. The one difference is that now your query's first line or paragraph headlines that you're a published novelist. You've already paid dues. You've proven yourself as a writer.

Managing Success

You may never have imagined a day when one of your problems would be managing your success. The challenge may begin with the ticking clock of a second-book deadline. It may begin when your agent negotiates a multiple-book contract. To this, you may presently be muttering, "Don't I wish", but the reality is that success comes with booby traps. Some novelists lose sleep worrying about whether they have one good book in them and that's it. They wonder if the success and acclaim of their first book was somehow a fluke. Whether you are a true overnight success or your success follows years or decades of privation and sacrifice, you may have to overcome negative internal messages of being an imposter, not really deserving of recognition. Give these worries their due—five minutes maximum. Then get on with what you do so well—writing what you must write. Trusting and counting on your years of skill to deliver another book reflective of your ability.

Monetary success is a second booby trap if it seduces you into changing your lifestyle prematurely. So well known is this trap that agents and editors often warn first-time novelists not to quit their jobs or make any other kind of sweeping change. Scale back hours, yes, but don't quit. Renovate the house, yes, but don't take on a horrendous mortgage in a new neighborhood that yanks you out of your present social circle and thrusts your kids into new schools.

Why? Especially if you can finally afford to do the things you have dreamed of for years? Because change produces stress, produces writer's block. Your life conditions prior to publication, however humble, contributed to the mental, emotional, and spiritual milieu that birthed your first book. Your environments, physical and social, have a more powerful influence on you and your writing than any of us can imagine. Don't get radical. Just write your next book. After a few books, when you have achieved a standard of reliability for publication and recognition, then you'll be in a better position to make and handle major life changes.

I was a sideline observer of one writer who had worked hard his whole life, developed his writing skills over several decades, and devoted most of his free time to writing. When his first novel was published, it became a modest bestseller. With his five-figure advance, more money than he'd ever seen at one time in his life, the author treated his friends to an extravagant vacation. Upon return, he bid them farewell and moved to the Bahamas with a multiple-book contract in his pocket. About six months later, he returned to his home state destitute, depressed, and desperate. He pulled through, met the deadlines, and is doing better. He did finally finish his second novel and it, too, was a bestseller. But for awhile, producing that second book was touch and go. Too much change too quickly. Don't quit your day job.

Remember what stirred you to take up the pen in the first place. Take a moment and feel the privilege of being a writer—even if you still await publication. You have the power to create worlds and characters that live in the imagination of your readers. Your words move others to feel and think, even to act. As you explore the wilderness of your own mind, heart, and soul, you satisfy the urges that compelled you to write in the first place. Guaranteed there will be days when you will curse your choice, question your sanity, stare into the white oblivion of a blank page, and wonder why. These days will be with you whether you write for your own pleasure or see your name on the spine of a book at the bookstore.

I hope this book ferries you across your impassable rivers, bridges your dark chasms, and frees you to take the next step in your writer's journey.

Appendices

SAMPLE AUTHOR/AGENT CONTRACT
LITERARY AGENCY AGREEMENT

(Provided with permission by Anne Sheldon and Michael Vidor of The Hardy Agency.)

This agreement is entered into on [date] by and between [agency name] a [state where agency is located] partnership [or sole proprietor business] hereinafter referred to as "Agent," and [author's name], hereinafter referred to as "Author."

This agreement is concerning the following manuscript: [title of book], hereinafter referred to as "the Work."

Author hereby appoints Agent as sole and exclusive agent of the Work, throughout the world pursuant to the following agreements and understanding:

1. Scope
Agent shall counsel and advise Author professionally and shall market all of the Author's literary rights in the Work, primary and subsidiary, including but not limited to print publishing, audio tape, video tape, motion picture, electronic, radio and television rights in the Work.

2. Sub-agents
Agent may, with prior notice to and approval by Author, appoint others to assist in fulfilling this agreement, including sub-agents.

3. Author's Approval
Agent agrees to submit to Author any offers received. No agreement shall bind Author without Author's consent and signature.

4. Collections
a) Agent agrees to collect and receive for Author all monies due from marketing and selling Author's literary rights, to hold money safely in a separate bank account while it is in Agent's possession and control, and to remit to Author, less agency commission and any uncollected expenses, within five (5) business days after funds clear Agent's account.

b) Author is responsible for Author's own tax liabilities and Agent is not responsible for the collecting or payment of taxes due by Author.

c) In the event any monies due Agent are paid directly to Author, Author will remit the appropriate commission, as defined in paragraph 7, within five business days.

5. Commissions
Agent shall be entitled to retain as Agent's full agency commission for the full life of the copyright and any renewals:

a) Fifteen percent (15%) of all monies collected from the sale of the primary or secondary rights in the Work for print publication within North America.

b) Twenty percent (20%) of all monies collected from the sale of the primary or secondary rights in the Work for print publication outside of North America.

c) Twenty percent (20%) of all monies collected from the sale of motion picture, audiotape, videotape, electronic, radio or television rights.

d) Whenever foreign taxes, fees, or commissions are deducted at the source of monies due, Agent's commission shall be based on the balance after said deductions.

6. Expenses

Author is responsible for out-of-pocket expenses relating to the marketing of the Work, limited to photocopying and postage for manuscript submission, and any bank charges for the collection and payment of the Author's royalties. Agent will not bill Author for other expenses unless previously approved by Author.

7. Records

Agent shall maintain accurate books and records of Author's royalty account and shall submit complete and accurate statements to Author semi-annually or when they are received from the publisher.

8. Term

a) This agreement shall have an initial term of six (6) months beginning upon the signing of this agreement. After the initial six-month period, this agreement may be terminated by either party upon thirty (30) days advance written notice.

b) If within three months after the date of termination, Author, or an agent representing Author, enters into a contract for the sale of literary rights with a buyer whom Agent had been negotiating prior to the termination, then that contract shall be deemed entered into during the term of this agreement.

c) Should the death of the Author occur during the term of this contract, the contract will remain in full force, and all of the Author's rights and monies due under this agreement shall transfer to the Author's heirs.

d) Should the death of the Agent occur during the term of this contract, the contract shall remain in full force and all monies due to Agent shall transfer to Agent's heirs or legal assignees.

e) Should Agent sell the business or make a change in ownership, Author shall have the right to cancel this contract upon written notice. Representation of any rights that remain unsold at that time will revert back to Author.

9. Indemnity

Author shall indemnify and hold Agent harmless against any suit, proceeding, action, claim, or liability of any nature that may arise from the creation, publishing, or marketing of the Work.

10. Mail

Mail addressed to the Author may be opened and processed by Agent unless marked "Personal" or is otherwise apparently personal in nature, in which event, it shall be forwarded promptly to Author.

11. Right to Contract

Both Agent and Author represent and warrant that they are free to enter into and fully perform this agreement and that they do not have nor shall have any contract or obligations which conflict with any of its provisions.

12. Modification of Waiver

This agreement represents the entire contract made by the parties. Its terms cannot be modified except by written document signed by the parties. A waiver of any form will not be construed as a continuing waiver of the other breaches of the same or other provision of the contract. If any part of this agreement is held to be illegal, void, or unenforceable, this shall not affect the validity of any other part of this contract.

13. Interpretation

This Agreement shall be governed by and interpreted in all respects in accordance with the Law of the United States, State of [location of agent's business].

_____

[signature of author] (Author)   Date

_____

[signature of agent(s)] (Agent) Date

Author's address and Social Security number for payments under this agreement:

_____

(address)

_____

(city, state, zip)

_____

(social security number)

RESOURCE DIRECTORY

A. On Craft & Technique

Bickham, Jack M. *Writing and Selling Your Novel.* Cincinnati, OH: Writer's Digest Books, 1996. Bickham is a gifted writing teacher with 80 novels to his credit. His instruction on the craft of writing a novel is lean and clear. It's thin on selling but because of his insights into scene and sequel, viewpoint, and stimulus-response, I consider this book a five-star, must-read, must-own book.

Bishop, Leonard. *Dare to Be a Great Writer: 329 Keys to Powerful Fiction.* Cincinnati, OH: Writer's Digest Books, 1988. This outstanding book is one to come back to again and again. Open it at any place, and you'll become deeply absorbed and unobtrusively learn about craft, technique, the writer's life, and publishing.

Brown, Rita Mae. *Starting From Scratch: A Different Kind of Writer's Manual.* New York: Bantam, 1988. This "manual" addresses concerns about craft, technique, and art that often fall in the cracks. My favorite is Brown's discussion of the way social class affects language use.

Carr, Robyn. *Practical Tips for Writing Popular Fiction.* Cincinnati, OH: Writer's Digest Books, 1992. Carr, a writing teacher with 14 published novels, addresses the special craft and technique needs of *genre* writers. This is an entire course in novel craft between two covers. Out of print. Available used.

Gary Provost's Writers' Workshop. Box 139, S. Lancaster, MA 01561. Attn: Gail Provost. So popular and effective a ten-day workshop (not conference) near Cincinnati, that most of the 30 participants return year after year. As a staff instructor, I now teach most of the master classes in novel craft. Website: www.writersretreatworkshop.com.

Guthrie, A.B. Jr. *A Field Guide to Writing Fiction.* New York: HarperCollins, 1991. Master of understatement and economy, this Pulitzer prize-winning author (for *The Big Sky*) takes one to three underpopulated pages—only!—to cover 40 aspects of craft, art, and the writer's life. He makes it look so simple…. I love this book. Out of print. Available used.

Hall, Oakley. *The Art & Craft of Novel Writing.* Cincinnati, OH: Writer's Digest Books, 1994. With nearly two dozen books to his credit, including a Pulitzer-prize nominee, Hall knows what he's talking about. This serious book on craft draws examples from classic literature but is packaged for the commercial as well as literary student of writing. This is a book to come back to throughout your career, gleaning different subtleties with every reading of it. A classic.

Kress, Nancy. *Beginnings, Middles, & Ends*. Cincinnati, OH: Writer's Digest Books, 1999. Kress takes the amorphous entity of a story and shows you how to give it form, direction, and logical development. For the motivated reader, her exercises will confirm whether you have mastery over the unique craft needs for beginnings, middles, and ends.

Maass, Donald. *Writing the Breakout Novel*. Cincinnati, OH: Writer's Digest Books. 2001. An author of a dozen novels, Donald Maass has served as president of the AAR and is one of the top literary agents in the U.S. This book is rich in practical advice, examples, and wisdom to help you get to the heart of your story.

McKee, Robert. *Story: Substance, Structure, Style, and the Principles of Screenwriting*. New York: HarperCollins, 1997. Although McKee wrote *Story* for screenwriting, all 480 pages illuminate every aspect of novel craft. You can read this book over and over for the rest of your life and find a useful nugget every time.

Stein, Sol. *Stein on Writing*. New York: Griffin, 2000. Like McKee, Stein knows craft, technique, and art. This master's knowledge and wisdom on writing fiction make his book another one to own and reread often.

B. Specific Aspects of Craft

Libraries, bookstores, and book clubs abound with how-to instruction on characterization, plot, dialogue, setting, theme, and on how to write mysteries, romances, science fiction, horror, thrillers, historical novels, and other categories of fiction. I will not mention these individually, except for a select few must-read, must-own titles. You will find your own way to other books that are right for you.

FOUR TECHNIQUES OF PLOT

Bickham, Jack M. *Scene and Structure*. Cincinnati, OH: Writer's Digest Books, 1993. While the hero's journey sets the foundation for a solid plot, scene and sequel development allow a writer to leapfrog from page to page. I call this book the graduate course in scene and sequel. It's technical and detailed. Read it; study it—after you have absorbed *Writing and Selling Your Novel*.

Vogler, Christopher. *The Writer's Journey: Mythic Structure For Writers*. Studio City, CA: Michael Wiese Productions, 1998. Because Joseph Campbell's mythic hero's journey defines the foundation of 98 percent of all novels, it's essential that novelists be thoroughly familiar with it. Vogler has translated Campbell's ideas with such clarity and relevance to writers that I recommend his work over Campbell's original, scholarly treatment, *The Hero With A Thousand Faces*.

Johnson, Bill. *A Story is a Promise*. Portland, OR: Blue Heron Publishing, 2000. This book provided the missing link in craft and understanding for many of my editing clients. Read Johnson's book to achieve laser-like clarity about story promise, theme, narrative tension, and movement.

* * *

The last of the fourfold techniques of plotting novels is the Big Scene, called the "Set-piece" by Ansen Dibell in Chapter Six of *Plot*, a Writer's Digest Book published in 1988. A further explanation of the Big Scene can be found in my article in *Writer's Digest* magazine, "Find Your Novel's Missing Links," by Elizabeth Lyon, reprinted in *The Complete Handbook of Novel Writing* (Writer's Digest Books, 2002).

CHARACTERIZATION

Many of the books listed above on novel craft in general have fine sections on characterization. I recommend two books that feature characterization.

Kress, Nancy. *Dynamic Characterization*. Cincinnati, OH: Writer's Digest Books, 1998. Practical, without fluff, this book, if you use it, virtually guarantees the development of three-dimensional, believeable, and memorable characters.

Pearson, Carol S. *Awakening the Heroes Within: Six Archetypes We Live By*. San Francisco, CA: Harper San Francisco, 1998. As if designed for novelists in mind, this book defines six archetypal characters on their journeys to self-discovery and personal transformation. Pearson defines the life goal for each, the fear, the dragon or problem, the response to the task, and the gift or virtue at the successful journey's end. Campbell's mythic hero's journey sets the stage; Pearson peoples it. If you want a guarantee of deep characterization in your work, read and apply Pearson's ideas.

C. On Editing & Revision

Bates, Jefferson D. *Writing With Precision: How to Write So That You Cannot Possibly Be Misunderstood*. New York: Penguin USA, 2000. This is a super book to guide you through self-editing. Checklists, clear headings, and exercises allow you to pull out what you need. Sections have been added for the computer age and include organizing, file management, and word processing.

Bickham, Jack M. *The 38 Most Common Fiction Writing Mistakes (and how to avoid them)*. Cincinnati, OH: 1997. This "list" book could have been titled "Don't." Great for self-editing and catching yourself in those bad writing habits.

Browne, Renni & King, Dave. *Self-Editing for Fiction Writers: How to Edit Yourself into Print*. New York: HarperPerennial, 1994. This carefully conceived book by two editors at William Morrow features clear instructional explanation on craft and technique, thoughtful examples, checklists you can use to direct revision, and cartoons to lift the spirit. By far, one of the best books on editing for fiction writers.

Cheney, Theodore A. Rees. *Getting the Words Right: How to Rewrite, Edit & Revise*. Cincinnati, OH: Writer's Digest Books, 1990. If you want to delve into editing, this book will take you on an extensive journey into craft. Less of a shopping mall of easy-fix editing ideas, this book will give you the fundamental concepts to make you an all-round better writer.

The Chicago Manual of Style, fourteenth edition. Chicago, IL: University of Chicago Press, 1993. Long considered the "last word" in editorial disputes, I couldn't live, i.e. edit, without it. While you can use other more reader-friendly guidebooks—like *Pinckert's Practical Grammar, The Chicago Manual of Style* gives you the security of answering every conceivable question and trusting the source.

Judd, Karen. *Copyediting, A Practical Guide*, second edition. Menlo Park, CA: Crisp Publications Inc., 1992. For authors, publishing personnel, writers, editors, journalists, teachers, desktop publishers, and computer software workers. Learn to recognize and use all those squiggly marks and produce clean, clear, copy.

Provost, Gary. *Make Your Words Work*. iUniverse, 2001. This on-demand reprint of a classic takes you beyond concerns of grammar and punctuation into the heart of writing. You'll gain help with style, music, pace, description, voice, characterization, viewpoint, unity, time, subtlety and much more. A must read.

D. On the World of Publishing

Balkin, Richard. *A Writer's Guide to Book Publishing*, third edition revised by Nick Bakalar and Richard Balkin. New York, NY: Plume/Penguin Group, 1994. The fact that this book has been revised, updated, and kept in print since 1977 speaks for itself. It's one of my favorite books for a comprehensive yet manageable overview of the publishing world.

Dessauer, John P. *Book Publishing: The Basic Introduction*. New York: The Continuum Publishing Company, 1996. Like Balkin's guide to book publishing, this book comprehensively covers the history of book publishing; its relationship to culture; how books are created, manufactured, marketed, stored, delivered, and financed. The books by Dessauer and Balkin are all you need for a complete education on publishing.

Gross, Gerald, editor. *Editors on Editing: What Writers Need to Know About What Editors Do*, third edition. New York: Grove Press, 1993. Comments by and about many of the most prestigious editors in the business.

Literary Market Place and *International Literary Market Place*. Annual. New Providence, NJ: R.R. Bowker, A Reed Reference Publishing Co. Not books you buy, most libraries carry these in their reference section. The *LMP* is the publishing industry's "bible": every writer should become familiar with it.

Maass, Donald, *The Career Novelist: A Literary Agent Offers Strategies for Success*. Portsmouth, NH: Heinemann (a division of Reed Elsevier Inc.), 1996. This book by an agent about the business is writer-friendly. Unique and especially helpful is an experienced agent's advice about managing a career from the first book to mid-career decisions and beyond.

Mandell, Judy. *Book Editors Talk to Writers*. New York, NY: John Wiley & Sons, Inc., 1995. Covering the most common and pressing questions about publishing, this book's question-and-answer format grants accessibility of information and speaks directly to the reader. Features penetrating interviews with 44 experienced editors.

E. Contracts & Publishing Law

Beren, Peter and Brad Bunnin. *Writer's Legal Companion: The Complete Handbook for the Working Writer.* New York: Perseus, 1998. Two lawyers offer explanations of publishing law, including contracts, copyrights, permissions, libel, subsidiary rights, agent agreements and more.

Kirsch, Jonathan. *Kirsch's Guide to the Book Contract: For Authors, Publishers, Editors and Agents.* Venice, CA: Acrobat, 1998. Written by a lawyer who is also a novelist, this handbook clarifies your rights and responsibilities as a writer. Explains contracts, documentation of research and sources, legal protections of confidential sources, copyright and "fair use" laws, defamation, and invasion of privacy. Also covers electronic and subsidiary rights, and often overlooked rights that occur with the end of your book's life. Kirsch includes a model publishing contract and breaks down the standard "boilerplate" contract and explains its terms.

Kopelman, Alexander. *National Writers Union Freelance Writers' Guide.* Cincinnati, OH: 2000. This indispensable book supports writers rights by informing you about better book contracts, standard book rates, royalties, advances, collaborations, new rules for electronic rights, and many other areas about which every writer should stay informed and aware.

Volunteer Lawyers for the Arts, 1 E. 53rd St., 6th Flr, New York, NY 10022; (212) 319-2787. Website: www.vlany.org. California Lawyers for the Arts. Website: www.californiawritersforthearts.org. A call to this organization will help you locate a nearby lawyer versed in publishing contracts or direct you to answers related to libel, slander, permissions, and publishing law.

F. Market Guides, Guilds, Associations of Publishers and Literary Agents

Association of Authors' Representatives (AAR), P.O. Box 237201, Ansonia Station, NY, NY 10003. Website: www.bookwire.com/aar.

Children's Writer's & Illustrator's Market. Annual. Cincinnati, OH: Writer's Digest Books. Comprehensive listing of children's book publishers and their specifications. Also includes book and magazine markets for writers and artists who are children.

Council of Literary Magazines and Presses. *Directory of Literary Magazines.* Annual. Wakefield, Rhode Island & London: Asphodel Press. Includes 600 magazines that publish short stories from the United States, Canada, and Europe.

Herman, Jeff. *Writer's Guide to Book Editors, Publishers, and Literary Agents.* Rocklin, CA: Prima Publishing, 2002-2003. Not just a directory, this book provides a brief history of 400 United States and Canadian publishers that include large, university, and religious/spiritual publishers. The guide is unique in listing current names of some 1000 editors at these houses, by specialty. Part II features questionnaire answers by some 80 agents, answers that tell agent education and personal preferences, in addition to statistics about rejection rates, numbers of new authors represented in the past year, and numbers of titles sold in the past year.

Guide to Literary Agents. Annual. Cincinnati, OH: Writer's Digest Books. Providing the listings, contact names, and specifications of some 400 agents, this directory also provides the helpful division of fee-charging and non-fee charging agents, script agents, articles by agents, and indexes by subject and geographic location.

International Directory of Little Magazines and Small Presses. Updated biannually. Paradise, CA: Dustbooks. Gives contact information and specifications on about 3500 markets, many of which are "tiny ventures" not listed elsewhere.

International Literary Market Place. Updated annually. New Providence, RI: R.R. Bowker.

Internet Directory of Literary Agents (and Writers). Lists agents (or writers) in 30 countries, incuding 362 in the USA and in Canada. Free membership. Website: www.writers.net/agents.html.

Literary Market Place. Annual. New York: R.R. Bowker. This tome of the publishing industry lists over 40,000 companies and individuals in U.S. and Canadian publishing. It is divided into headings for book publishers, editorial services, literary agents, advertising, marketing, and publicity (including book clubs), direct-mail specialists, magazines that feature books, book manufacturing, book distributors, wholesalers, book producers, services and supplies, awards, contests, and grants, book-trade events, and much more.

Paludan, Eve. *Romance Writer's Pink Pages: The Insider's Guide to Getting Your Romance Novel Published.* Annual. Rocklin, CA: Prima Publishing, 1996-1997. This directory includes about 100 agents, a directory listing of romance publishers, and many more resources for the romance writer. Out of print. Available used.

Writer's Digest Books. Besides the obvious, this directory also contains listings of contests and awards, conferences and workshops, retreats and colonies, organizations, websites, and interview articles.

Writers Resource. An internet site that offers comprehensive resources and links. Website: www.indranet.com/writinginfo.html

Writers Guild of America (West); 7500 members; 700 W. Third St., Los Angeles, CA 90048; (323)951-4000 or 1-800-548-4532. This organization is the depository for registration of novels, treatments, and screenplays for protection when marketing to the movie industry. List of WGA signatory literary agents on website. Website:www.wga.org

Writers Guild of America (East); 3000 members; 555 W. 57th St., Ste. 1230, NY, NY 10019; (212) 767-7800. See former description. List of signatory agent members on website. Website: http://www.wga.org

Writers Guild of Alberta; 750 members; 11759 Groat Rd., Edmonton, AB T5M 3K6 Canada; (403) 422-8174. Website: www.writersguild.ab.ca

Writer's Northwest Handbook, sixth edition. Biennial. Portland, OR: Media Weavers, 1995. Essays and how-to articles by writers comprise about one third of this handbook, while the rest offers the listings and specifications of some 3000 book and magazine publishers and individuals, as well as other Pacific Northwest resources for writers.

Writer's Market. Annual. Cincinnati, OH: Writer's Digest Books. Lists more than 8000

editors to whom freelance writers can sell articles, books, novels, stories, fillers, scripts, and more. In addition to specifications and editor names for about 800 publishers, the "Market" includes some agent listings.

G. General Interest Writers' Magazines and Trade Publications

Authorship, bimonthly magazine of National Writers Association, Circulation: 4000. 1450 S. Havana, Ste 424, Aurora, CO 80012. General interest on craft and marketing.

Fiction Writer's Guideline, The Newsletter of Fiction Writer's Connection (FWC), Circulation: 1000. P.O. Box 7230, Albuquerque, NM 87195. Bimonthly. General interest on craft and marketing. Webite: www.fictionwriters.com/

Horn Book Magazine, 11 Beacon St., Boston, MA 02108. Bimonthly magazine covering children's literature. Website: www.hbook.com

Poets & Writers. Circulation: 60,000. 72 Spring St., 3rd Flr, New York, NY 10012. Bimonthly professional trade journal for poets and fiction writers. General interest on craft, technique, writer's life, and marketing. Website: www.pw.org

Publishers Weekly, 249 W. 17th St., 6th Flr, New York, NY 10011. Weekly magazine covering the book-publishing industry. Industry bible for 125 years: who's who, what's what, and why. Interviews, trends, problems, personnel changes, mergers, crashes, successes, and book reviews. Website: www.publishersweekly.com

Small Press Review/Small Press Magazine. Circulation: 3500. P.O. Box 100, Paradise, CA 95967. Monthly review of small presses and magazines, current trends and data. Website: www.dustbooks.com

The Writer. Circulation n/a. 120 Boylston St., Boston, MA 02116-4615. General interest on craft, technique, and marketing. Website: www.writermag.com/thewriter.html

Writers Connection. Circulation: 1500. P.O. Box 24770, San Jose, CA 95154-4770. Monthly newsletter covering writing and publishing.

Writer's Digest. Circulation: 225,000. Monthly magazine about writing and publishing. Website: writersdigest.com

Writer's Forum. Circulation: 13,000. Quarterly newsletter for students of Writer's Digest School covering writing techniques, marketing, and inspiration.

Writers Information Network, The Professional Association for Christian Writers. Circulation: 1000. P.O. Box 11337, Bainbridge Island, WA 98110. Bimonthly newsletter covering the religious publishing industry.

Writers' Journal. P.O. Box 394, Perham, MN 56573. Bimonthly general interest on craft, technique, and marketing. Publishes short fiction and hosts many contests. Website: www.sowasho.com/writersjournal

H. Writers' Conferences, Colonies, and Contests

In addition to the following books' listings of hundreds of writers' conferences in the United States and Canada, you can find contact information for conferences in *The Literary Market Place* (under "Book Trade Workshops") and in directories like *Writers Market*. Also note that the May issues of *The Writer* and *Writer's Digest Magazine* list hundreds of conferences by state. Even so, you are likely to find many other conferences, retreats, and workshops in your region that are not listed in these guides.

Many conferences host writers' contests. You may also find information about contests, awards, and grants listed in nearly every directory.

Middleton, Loomis, and Seale. *Artists and Writers Colonies: Retreats, Residencies, and Respites for the Creative Mind.* Portland, OR: Blue Heron Publishing Inc., 2000. Provides full descriptions of 175 domestic residencies, retreats, fellowships and grants, opportunities for playwrights, and artists-in-residence programs, domestic and foreign. Thoroughly researched.

The Complete Guide to Literary Contests 2001. Compiled by Literary Fountain. New York: Prometheus, 2001. Features alphabetical listings, full descriptions, and a separate list for fiction, nonfiction, poetry, plays, children writers, grants, and fellowships. Includes nearly 700 listings.

Grants and Awards Available to American Writers, A Publication of Pen American Center. New York: PEN American Center. 568 Broadway, New York, NY 10012-3225; Fax: (212) 334-2181. Biennial. Includes a section of awards and grants available to Canadian writers.

ShawGuides. Most comprehensive online directory of writers' conferences and worshops, domestic and foreign. Lists and links to nearly 700 organizations. Website: www.shawguides.com

Mettee, Stephen Blake, ed. *The Portable Writers Conference: Your Guide to Getting and Staying Published.* Fresno, CA: Quill Driver Books, 1997. Can't get to a writers' conference? No problem. This 444-page book replicates the best workshops of any conference I've been to. Featuring essays and articles written by writing and publishing professionals, this book is a companion to every chapter in the *Sell-Your-Novel Toolkit.*

Noble, William. *The Complete Guide to Writers' Conferences and Workshops.* Forest Dale, VT: Paul S. Ericksson, 1995. Sketching 150 conferences throughout the United States and listing contact information alone for another 60, this guide is little more than a weak expansion of a list.

Poets and Writers, Inc. *Writers' Conferences 1997.* Dept. CONF97, 72 Spring St., New York, NY 10012, (212) 226-3586, e-mail: PWSubs@pw.org. Over 200 listings in the United States and abroad. Dates, addresses, fees, deadlines, and workshop leaders. New at the time of this book's publication, I haven't seen this resource to know if it is a mere listing or fuller description.

I. Writers' Organizations, Trade Groups, Internet Web Sites

This is a list of national and Canadian organizations for writers and booksellers, many of which have regional and local chapters. Most of these organizations publish newsletters, magazines, or handbooks that can be purchased by nonmembers. Many of these organizations host annual conferences and other workshops. They may also publish newsletters or magazines available for purchase by nonmembers.

CRIME AND MYSTERY

International Association of Crime Writers Inc., North American Branch; 225 members; JAF Box 1500, NY, NY, 10116; (212) 753-3915.

Crime Writers of Canada; 150 members; 3007 Kingston Rd., Box 113, Scarborough, ON M1M 1P1 Canada; (416) 782-3116; e-mail: info@crimewriterscanada.com

Sisters in Crime, P.O. Box 442124, Lawrence, KS 66044; (913) 842-1325; Website: www.sistersincrime.org

American Crime Writers League, 12 St. Ann Dr., Santa Barbara, CA 93109; Website: www.acwl.org/

Mystery Writers of America; 2600 members; 17 East 47th St., 6th Flr., New York, NY 10017; (212) 888-8171; Website: http://www.mysterywriters.net

Police Writers Club, P.O. Box 738, Ashburn, VA 20146; (703) 723-4743; Website: www.policewriter.com/

ROMANCE

Alberta Romance Writers Association, 223 12th Ave. SW, Calgary, Alberta T2R OG9, Canada; Fax: (403) 283-7325; Website: www.albertaromancewriters.homestead.com/

Romance Readers Association, P.O. Box 24584, San Jose, CA 95154; Fax: (408) 978-9863; Website: www.theromancereader.com

Romance Writers of America; 7900 members with hundreds of regional chapters; 3707 FM 1960 West, Suite 555, Houston, TX 77068; (281) 440-6485; Website: www.rwanational.org/

SCIENCE FICTION, FANTASY, HORROR

Hatrack River; Website created by Orson Scott Card, including a writers group and young writers group; Website: www.hatrack.com

Horror Writers Association; 700 members; P.O. Box 50577, Palo Alto, CA 94303; e-mail: hwa@horror.org; Website: www.horror.org/

InterZone; monthly British magazine of science fiction and fantasy. Website offering reviews, texts of sci-fi books, listings of publishers, etc. Website: wwwsfsite.com/interzone

Mylanders; Website message board with real-time chat for writers of fantasy and sci-fi; www.mylanders.com

Science Fiction and Fantasy Writers of America; 1250 members; Suite 1B, 5 Winding Brook Dr., Guilderland, NY 12084; (518) 869-5361; Website: www.sfwa.org

WESTERN

Western Writers of America; 600 members; 1012 Fair St., Franklin, TN 37064. Website: www.westernwriters.org

CHILDREN'S

Canadian Society of Children's Authors, Illustrators and Performers, 35 Spadina Rd., Toronto, ON M5R 2S9 Canada; (416) 515-1559; The Canadian Children's Centre; 1200 members; (same address); (415) 975-0010; Website: www.canscaip.org

The Children's Book Council, 568 Broadway, Suite 404, New York, NY 10012; (212) 966-1990; e-mail: info@cbcbooks.org. Website: www.cbcbooks.org

The Children's Writing Resource Center; provides information to children's writers; Website: www.write4kids.com

Society of Children's Book Writers and Illustrators; 10,000 members; 8271 Beverly Blvd., Los Angeles, CA 90048; Website: www.scbwi.org

CHRISTIAN

Christian Writers Information Network; the "professional association for Christian writers," with links to conferences, publishers, critique groups, and regional writers' guilds. Website: www.bluejay pub.com/win

WOMEN'S

International Women's Writing Guild; 5000 members; Gracie Station, Box 810, New York, NY 10028-0082; (212) 737-7536; e-mail: iwwg@iwwg.com. Website:www.iwwg.com

Women's National Book Association, Inc.; Over 900 members; 160 Fifth Ave., New York, NY 10010; (212) 675-7805; Website: www.wnba-books.org

ETHNIC, MULTICULTURAL

American Black Book Writers Association, 4000 members; P.O. Box 10548, Marina Del Rey, CA 90295; Website: www.iwaysoul.com

Asian American Writers Workshop, 16 W. 32nd St., Suite 104, New York, NY 10003; (212) 494-0061; Website: www.aaww.org

Black Writers Alliance; P.O. Box 700065, Dallas, TX 75370-0065; Website: www.black-writers.org

Multicultural Publishing and Educational Catalog; 250 members; 2280 Grass Valley Hwy, Suite 181, Auburn, CA 95603; (916) 889-4438; Website: www.mpec.org

NATIONAL AND INTERNET SITES

The American Booksellers Association; 8427 members; 828 S. Broadway, Tarrytown, NY 10591; (914) 571-2665; Website: www.bookweb.org

The Art of Writing, "a Webzine about writing for writers." A great site for great links; Website: www.webcom.com/wordings/artofwrite/

The Authors Guild, 31 E. 28th St., 10th Flr, New York, NY 10016; (212) 563-5904; Website:www.authorsguild.org

The Authors League of America, Inc. (sister organization to the Author's Guild), 330 W. 42nd St., New York, NY 10036; (212) 564-8350.

National Writers Association; 3500 members; 3140 S. Peoria Ave., PMB 295, Aurora, CO 80014, (303) 841-0246; Webite: www.nationalwriters.com

National Writers Union; 4000 members; 873 Broadway, #203, New York, NY 10003, 212-254-0279; West-coast Office: 337 W. 17th St., Ste 101, Oakland, CA 94612; (510) 839-0110; Website: http://www.nwu.org/

PEN American Center; 3000 members; 568 Broadway, New York, NY 10012; (212) 334-1660; Website: www.pen.org

PEN Center West; 1000 members; 672 S. Lafayette Park Pl., #41, Los Angeles, CA. 90057; (213) 365-8500; Website: www.pen-wa-west.org

PEN Canada; 500 members; The Writer Centre, 24 Ryerson Ave., Suite 214, Toronto, ON M5T 2P3, Canada; (416) 703-8448; Website: www.pencanada.ca

Poets & Writers, 72 Spring St., Suite 301, New York, NY 10012; (212) 226-3586; Website;www.pw.org/

ZuZu's Petals Literary Resource. Superb site for finding the full spectrum of writing resources and links, including a fiction writers' resource page. Website: www.zuzu.com

CANADIAN

Canadian Authors Association, Box 419, Campbellford, ON K0L 1L0 Canada; (705) 653-0323; Website: www.canauthors.org

The Federation of British Columbia Writers; 700 members; Suite 905, 626 W. Pender St., Vancouver, BC V6B 1V9, Canada; (604) 683-2057; Website: www.bcwriters.com

Manitoba Writer's Guild Inc.; 500 members; 206-100 Arthur St., Winnipeg, MB R3B 1H3, Canada; (204) 947-3168; Website: www.mbwriter.mb.ca/

Saskatchewan Writers' Guild. 700 members. P.O. Box 3986, Regina, SK, Canada; (306) 757-6310; Website: www.skwriters.com

Writers' Federation of New Brunswick, 250 members, Box 37, Station A, Fredericton, Nova Scotia E 38 4Y2 Canada; Website: sjfn.nb.ca

Writers Guild of Alberta, 700 members, 11759 Groat Rd., 3rd Flr, Percy Page Centre, Edmonton, Alberta T5M 3K6 Canada; (780) 422-8174; Website: www.writersguild.ab.ca/, Calgary office: (800) 665-5354

NORTHEAST

Bookbuilders of Boston; 1915 members, 27 Wellington Dr., Westwood, MA 02090; (781) 326-3275; Website: www.bbboston.org

League of Vermont Writers; 450 members; P.O. Box 179, South Pomfret, VT 05067-0179; (802) 457-1637; e-mail: constance.h.fitz@valley.net

Maine Writers and Publishers Alliance; 1500 members; 14 Maine St., Brunswick, ME 04011-2201; (207) 729-6333; Website: www.mainewriters.org/

The Writer's Center; 2600 members; 4508 Walsh St., Bethesda, MA 20815; (301) 654-8604; Website: www.writer.org

EAST

Brooklyn Writers' Network (BWN); 500 members; 2509 Ave. "K", Brooklyn, NY 11210; (718) 377-4945.

Brooklyn Writers' Club; 500 members; P.O. Box 184, Bath Beach Station, Brooklyn, NY 11214-0184; (718) 837-3484.

Washington Independent Writers, 220 Woodward Bldg., 733 15th St., NW, Room 220, Washington DC 20005; (202) 347-4973; Website: www.washwriter.org

Writers & Books, 329 East Ave., Suite 302, Rochester, NY 14607; (716) 232-1070. (Second largest community-based literary arts organization in the United States) Website: www.wab.org

SOUTH

The Knoxville Writers' Guild, P.O. Box 10326, Knoxville, TN 37939; Website: www.knoxvillewritersguild.org

Space Coast Writers Guild, Inc.; 375 members; Box 804, Melbourne, FL 32902; (407) 727-0051.

MIDWEST

The Loft Literary Center, Suite 200, Open Book, 1011 Washington Ave. S., Minneapolis, MN 55415; Website: www.loft.org

Midwest Writers; c/o Dr. Earl Conn, College of Communication, Information & Media, Ball State University, Muncie, IN 47306.

Nebraska Writers Guild; 235 members; 515 N. 87th St., Omaha, NE 68114; (402) 391-7888.

Society of Midland Authors; 190 members; P.O. Box 10419, Chicago, IL 60610-0419; (312) 337-1482.

The Writers Place, 3607 Pennsylvania, Kansas City, MO 64111; (816) 363-8010.

SOUTHWEST

Arizona Authors Association, 3509 E. Shea Blvd., Suite 117, Phoenix, AZ 85028; (602) 867-9001.

Book Publishers of Texas; 150 members; 3404 S. Ravina Dr., Dallas, TX 75233; (214) 330-9795; e-mail: pamlange@aol.com

New Mexico Book League; 500 members; 8632 Horacio Pl. N.E., Albuquerque, NM 87111; (505) 299-8940.

The Society of Southwestern Authors; 125 members; Box 30355, Tucson, AZ 85751-0355; (520) 296-5299.

Southwest Writers Workshop; 1338-B Wyoming Blvd. N.E., Albuquerque, N.M. 87112; fax: (515) 237-2665; e-mail: swriters@aol.com; Website: www.us1.net/sww

Writers League of Texas (formerly Austin Writers League); 1600 members; 1501 W. Fifth St., Suite E-2, Austin, TX 78703; (512) 499-8914; Website: www.writersleague.org

NORTHWEST

Idaho Writers' League; P.O. Box 492, Kootenai, ID 83840; (208) 263-7207; Website: www.idahowritersleague.com

Oregon Writers Colony, P.O. Box 15200, Portland, OR 97293-5200; (503) 827-8072; Website: www.oregonwriterscolony.org

Pacific Northwest Writers; 900 members. 2033 Sixth Ave., Suite 804; Seattle, WA 98121; (206) 443-3807; Website: www.pnwa.org

Seattle Writers Association; P.O. Box 33265, Seattle, WA 98133; (206) 789-7288 or (206) 728-5819.

Willamette Writers; 600 members; 9045 S.E. Barbur Blvd., Suite 5-A, Portland, OR 97219; (503) 452-1592; Website: www.willamettewriters.com

WEST

California Writers' Club; 900 members; P.O. Box 1281, Berkeley, CA 94701; 91-year-old club with ten branches throughout California; (760) 446-4350; Website; www.cal-writers.com

Rocky Mountain Fiction Writers; P.O. Box 260244, Denver, CO. 80226-0244; (303) 331-2608; Website: www.rmfw.org

Writers' Haven Writers; 200 members; 2244 Fourth Ave., San Diego, CA 92101; (619) 696-0569.

INDEX

ABOUT THE AUTHOR

As an independent book editor, Elizabeth Lyon serves writers in the United States and abroad through her company, Editing International, LLC, *www.4-edit.com*. Scores of writers credit her help with their success in getting published, winning contests, and securing movie options.

Lyon's first book for writers, *Nonfiction Book Proposals Anybody Can Write*, is considered a standard reference on preparing proposals. As an instructor and keynote speaker, Elizabeth Lyon is known for her clear, practical instruction, inspirational encouragement, and good humor. A contributor to *Writers Digest* magazine and *The Writer*, Lyon also writes columns, essays, and articles for newsletters and online e-zines. In addition, readers may find helpful tips posted at her author web site: *www.elizabethlyon.com*.

Born in Toledo, Ohio, she lives in Eugene, Oregon, with Riley, her beloved border collie.